HOW TO BUILD MODERN FURNITURE

MARIO DAL FABBRO

VOL. I PRACTICAL CONSTRUCTION METHODS

PUBLISHED BY F. W. DODGE CORPORATION, NEW YORK

FOREWORD

WHEN IT WAS DECIDED THAT I SHOULD PREPARE THIS VOLUME ON THE CONSTRUCTION OF FURNITURE I WAS GREATLY PLEASED. I SAW THE OPPORTUNITY TO EXPLAIN MY IDEAS IN A FIELD THAT IS PARTICULARLY DEAR TO ME. IN PREPARING THIS BOOK I HAD THE FULL COOPERATION OF MR. JEFFREY LIVINGSTONE, EDITOR OF THE BOOK DEPARTMENT OF THE F. W. DODGE CORP. WITH HIS ASSURANCE THAT THERE WAS A NEED FOR SUCH A BOOK, I PROCEEDED IN ITS PREPARATION GIVING THE BEST KNOWLEDGE WITHIN ME, A KNOWLEDGE GAINED FROM LONG EXPERIENCE IN THIS WORK IN EUROPE AND MORE RECENTLY IN AMERICA. DUE TO MY LIMITED KNOWLEDGE OF THE ENGLISH LANGUAGE, DR. RUDOLPH PAROLA OF NEW YORK CITY TRANSLATED MY ORIGINAL TEXT, SO THAT I MIGHT MORE FULLY EXPLAIN WHAT I HAD IN MIND.

I BEGAN MY TASK BY FINDING OUT WHO WOULD BE MOST INTERESTED IN A BOOK OF THIS SORT. AFTER CONTACTING PEOPLE IN DIFFERENT BRANCHES OF THE FURNITURE FIELD I FOUND THAT THERE WAS A KEEN INTEREST AMONG ARCHITECTS, DRAFTSMEN, INTERIOR DECORATORS, CABINET MAKERS, AMATEURS, HOBBYISTS, AND COLLEGE STUDENTS.

TO PREPARE A VOLUME THAT WOULD SERVE THOSE INTERESTED IN THE VARIOUS BRANCHES OF THE FURNITURE DESIGN WAS NOT AN EASY ACCOMPLISHMENT. I DISCARDED ONE METHOD AFTER ANOTHER. I REALIZED THAT A BOOK WITH TOO MUCH WRITTEN MATERIAL WOULD NOT SERVE THE INTENDED PURPOSE, SO I THOUGHT IT WOULD BE BEST IF I CONFINED MYSELF TO ILLUSTRATIVE MATERIAL WHERE POSSIBLE. IN THIS WAY I WAS SURE THAT THE ILLUSTRATIONS WOULD EXPLAIN THE DESIGNS SIMPLY WHILE THE SHORT FOOTNOTES UNDER EACH WOULD GIVE A BRIEF BUT DETAILED EXPLANATION.

IN THIS BOOK I HAVE TRIED TO GIVE A STEP BY STEP COVERAGE OF ALL PHASES OF FURNITURE CONSTRUCTION. MANY METHODS OF JOINING PLANKS, RAILS AND FRAMES HAVE BEEN EXPLAINED. IN OTHER SECTIONS VENEERS, PLYWOODS, CURVES AND DOORS ARE DESCRIBED. HARDWARE IS THE SUBJECT OF ANOTHER PART. METHODS OF JOINING WOOD TO OTHER MATERIALS SUCH AS GLASS, METAL AND PLASTICS ARE SHOWN. UPHOLSTERING PROCEDURES ARE ILLUSTRATIVELY DESCRIBED IN A WAY THAT THE AMATEUR WILL BE ABLE TO FOLLOW.

THE LAST 15 PAGES OF THE TEXT HAVE BEEN DEVOTED TO DRAWINGS OF FURNITURE PIECES WHICH MAY BE BUILT BY THE HOME CRAFTSMAN. THIS SECTION IS ESSENTIALLY A PRELUDE TO VOLUME TWO.

IN THE SECOND VOLUME WHICH I HAVE UNDERTAKEN TO DO FOR THE F. W. DODGE CORPORATION I WILL FULLY DESCRIBE THE TOOLS WHICH SHOULD BE USED IN FURNITURE CONSTRUCTION, THE STANDARD MEASUREMENTS OF FURNITURE AND A SERIES OF FURNITURE DESIGNS WHICH WILL ENABLE THE UNSKILLED TO ACHIEVE SUCCESS IN WHAT HE BUILDS. THIS SECOND VOLUME WILL ALSO SHOW EXAMPLES OF ASSEMBLED FURNITURE IN MODERN GROUPINGS.

IT IS MY PERSONAL BELIEF THAT A BOOK OF THIS TYPE WILL BE FOUND USEFUL BY ALL THOSE INTERESTED IN FURNITURE. FOR THOSE WHO HAVE A DESIRE TO BUILD, THIS VOLUME IS AN INDISPENSABLE ASSET. IT IS MY HOPE AND DESIRE THAT ALL THOSE WHO USE THIS BOOK ARE SUCCESSFULLY SERVED.

Mario Dal Fabbro

THE AUTHOR

MARIO DAL FABBRO WAS BORN IN ITALY IN 1913. AFTER COMPLETING HIS STUDIES AT THE R. SUPERIOR INSTITUTE FOR DECORATIVE AND INDUSTRIAL ARTS AT VENICE, HE ATTENDED THE R. MAGISTERO ARTISTICO, FROM WHICH HE WAS GRADUATED WITH HIGH HONORS IN 1937.

FOLLOWING A LONG-ESTABLISHED TRADITION, MARIO WORKED FROM CHILDHOOD IN HIS FAMILY'S FURNITURE DESIGN SHOP. THIS EARLY EXPERIENCE PROBABLY ACCOUNTS FOR HIS SUCCESS IN THE TECHNICAL AND CREATIVE FIELD OF FURNITURE DESIGN, FOR HE HAS ALWAYS BEEN ABLE TO COMBINE THE THEORETICAL WITH THE PRACTICAL ASPECTS OF CONSTRUCTION. MARIO HAS ALSO BEEN AFFILIATED WITH ONE OF THE LARGEST FURNITURE HOUSES IN ITALY.

BETWEEN 1938 AND 1948 MARIO CREATED DESIGNS FOR PRIVATE INDIVIDUALS AND VARIOUS FURNITURE HOUSES IN MILAN. HE HAS CONTRIBUTED TO THE ITALIAN MAGAZINES *DOMUS* AND *STILE*, AND THE FRENCH MAGAZINE *L'ARCHITECTURE D'AUJOURD'HUI*, AND IS THE AUTHOR OF SEVERAL BOOKS ON FURNITURE CONSTRUCTION PUBLISHED BY HOEPLI AND GORLICH IN MILAN. IN 1939 AND 1947 HE PARTICIPATED IN THE TRIENALI INTERNATIONAL COMPETITION AND WON THE GARZANTI CONTEST FOR THE STANDARDIZATION OF FURNITURE.

IN 1948 HE TRANSFERRED HIS DESIGN ACTIVITIES TO THE UNITED STATES. HIS FIRST WORK PUBLISHED IN THIS COUNTRY WAS MODERN FURNITURE, A BOOK WHICH HAS ACHIEVED INTERNATIONAL RECOGNITION. THE AUTHOR NOW DESIGNS FURNITURE FOR MASS PRODUCTION. HE HAS ALSO CONTRIBUTED TO VARIOUS NEWSPAPERS AND MAGAZINES, INCLUDING *THE NEW YORK TIMES* AND *HOUSE AND GARDEN*.

Jeffrey H. Livingstone

CONTENTS

GENERAL NOTES ABOUT WOOD

IN ORDER TO SELECT THE TYPE OF WOOD BEST ADAPTED TO SPECIFIC NEEDS, IT IS ESSENTIAL TO UNDERSTAND THE CHARACTERISTICS OF THE MATERIAL. I HAVE, THEREFORE, OUTLINED SOME BASIC INFORMATION REGARDING ITS STRUCTURE AND DEFECTS, AS WELL AS METHODS OF SAWING AND HANDLING.

STRUCTURE OF WOOD

WOOD IS DERIVED FROM A TREE. IT IS MADE UP OF BUNDLES OF FIBERS OR LONG TUBES THAT RUN PARALLEL TO THE STEM OF THE TREE. THESE ARE CROSSED BY OTHER FIBERS THAT FORM THE MEDULLARY RAYS. THESE MEDULLARY RAYS PASS FROM THE CENTER OR PITH TO THE BARK AND SERVE TO BIND THE UNITS TOGETHER. THE ARRANGEMENT OF THE WOOD IN CONCENTRIC RINGS IS DUE TO THE TREE'S GRADUAL FORMATION. ONE LAYER OR RING IS ADDED EACH YEAR, AND FOR THIS REASON THE LAYERS ARE CALLED ANNUAL RINGS.

NATURE OF WOOD

SHOWN BELOW IS A PARTIAL SECTION OF A TREE. NOTE THE LOCATION OF ITS PARTS AS DESCRIBED BELOW. MEDULLA OR PITH: THIS IS THE CENTER OF THE TREE. IT IS LIGHTER IN COLOR AND LESS STRONG THAN HEARTWOOD.

HEARTWOOD: LOCATED BETWEEN THE MEDULLA AND SAPWOOD, THIS PART OF THE TREE ALWAYS GIVES US THE BEST BUILDING MATERIAL.

SAPWOOD: THIS PART OF THE TREE CONTAINS THE RECENT ANNUAL RINGS. IT IS SITUATED BETWEEN THE HEARTWOOD AND CAMBIUM.

CAMBIUM: THIS IS THE MOST RECENT ANNUAL RING.

BARK: THIS EXTERNAL LAYER SERVES AS A PROTECTION TO THE TREE.

DEFECTS IN WOOD

THE VARIOUS DEFECTS IN WOOD MAY BE DIVIDED INTO TWO CLASSES. FIRST ARE THOSE WHICH COME

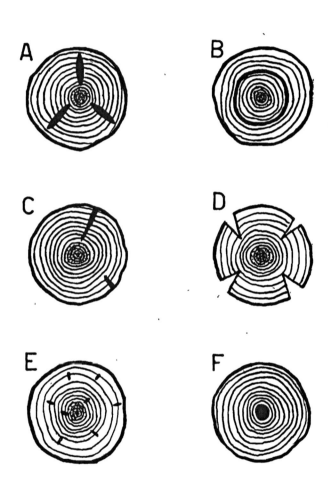

FROM ABNORMAL GROWTH SUCH AS HEART SHAKES, WIND OR CUP SHAKES AND KNOTS. SECOND ARE THOSE CAUSED BY DETERIORATION SUCH AS DRY AND HEART ROT. IN THE SECTIONS ABOVE YOU WILL NOTE THE FOLLOWING DEFECTS:

A — HEART SHAKES   D — STAR SHAKES
B — WIND OR CUP SHAKE   E — DRY ROT
C — HARD KNOTS   F — HEART ROT

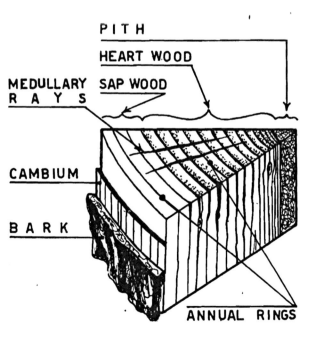

PITH
HEART WOOD
MEDULLARY RAYS
SAP WOOD
CAMBIUM
BARK
ANNUAL RINGS

SAWING THE TREE INTO PLANKS

A TREE IS USUALLY CUT DURING THE WINTER SEASON WHEN THERE IS LITTLE SAP IN THE WOOD. AT THIS TIME THE WOOD IS LESS SUBJECT TO FUNGI ATTACK. AFTER THE BARK HAS BEEN STRIPPED, THE TRUNK IS WASHED TO PREVENT FUNGI, MOLD OR OTHER GROWTH. THIS PROCESS ALSO HELPS TO SEASON THE WOOD. AT THE END OF THE SEASONING PERIOD THE TRUNK MAY BE SAWED INTO PLANKS IN A NUMBER OF DIFFERENT WAYS. ONE OF THE MOST PRACTICAL METHODS IS SAWING PARALLEL TO THE GRAIN. ANOTHER METHOD WHICH IS USED FOR BETTER WORK IS QUARTER SAWING.

A — PLAIN (OR BASTARD) SAWING OF A TRUNK INTO PLANKS PARALLEL TO THE GRAIN.

B — CURVATURE OF PLANKS AFTER THEY HAVE BEEN SAWED.

C — SAWING OF PLANKS PARALLEL TO THE GRAIN FROM A TRUNK THAT HAS HAD TWO SIDES REMOVED.

D — SAWING A TRUNK INTO PLANKS AFTER REMOVING THE PITH PLANK.

E — SAWING OF PLANKS FROM TRUNK THAT HAS BEEN SQUARED AND PITH PLANK REMOVED.

F — SAWING A TRUNK INTO PLANKS BY FOLLOWING THE MEDULLARY RAYS.

A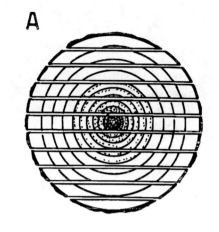

B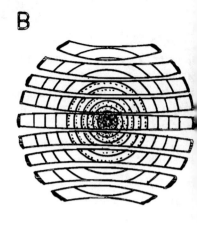

C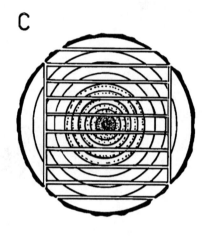

D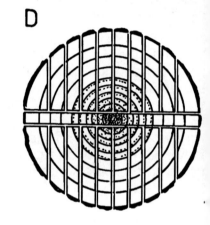

E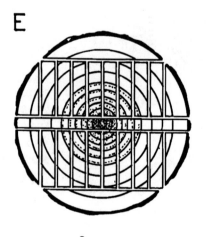

F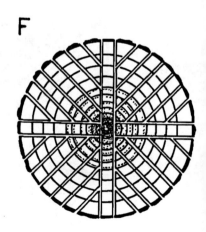

2

WOOD CHANGES

PLANKS UNDERGO SOME CHANGES DURING THE SEASONING PROCESS. THESE CHANGES ARE CALLED WARPING AND SHRINKING. SHRINKING IS MOST NOTICEABLE AT THE OUTER EDGES OF THE PLANK BECAUSE THE ANNUAL RINGS OF THE SAPWOOD ARE FRESHER AND LESS DENSE. THE GENERAL CHANGE THE PLANK UNDERGOES AFTER BEING CUT IS CALLED WARPING.

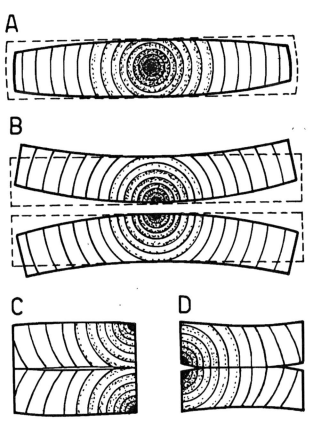

A — WARPING WHICH TAKES PLACE IN A PLANK WHICH INCLUDES THE PITH.
B — WARPING AND CURVATURE OF PARALLEL SAWED PLANKS. NOTE HOW THE CURVATURE RUNS IN A DIRECTION OPPOSITE TO THE ARC FORMED BY THE ANNUAL RINGS.
C — ALIGNING OR JOINING OF TWO PLANKS MUST BE DONE ON THEIR CONCAVE SIDES.
D — JOINING TWO PLANKS ON THEIR CONVEX SIDES WILL PRODUCE A WEAK JOINT.

SEASONING OF LUMBER

IT IS ESSENTIAL THAT LUMBER BE WELL SEASONED BEFORE IT IS USED. THE USUAL METHODS ARE AS FOLLOWS:

NATURAL SEASONING: IN THIS METHOD SAWED LUMBER IS EXPOSED TO FREE AIR AFTER IT HAS BEEN CAREFULLY STACKED. WHILE THE PROCEDURE IS SLOW, THE LUMBER PROCESSED IN THIS WAY IS THE LEAST SUBJECT TO SPLIT OR DECAY.

WATER SEASONING: A SOMEWHAT QUICKER METHOD OF SEASONING CONSISTS OF IMMERSING THE LUMBER IN RUNNING WATER FOR ABOUT ONE MONTH. THE WATER ENTERING THE PORES OF THE WOOD WASHES OUT THE SAP. THE LUMBER IS DRIED IN THE OPEN AIR.

ARTIFICIAL SEASONING: IN THIS METHOD THE LUMBER IS PLACED IN A DRYING KILN. A CURRENT OF HOT AIR IS ALLOWED TO CIRCULATE CONTINUOUSLY BETWEEN THE LAYERS OF LUMBER. IN SOME CASES STEAM IS USED. THIS IS THE QUICKEST METHOD.

GLUING WOOD

ONE OF THE ADVANTAGES OF WOOD IS THAT PIECES MAY BE JOINED TOGETHER BY GLUE.

AMONG THE OLDER ADHESIVES STILL USED IN WOODWORKING ARE THE PROTEIN ADHESIVES WHICH ARE WATER SOLUBLE, NON-STAINING AND EASY TO HANDLE. CASEIN GLUE MADE FROM SKIM MILK IS ALSO USED. FISH BASE AND BLOOD ALBUMIN GLUES ARE SUITABLE, BUT REQUIRE HEATING TO 140° TO 180° F BEFORE APPLICATION.

AMONG THE SYNTHETIC GLUES NOW USED ARE THE PHENOLS, RESORCINOL, MALAMINE AND UREA ADHESIVES. RUBBER BASE ADHESIVES, ANOTHER GROUP, ARE OFTEN USED TO JOIN WOOD AND METAL.

IN ORDER TO JOIN TWO PIECES OF WOOD IT IS NECESSARY THAT THEY BE PLACED TOGETHER SO THAT THE GRAIN IS PARALLEL. AFTER THE PIECES ARE PREPARED, THE GLUE IS APPLIED TO THE SURFACE OF EACH PIECE AND IN TURN THEY ARE CLAMPED OR PRESSED TOGETHER FOR FOUR TO TWELVE HOURS ACCORDING TO THE TYPE OF GLUE USED.

COLORING WOOD

BEST RESULTS DEPEND UPON THE ABILITY OF THE PERSON APPLYING THE COLOR. AFTER INITIAL SANDPAPERING, A STAIN MAY BE USED TO CHANGE THE NATURAL COLORING OF THE WOOD. THIS COLORING MATERIAL MAY BE MADE BY ADDING CHROMA IN TUBES, POWDER OR GRANULES TO WATER OR ALCOHOL. THIS MATERIAL IS THEN BRUSHED, RUBBED OR SPRAYED ON THE WOOD SURFACE.

FINISHING WOOD

GENERALLY, WOOD IS FINISHED WITH LACQUER APPLIED BY SPRAY IN THIN LAYERS OVER THE PREPARED SURFACE. WHEN DRY, THE LACQUER WILL FORM A SOLID TRANSPARENT LAYER. A FINAL FINISH MAY BE ADDED BY RUBBING WITH A PREPARED COMPOUND EITHER BY HAND OR BY USE OF A BUFFING WHEEL. ONE OF THE OLDEST METHODS OF FINISHING IS FRENCH POLISHING, WHICH CONSISTS OF RUBBING A MIXTURE OF ONE PART SHELLAC TO THREE PARTS ALCOHOL OVER THE SURFACE WITH A RUBBER BLOCK.

METHODS OF JOINING BOARDS

PARALLEL BUTT JOINT

WHEN PLANKS ARE SAWED FROM THE TRUNK, IT IS OFTEN FOUND THAT THEY ARE NOT LARGE ENOUGH FOR THE PARTICULAR WORK INVOLVED. IN ORDER TO OBTAIN THE DESIRED WIDTH OR LENGTH IT IS NECESSARY TO GLUE ONE OR MORE PIECES TOGETHER WITH WHAT IS CALLED A SIDE OR END JOINT.

IN ORDER TO OBTAIN AN INVISIBLE JOINT IN EXPOSED PANELS IT IS NECESSARY THAT A UNION OF PARALLEL JOINTS BE MADE BY AN ACCURATE ALIGNMENT OF THE GRAIN. AS IN ALL OTHER TYPES OF JOINTS, THERE ARE MANY WAYS OF JOINING THESE PARTS. EACH METHOD HAS ITS OWN PARTICULAR USE, DEPENDING ON THE TYPE OF WORK INVOLVED.

A — BECAUSE THE PLANKS SAWED FROM THE CENTER OF THE TREE TRUNK ARE CONSIDERED THE WEAKEST, IT IS ADVISABLE TO SAW THEM IN TWO AND GLUE THEM TOGETHER TO GIVE THEM STABILITY AND STRENGTH.

B — TO OBTAIN BEST RESULTS, THE JOINING OF TWO PLANKS SHOULD BE ACCOMPLISHED BY MATCHING THE EXTERNAL RINGS, OR INTERIOR RINGS, IN ORDER TO EQUALIZE WHATEVER SHRINKING OR WARPING TAKES PLACE.

C — IF THE EXTERNAL PART OF THE LUMBER IS CONNECTED WITH THE INTERNAL PART, A VERY BAD JOINT MAY BE THE RESULT. THERE WILL BE NO PROPER SEASONING OF THE TWO PIECES AND AFTER A PERIOD OF TIME THERE WILL BE A NOTICEABLE DEMARCATION OF THE WHOLE JOINT.

D — TO OBTAIN BEST RESULTS IN A SOLID PANEL IT IS NECESSARY TO HAVE THE EDGE STRAIGHT TO FORM A PERFECT JOINT. IT IS OF UTMOST IMPORTANCE TO SEE THAT THE GRAIN OF EACH PLANK IS ALTERNATED WITH THE NEXT IN ORDER TO EQUALIZE THE STRAIN MADE BY THE ANNUAL RINGS.

E — HERE IS AN EXAMPLE OF WHAT WOULD HAPPEN IF ATTENTION WERE NOT PAID TO PARAGRAPH D. THE PLANK WOULD HAVE A TENDENCY TO CURVE.

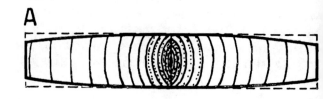

A

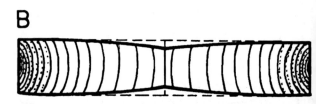

B

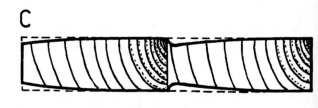

C

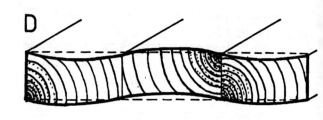

D

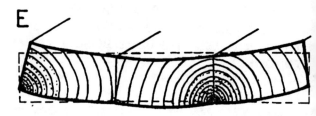

E

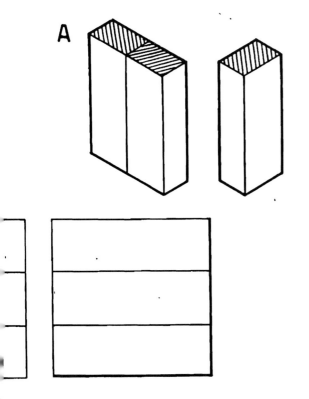

A

STRAIGHT JOINT: THIS IS ONE OF THE SIMPLEST AND MOST FREQUENTLY USED JOINTS.

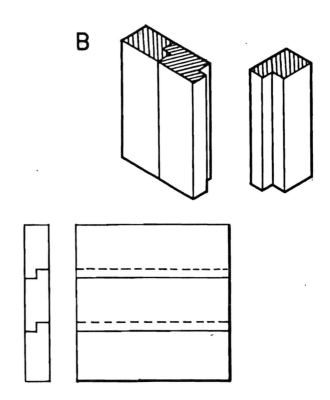

B

RABBET JOINT: SIMILAR TO THE PRECEDING METHOD, BUT SELDOM USED BECAUSE IT IS MORE DIFFICULT.

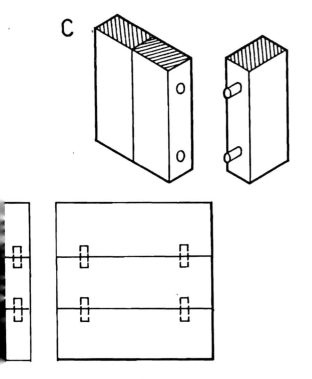

C

DOWEL JOINT: A COMMON METHOD, OFTEN USED WHERE THE TOTAL AREA IS LARGE.

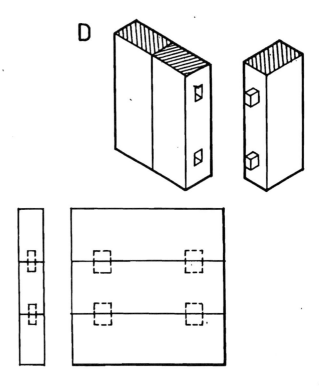

D

MORTISE AND TENON JOINT: THIS METHOD IS LESS OFTEN USED THAN THE JOINT AT LEFT.

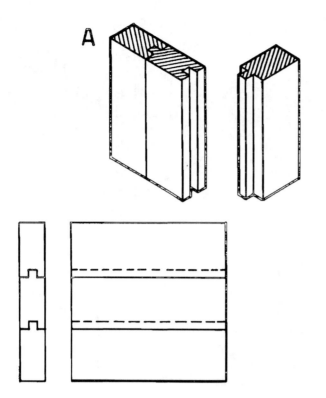

TONGUE AND GROOVE: FLOORING IS USUALLY MADE THIS WAY. IT IS ALSO PRACTICAL IN FURNITURE WORK.

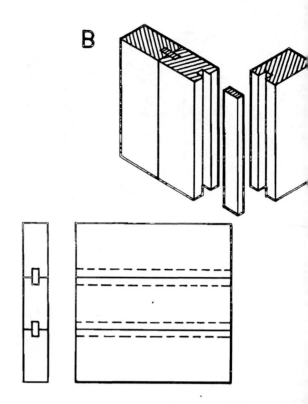

FEATHER JOINT: THIS IS ONE OF THE BEST AND MOS PRACTICAL WAYS OF JOINING PARALLEL PLANES.

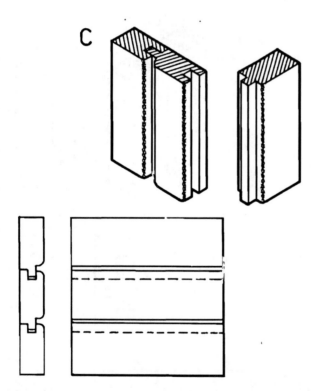

LOOSE TONGUE AND GROOVE: WITH ROUNDED OR BEVELED EDGES, THIS JOINT IS OFTEN USED IN WALL PANELING.

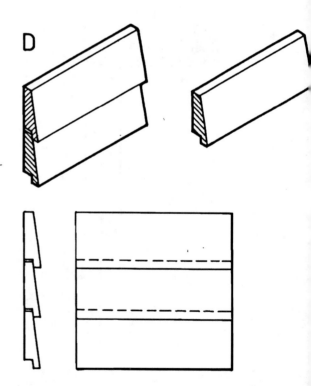

SHIP LAP JOINT: THIS METHOD IS USED EXTENSIVELY FOR SIDING ON HOMES. IT IS EASY TO MAKE A WATER TIGHT JOINT IN THIS WAY.

6

DRAWING BOARD USING A TONGUE AND GROOVE JOINT. THE TRANSVERSE RAIL IS USED TO AVOID WARPING IN THE PLANK.

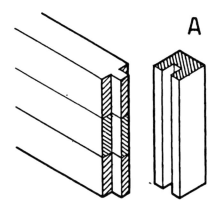 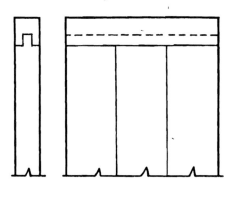

A

WEDGE MORTISE AND TENON: THIS METHOD IS USED WHEN WORK IS TO BE EXPOSED TO INCLEMENT WEATHER.

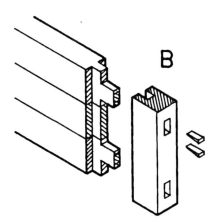 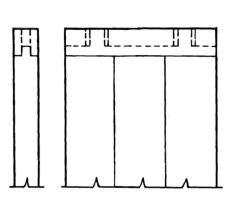

B

STRAIGHT JOINT WITH WEDGES.

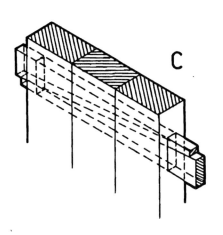 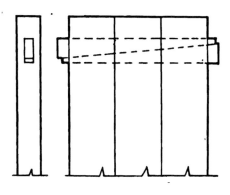

C

STRAIGHT JOINT WITH DOVE-TAIL WEDGE: THIS IS A GOOD METHOD TO USE WITH A STRAIGHT JOINT AND FOR OUTSIDE WORK.

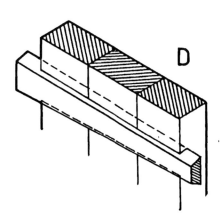 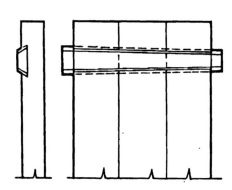

D

7

BUTT JOINTS

THE END BUTT JOINT IS NOT OFTEN USED IN FURNI-
TURE WORK FOR PRACTICAL REASONS: IT IS NOT
STRONG, GLUE WILL NOT ADHERE EASILY TO ITS SUR-
FACES, AND THE JOINT IS ALWAYS VISIBLE. WHEN
POSSIBLE, IT IS BEST TO AVOID THIS TYPE OF CON-
STRUCTION IN CABINET WORK.

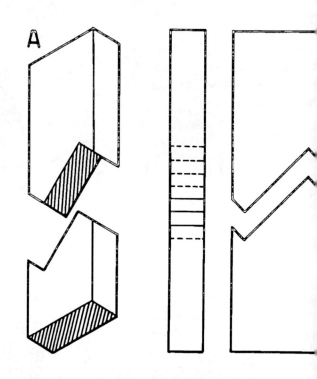

ZIG ZAG BUTT JOINT: THIS JOINT HAS GREATER CON-
TACT WITH THE WOOD GRAIN AND IS, THEREFORE,
STRONGER THAN A RIGHT ANGLE BUTT JOINT.

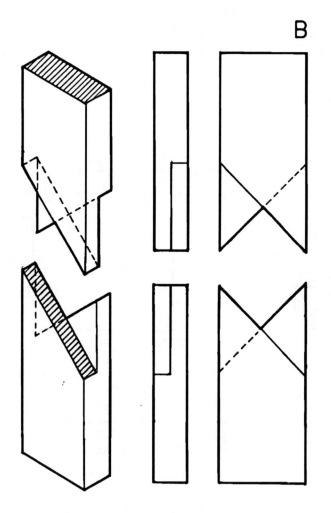

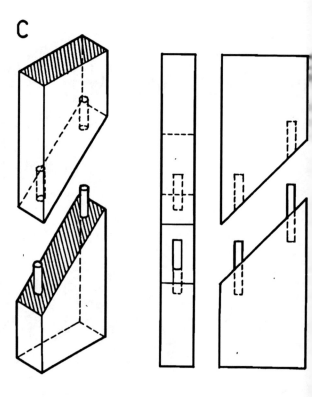

FORK BUTT JOINT: A GOOD JOINT IS OBTAINED BE-
CAUSE THE NATURAL CONTACT OF THE SURFACES
PERMITS GOOD GLUE ADHESION.

DOWEL BUTT JOINT: THE DOWELS STRENGTHEN THE
JOINT. GLUE IS USED WITH ALL OF THESE JOINTS.

DOUBLE DOVETAIL BUTT JOINT:
THIS IS USED IN CASES WHERE
THE JOINT IS SUBJECT TO STRAIN.

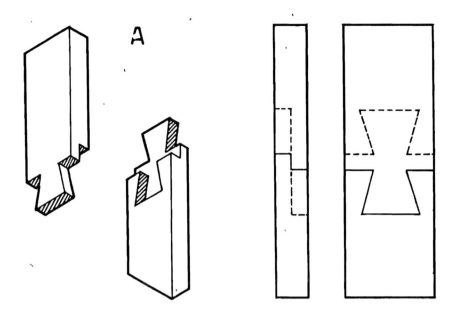

A

TENSION SCARF JOINT: THIS
JOINT IS HELD IN PLACE BY
WOODEN WEDGES, AND IS USED
MOSTLY IN ORDINARY CAR-
PENTRY.

WEDGES

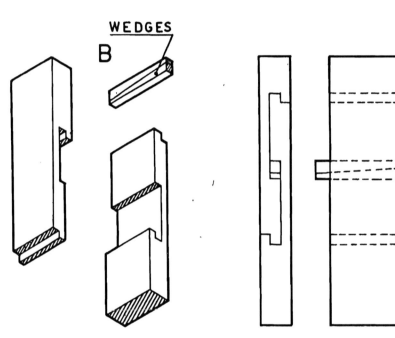

B

C

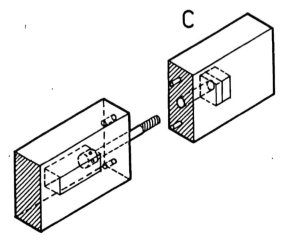

DOWEL AND BOLT BUTT JOINT: THIS IS DONE WITH DOWELS AND
CLOSED WITH BOLTS INCASED IN THE WOOD.

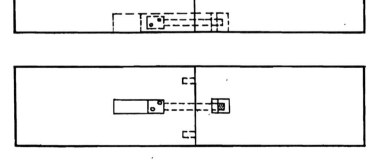

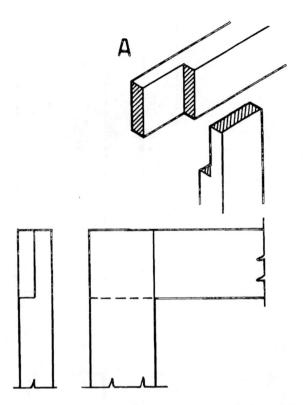

ANGLE RAIL JOINTS

THE PREPARATION FOR ANGLE RAIL JOINTS IS OF GREAT IMPORTANCE. THEY REPRESENT THE BASIC ELEMENT IN THE CONSTRUCTION OF FURNITURE PIECES. VARIOUS TYPES OF STRAIGHT RAILS AND TRANSVERSE RAILS MAY BE USED TO FORM VARIOUS TYPES OF FRAMES. EACH OF THESE JOINTS HAS INDIVIDUAL CHARACTERISTICS WHICH NECESSITATE CHOOSING THE RIGHT TYPE FOR THE WORK TO BE DONE. YOU MUST CONSIDER THE THICKNESS OF THE STRAIGHT AND TRANSVERSE RAILS, THE QUALITY OF WOOD, AND THE POSITION OF THE FRAME — WHETHER VISIBLE OR OBSCURED. AT TIMES A MIDDLE RAIL IS ADDED TO THE STRAIGHT AND TRANSVERSE RAILS FOR EXTRA SUPPORT. THE SERIES OF ILLUSTRATED EXAMPLES WILL GIVE YOU AN IDEA OF THE VARIOUS TYPES, AND EXPLAIN THE INDIVIDUAL CHARACTERISTICS OF EACH.

END HALF LAP JOINT: THIS JOINT IS EASILY CONSTRUCTED. UNLESS REINFORCED WITH PINS AND BOLTS OR SCREWS, IT DOES NOT MAKE A VERY DURABLE JOINT. IT IS USED MOSTLY IN REPAIR WORK.

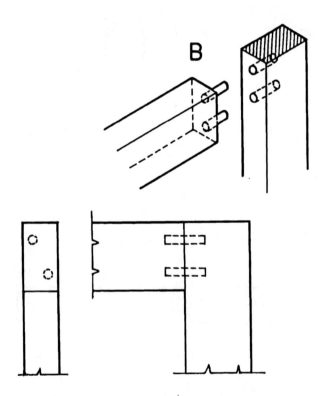

DOWEL JOINT: A COMMON JOINT AND USED IN ORDINARY REPAIR WORK.

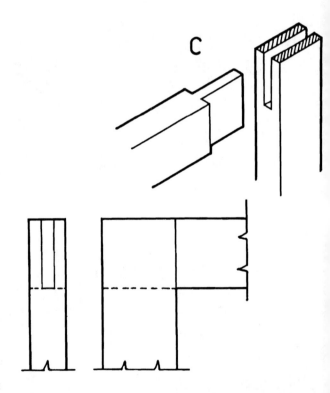

THROUGH MORTISE AND TENON JOINT: THIS IS A JOINT OFTEN USED BY THE AMATEUR CRAFTSMAN.

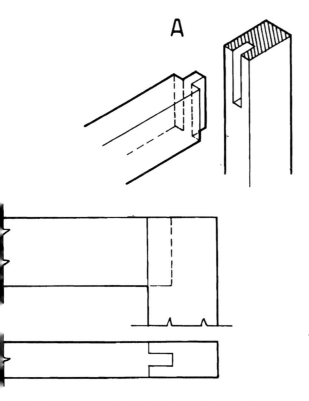

A

OPEN MORTISE AND TENON JOINT: THIS JOINT IS
EASY TO MAKE AND IS USED FOR ORDINARY WORK.

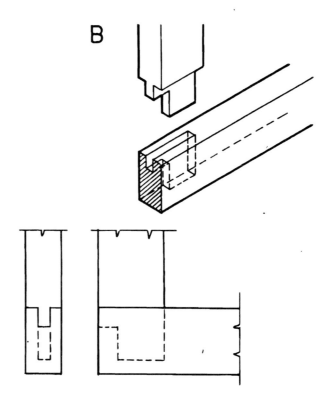

B

RABBET MORTISE AND STUB TENON JOINT: THIS IS THE
MOST USED JOINT IN THE FURNITURE FIELD. IT HAS
ALL THE REQUISITES OF THE PERFECT JOINT.

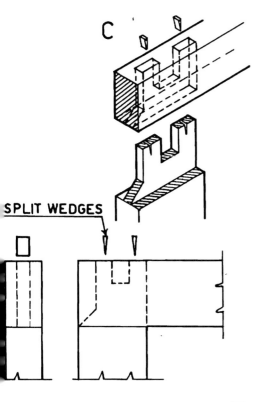

C

SPLIT WEDGES

DOUBLE MORTISE AND TENON WITH MITER RABBET:
THESE JOINTS ARE VERY STRONG AND PREFERRED
WHERE THE WORK IS EXPOSED TO THE ELEMENTS.

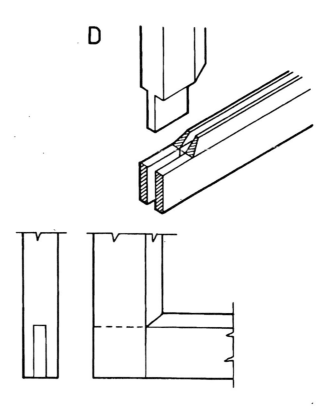

D

THROUGH MORTISE AND TENON WITH GROOVE END
MITER ON THE INNER EDGE.

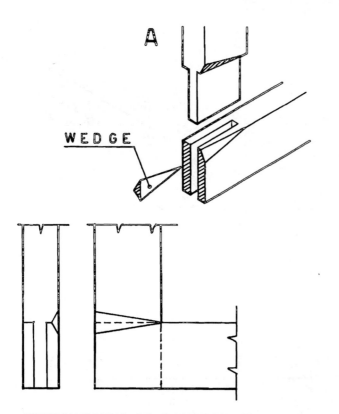

THROUGH MORTISE AND TENON WITH WEDGE IN THE SIDE JOINT USED FOR VENEER COVER. THE WEDGE ELIMINATES ANY MARK ON THE OUTSIDE OF THE VENEER.

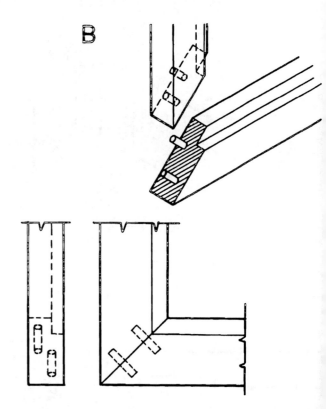

DOWEL MITER JOINT IS USED IN EVERY TYPE OF WORK.

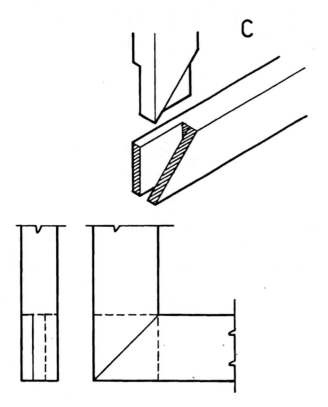

OPEN MORTISE AND TENON WITH MITER.

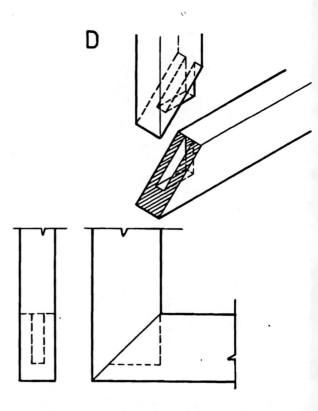

MITER WITH BLIND MORTISE AND TENON.

12

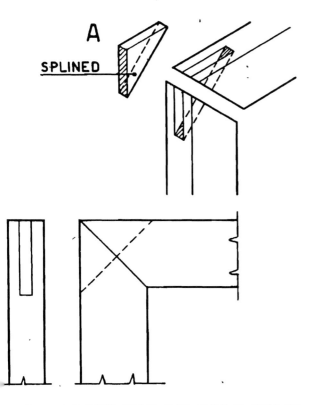

A

SPLINED

MITER JOINT WITH SPLINE: THIS JOINT IS EASY TO MAKE AND USED IN WORK DONE BY THE AMATEUR CRAFTSMAN.

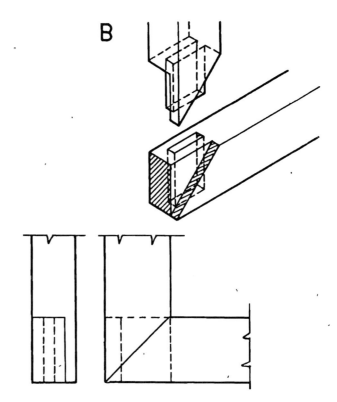

B

MITER MORTISE AND TENON JOINT: A VERY STRONG JOINT USED FOR WORK EXPOSED TO HUMIDITY.

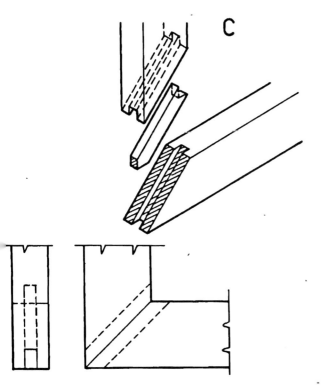

C

MITER TONGUE JOINT: THIS IS VERY COMMON IN STANDARD PRODUCTION.

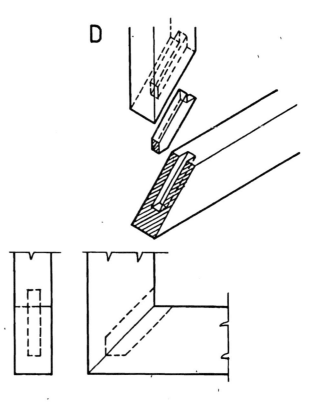

D

MITER STUB TONGUE JOINT: SAME AS PRECEDING ONE EXCEPT THAT FEATHER JOINT IS INVISIBLE.

MIDDLE RAIL JOINTS

LAP TEE JOINT: OFTEN USED
BY THE AMATEUR CRAFTSMAN;
ALSO IN REPAIR WORK.

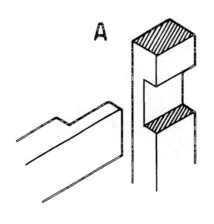
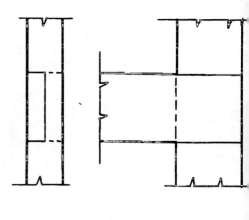

DOWEL JOINT: VARIOUS TYPES
OF WORK REQUIRE THIS TYPE
OF JOINT.

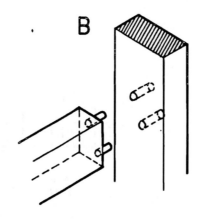
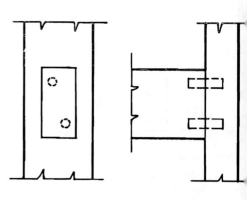

BLIND MORTISE AND TENON:
THIS IS AN EASILY MADE JOINT
THAT IS USED EXTENSIVELY.

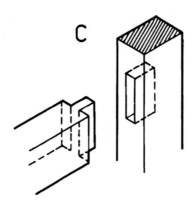
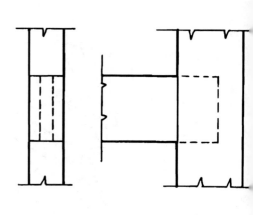

THROUGH MORTISE AND TEN-
ON JOINT: WITH THE ADDI-
TION OF THE WEDGE THIS IS
A VERY STRONG JOINT. IT IS
USED IN WORK EXPOSED TO
WEATHER.

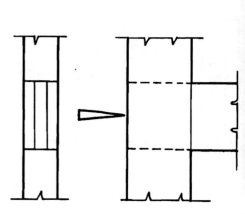

DOVETAIL STUB JOINT: THIS METHOD IS USED TO STRENGTHEN THE FRAME WHERE UNUSUAL STRAIN TAKES PLACE.

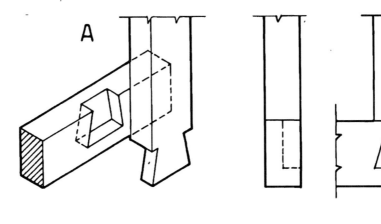

OBLIQUE DOVETAIL JOINT: SAME AS ABOVE EXCEPT THAT TONGUE RUNS THROUGH AND JOINT IS IN OBLIQUE POSITION.

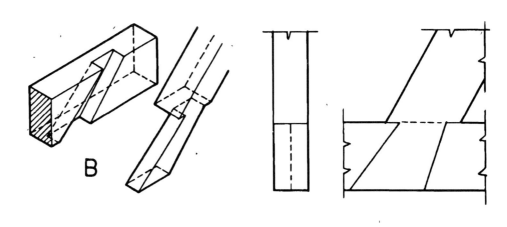

SPECIAL DOVETAIL JOINT: THIS IS DIFFICULT TO MAKE AND IS USED ONLY WHEN PRECISION WORK IS REQUIRED.

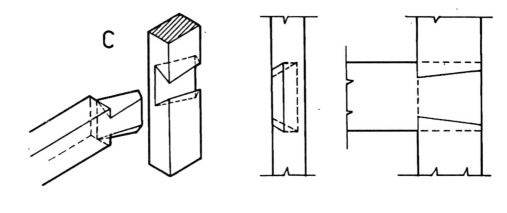

DOUBLE DOVETAIL JOINT: THE PRINCIPLE HERE IS THE SAME AS IN A SINGLE DOVETAIL JOINT. BOTH SYSTEMS ARE USED WHERE THERE IS GREAT STRAIN.

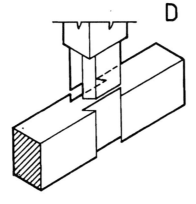

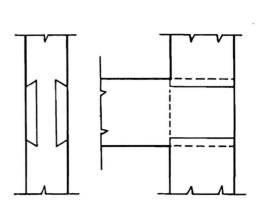

MORTISE AND TENON WITH RAB-
BET: HERE IS ONE WAY OF JOIN-
ING A RAIL AND A PANEL.

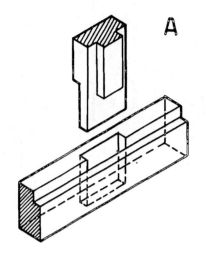

A

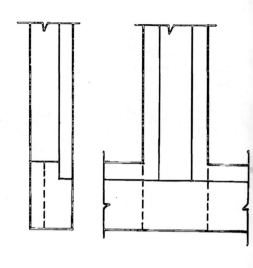

MORTISE AND TENON JOINT
WITH GROOVE: SAME AS PRECED-
ING METHOD BUT WITH GROOVE
FOR PANEL. NOTE THAT THE MOR-
TISE AND TENON ARE REDUCED
IN WIDTH.

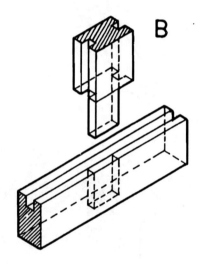

B

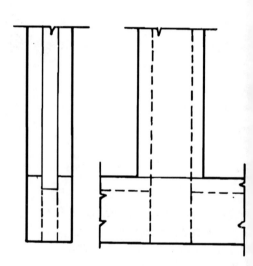

MORTISE AND TENON WITH MI-
TERED RAIL AND FRAME: SAME
AS ABOVE BUT SQUARED AT IN-
TERSECTION. THE ANGLE JOINT
MUST BE MITERED.

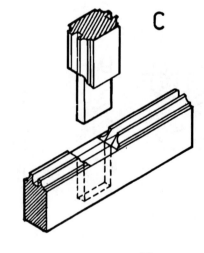

C

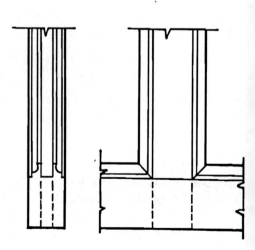

CROSS LAP JOINT: EASY TO MAKE AND USED IN ALL TYPES OF WORK; ONE OF THE MOST COMMONLY USED ELEMENTS IN FURNITURE CONSTRUCTION.

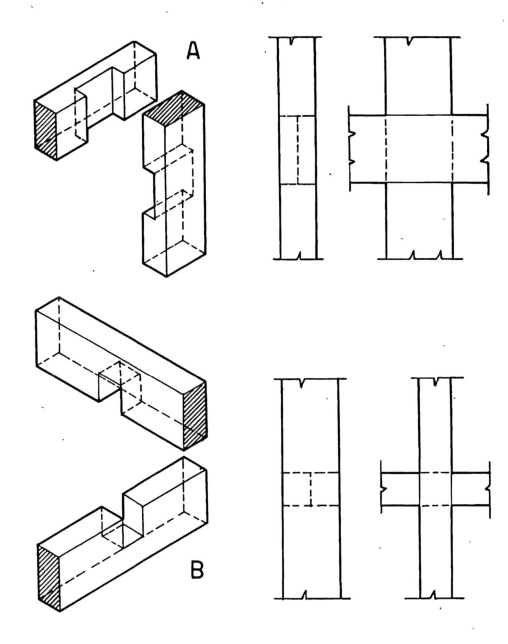

A

CROSS LAP JOINT: THE SAME METHOD AS ABOVE WITH JOINT IN DIFFERENT POSITION.

B

MORTISE AND TENON: THIS CROSS RAIL JOINT HAS MANY APPLICATIONS AND USES.

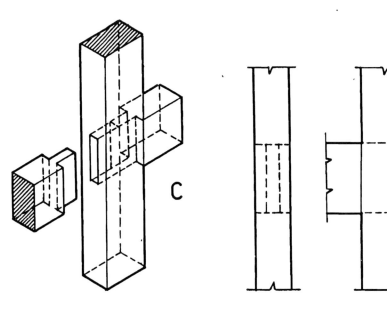

C

17

RAIL TO FRAME JOINTS

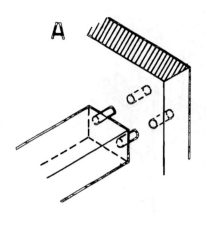

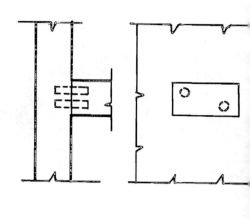

DOWEL JOINT: THIS IS ONE OF THE EASIEST UNIONS TO MAKE.

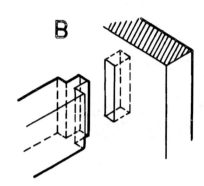

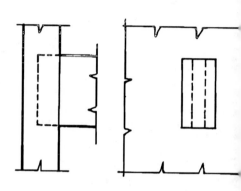

MORTISE AND TENON JOINT: GOOD RESULTS ARE OBTAINED BY THIS METHOD. THE JOINT MAY BE GLUED AT THE ENDS.

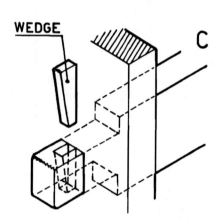

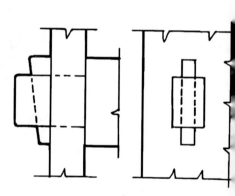

EXPOSED WEDGE JOINT: THE WEDGE TIGHTENS THE RAIL AND PANEL TOGETHER, MAKING A VERY SOLID JOINT.

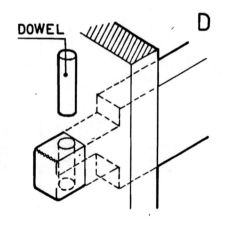

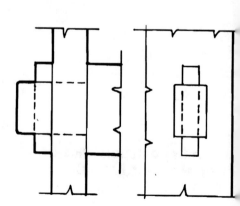

EXPOSED DOWEL JOINT: SIMILAR TO THE WEDGE JOINT (ABOVE) EXCEPT THAT THE DOWEL DOES NOT TIGHTEN THE PANEL AND RAIL.

PANEL TO FRAME JOINTS

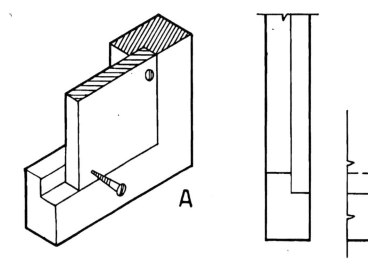

PANEL IN RABBET: PANEL IS AT-
TACHED TO FRAME WITH
SCREWS. THIS IS A SATISFAC-
TORY METHOD OF JOINING A
PANEL AND FRAME.

A

MOLDING

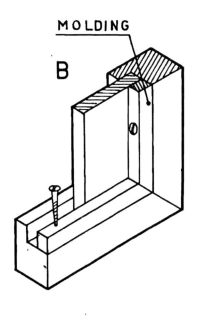
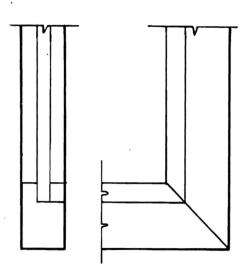

B

PANEL IN RABBET WITH MOLD-
ING: THE MOLDING IS ATTACH-
ED WITH SCREWS OR NAILS
AFTER THE PANEL IS IN PLACE.

COVE MOLDING

C

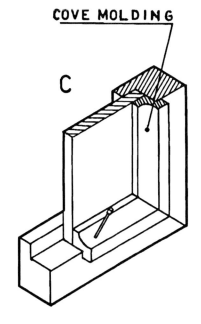
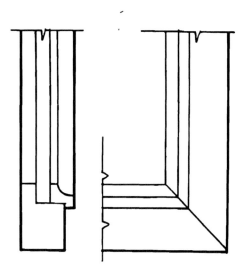

PANEL IN RABBET WITH COVE
MOLDING: THIS IS SIMILAR TO
"B" ABOVE, EXCEPT FOR THE
TYPE OF MOLDING USED.

PANEL IN DADO GROOVE: THIS IS A SIMPLE METHOD OF JOINING A PANEL AND FRAME. THE FRAME MUST REMAIN INDEPENDENT OF THE PANEL TO ALLOW FREE MOVEMENT IN THE WOOD.

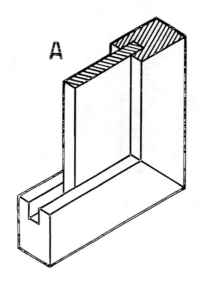

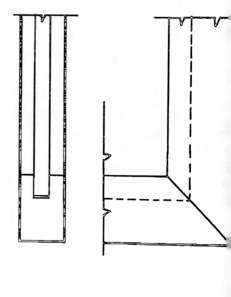

BEVELED PANEL IN DADO GROOVE: THE BEVELING OF THE PANEL PERMITS GREATER STABILITY. PANEL WILL NOT RATTLE AS ONE WALKS ACROSS THE FLOOR.

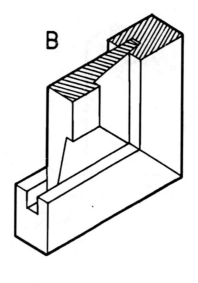

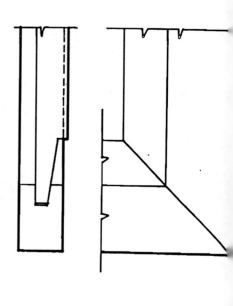

PANEL LOCK JOINT: THE PANEL AND FRAME ARE INDEPENDENT MEMBERS.

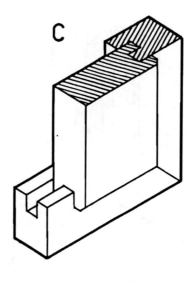

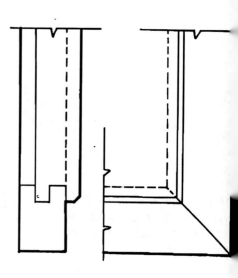

ANGLE FRAME JOINTS

JOINING FRAME MEMBERS IS ONE OF THE MOST IM-
PORTANT PHASES OF FURNITURE CONSTRUCTION.
AFTER MAKING THE FRAME PIECES TO THE DESIRED
SIZE, YOU WILL WANT TO ASSEMBLE THEM. ALWAYS
BEAR IN MIND THAT SOLID WOOD SECTIONS HAVE
A TENDENCY TO SHRINK, AND THAT SHRINKAGE
CAUSES CRACKS IN THE DIRECTION OF THE GRAIN.
YOU WILL WANT TO SELECT THE PROPER JOINT IN
ACCORDANCE WITH THE CHARACTER OF THE WORK
AND THE STRENGTH REQUIRED FOR THE FINAL PIECE
OF FURNITURE.

IN LARGE FURNITURE PIECES WHICH WILL BE DIFFICULT
TO MOVE, IT IS ADVISABLE TO USE JOINTS THAT CAN
BE EASILY REASSEMBLED (SOMETIMES REFERRED TO
AS DEMOUNTABLE JOINTS). IN THESE CASES THE
FRAME WILL PROBABLY HAVE TO BE CONSTRUCTED
WITH SPECIAL BOLTS OR DOVETAIL JOINTS. BELOW
ARE SEVERAL EXAMPLES SHOWING WAYS THIS CAN
BE DONE.

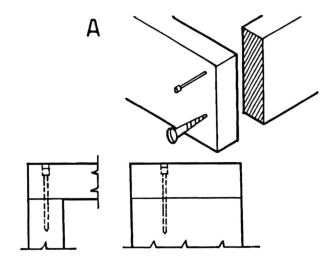

A

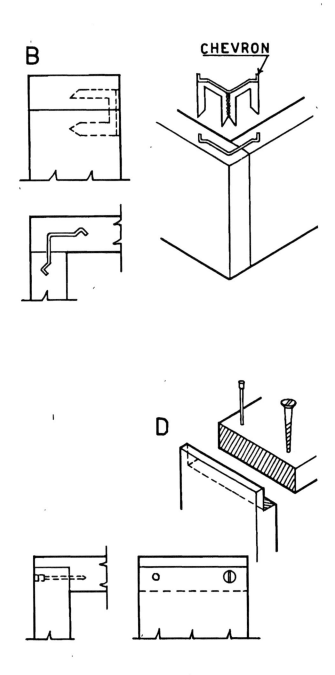

B

CHEVRON

D

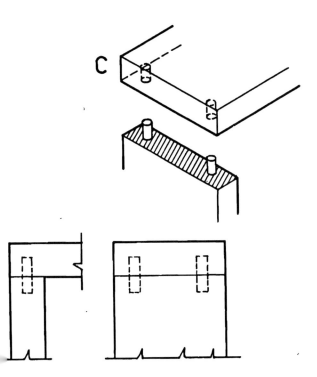

C

A – BUTT JOINT ATTACHED WITH NAILS OR SCREWS.
B – BUTT JOINT ATTACHED WITH CHEVRONS ON THE
BOARD.
C – DOWEL JOINT WHICH IS COMMONLY USED IN
THIS TYPE WORK.
D – RABBET JOINT ATTACHED WITH GLUE AND NAILS
OR SCREWS.

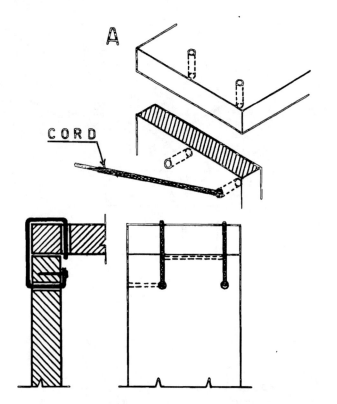

BUTT JOINT WITH CORD OR LEATHER: USED IN SPECIAL CONSTRUCTION SUCH AS CHILDREN'S FURNITURE.

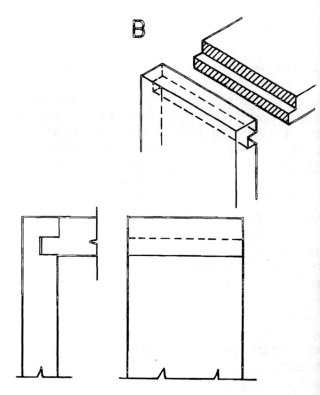

BOX CORNER JOINT: THIS JOINT IS LESS USED DUE TO POSSIBILITY OF CRACKS AT EDGES.

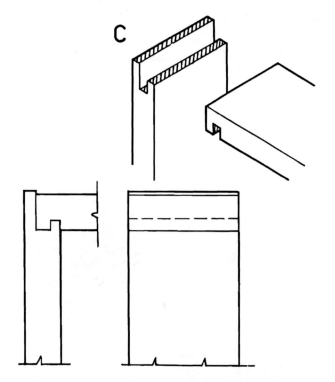

MILLED CORNER JOINT: EXTENSIVELY USED IN BUILD-ING DRAWERS. IT DIFFERS FROM THE PRECEDING JOINT IN HAVING CLOSED EDGES, WHICH AVOID CRACKS.

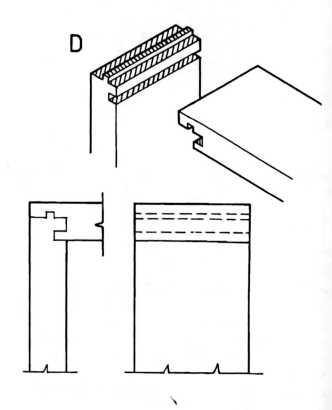

LOCK BUTT JOINT: EXCELLENT WHERE ACCURATE WORK IS DESIRED.

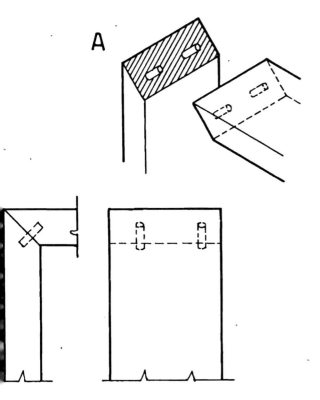

A

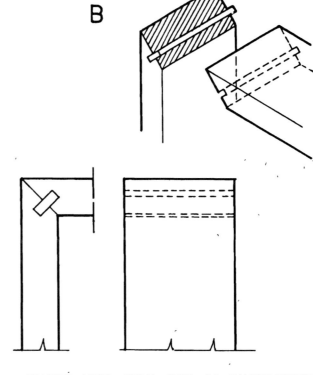

B

DOWEL MITER JOINT: OFTEN USED BY THE AMATEUR CRAFTSMAN AND CARPENTERS.

FEATHER MITER JOINT: USED IN MANUFACTURED WORK.

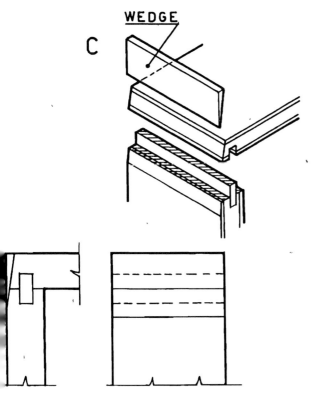

C

WEDGE

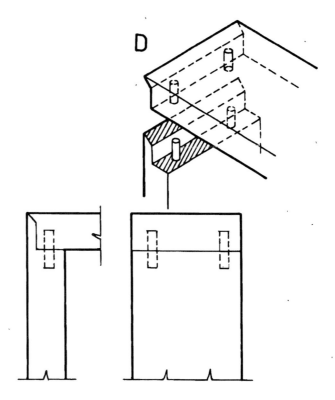

D

FEATHER JOINT: COVERED WITH A WEDGE AND USED WHEN VENEER IS APPLIED. THE WEDGE ELIMINATES ANY MARK ON THE VENEER OUTSIDE.

DOWEL MITER JOINT: THIS METHOD IS COMMON IN MANUFACTURED PIECES.

SPLINED MITER JOINT: USED BY
AMATEUR CRAFTSMEN.

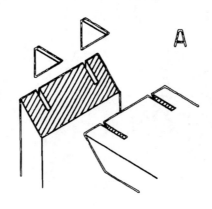
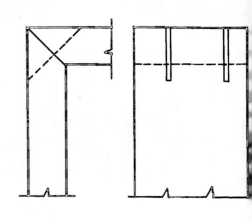

A

MITER WITH METAL CLAMP: THIS
CLAMP IS EASY TO APPLY AND
GIVES GOOD RESULTS.

METAL CLAMP

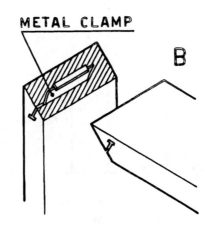
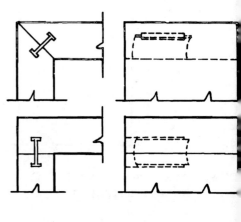

B

MITER TONGUE AND GROOVE
JOINT USED IN GOOD STANDARD
PRODUCTION.

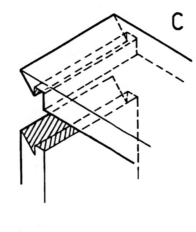
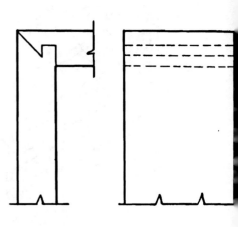

C

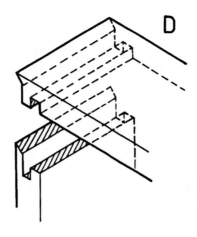
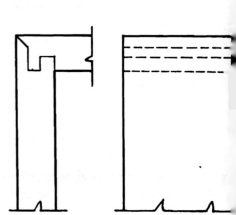

D

LOCK MITER JOINT IS ONE OF
BETTER CONSTRUCTION.

24

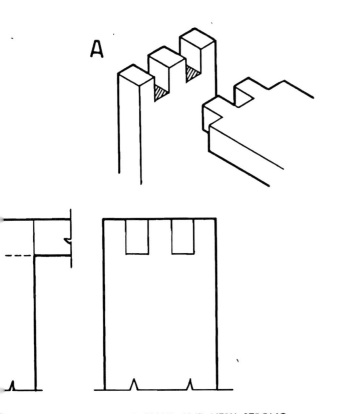

A

OX JOINT: AN EASY TO MAKE AND VERY STRONG OINT.

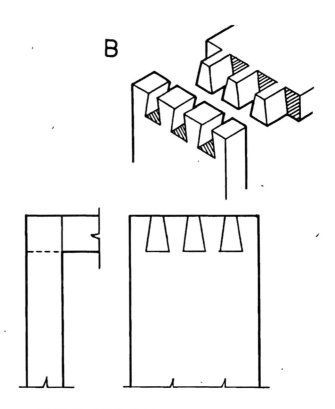

B

DOVETAIL JOINT: THIS IS ONE OF THE STRONGEST TERMINAL TYPE JOINTS.

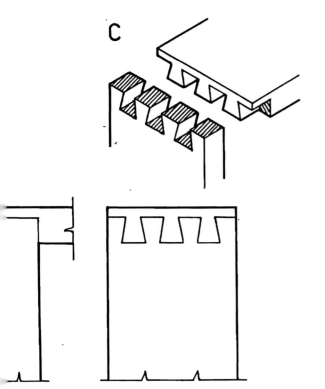

C

ALF BLIND DOVETAIL JOINT.

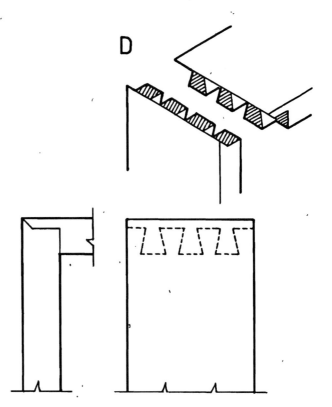

D

BLIND DOVETAIL JOINT: USED WHEN THE TWO SIDES ARE TO BE LEFT EXPOSED.

DEMOUNTABLE JOINTS

OLD TYPE OF DEMOUNTABLE
JOINT. THIS TYPE IS SELDOM USED
ANY MORE IN STANDARD PRO-
DUCTION.

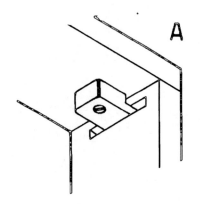
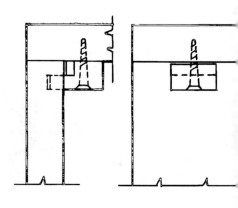

BUTT JOINT USING EXPOSED
HARDWARE.

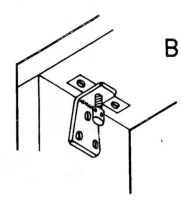
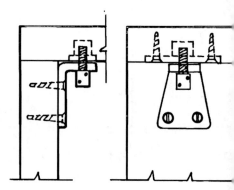

ENCASED BOLT: NOTE THAT HOLE
MUST BE CUT SO THAT BOLT MAY
BE TIGHTENED.

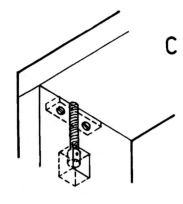
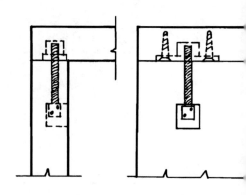

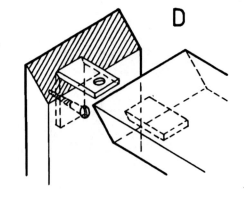
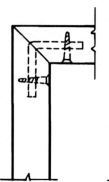
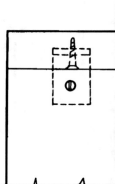

MITER JOINT WITH BLIND ANGLE
IRON: ONLY TWO SCREWS ARE
NEEDED AT EACH JOINT.

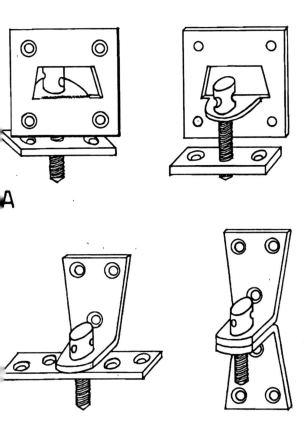

A

VARIOUS TYPES OF BOLTS USED WITH FURNITURE
WHICH MUST BE REASSEMBLED OCCASIONALLY.

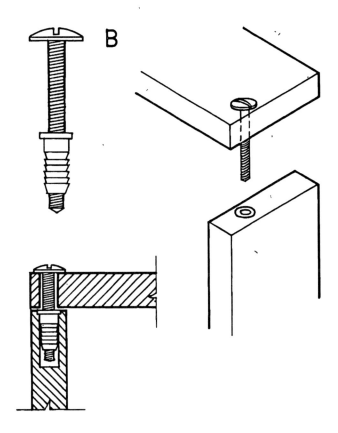

B

BUTT JOINT WITH AN ENCASED BOLT: NOTE THAT
BOLT HEAD WILL BE EXPOSED.

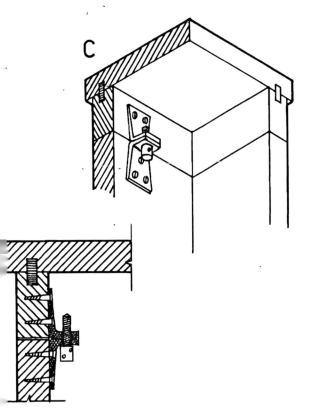

C

SIDE JOINT WITH EXPOSED BOLTING ARRANGEMENT:
THIS IS A SIMPLE METHOD FOR THE NOVICE.

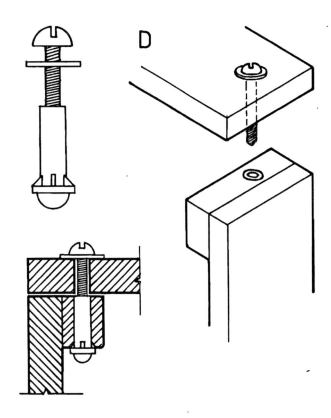

D

BOLT TO RAIL JOINT: RAIL SHOULD BE FIRMLY AT-
TACHED TO SIDE BEFORE BOLT IS INSTALLED.

27

MIDDLE FRAME JOINTS

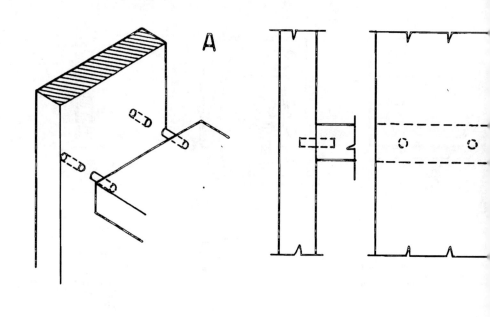

DOWEL JOINT: THIS IS AN EASY JOINT OFTEN USED BY THE AMATEUR CRAFTSMAN.

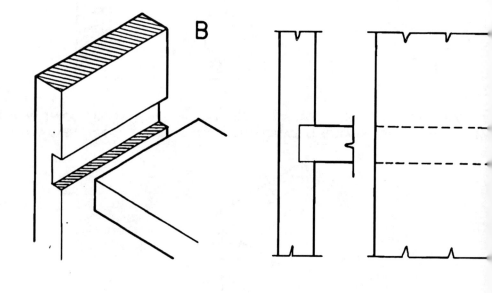

DADO JOINT: USED IN ORDINARY WORK, ESPECIALLY WHERE PRODUCT IS TO BE PAINTED.

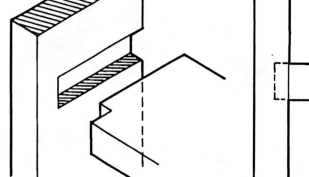

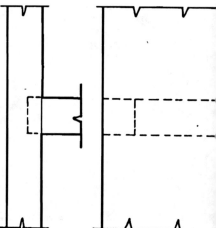

STOPPED DADO JOINT: EXCELLENT METHOD OF JOINING CERTAIN TYPES OF WOODWORK.

THROUGH AND STOPPED FEATHER
JOINT: WHEN PROPERLY GLUED,
THIS IS A GOOD JOINT.

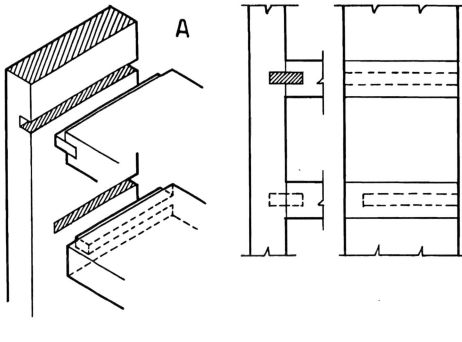

DOVETAIL SLIP JOINT: SIDES JOIN-
ED BY THIS METHOD CANNOT
PULL APART.

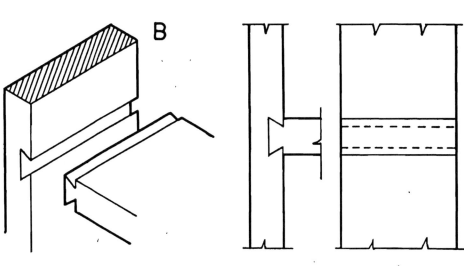

METAL CLAMP JOINT: THIS IS A
PATENTED CLAMP THAT IS EASY
TO INSTALL.

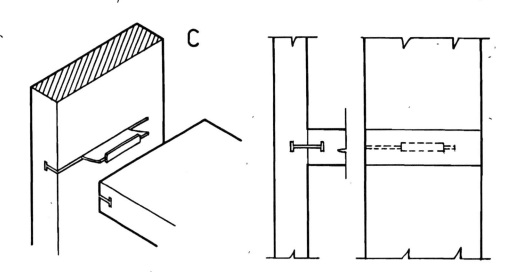

BACK PANEL JOINTS

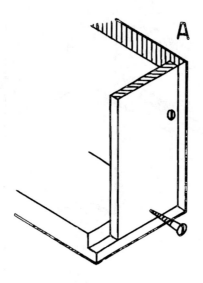
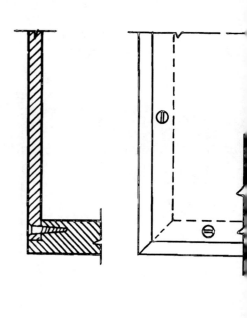

BACK IN RABBET JOINT: THIS IS A COMMON METHOD OF AT-TACHING A BACK PANEL BY MEANS OF NAILS OR SCREWS.

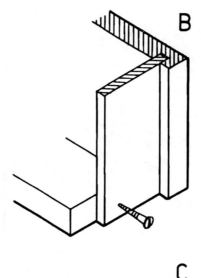
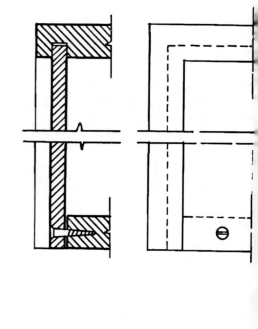

BACK IN GROOVE: NOTE THAT THE BOTTOM OF THE PANEL IS HELD IN PLACE WITH SCREWS.

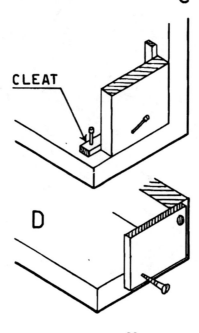

CLEAT

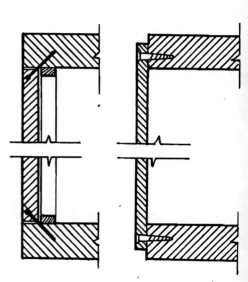

THESE TWO METHODS OF AT-TACHING THE BACK PANEL ARE IDEAL FOR AMATEUR CRAFTSMEN.

JOINING OF
THREE PIECES

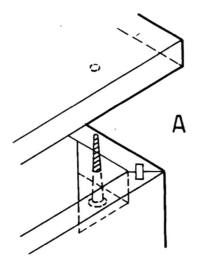

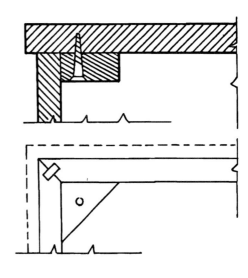

A

TOP ATTACHED WITH SCREWS FROM UNDER SIDE. BOLTS OR DOWELS MAY BE SUBSTITUTED FOR SCREWS.

TOP ATTACHED TO SIDES WITH DOWELS.

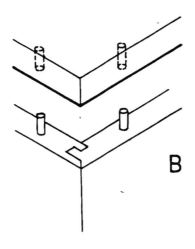

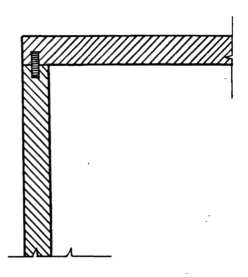

B

TOP RABBET JOINT: THIS MAKES A LOOSE JOINT IF PLATE GLASS OR MARBLE IS USED, AND A FIXED JOINT IF WOOD. IF GLASS IS USED, IT IS WELL TO COVER THE PLATFORM EDGE OF THE RABBET WITH FELT.

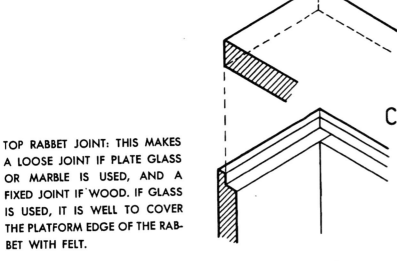

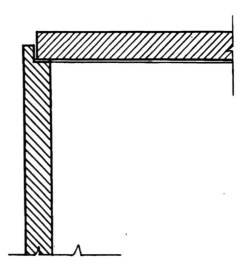

C

31

PLYWOOD, LUMBER CORE PLYWOOD, AND LAMINATED WOOD

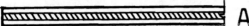

A

A — FORMATION OF A PANEL OF PLYWOOD WITH THREE-PLY VENEER.

B

B — FORMATION OF PLYWOOD WITH FIVE-PLY VENEER.

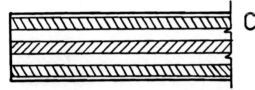

C

C — FORMATION OF PLYWOOD WITH SEVEN-PLY VENEER.

PLYWOOD IS PRODUCED BY PLACING 3-5-7 OR MORE LAYERS OF WOOD ONE ON TOP OF THE OTHER WITH GRAIN CROSSED. EACH LAYER IS GLUED TO THE PREVIOUS LAYER AND PUT UNDER HEAVY PRESSURE. THE FACE VENEER GENERALLY IS IN ONE CONTINUOUS SHEET STRIPPED OR PEELED FROM THE SURFACE OF A SINGLE LOG AFTER THE LOG HAS BEEN REDUCED TO UNIFORM DIAMETER.

LUMBER CORE PLYWOOD CONSISTS OF GLUED STRIPS OF SOLID HEARTWOOD COVERED ON EACH SIDE WITH A THIN PANEL OF PLYWOOD. THIS METHOD HAS DONE MUCH TO CHANGE FURNITURE CONSTRUCTION.

IN ADDITION TO PLYWOOD AND LUMBER CORE PLYWOOD WE HAVE TODAY THE POSSIBILITY OF PRODUCING DIFFERENT TYPES OF PANELS BY GLUING WITH SPECIAL GLUES ONE OR MORE LAYERS OF WOOD AND UNITING THEM WITH VARIOUS OTHER MATERIALS SUCH AS LIGHT METAL (page 107 D.E.; page 108 fig. A), AND PLASTIC MATERIALS, EACH HAVING ITS OWN PARTICULAR CHARACTERISTIC.

LAMINATED WOOD IS PRODUCED BY GLUING THIN SHEETS OF HARDWOOD WITH THE GRAIN RUNNING IN THE SAME DIRECTION. IT IS USED TO OBTAIN A SOLID CURVATURE IN THE WOOD (see page 46, fig. A).

GRAIN DIRECTION

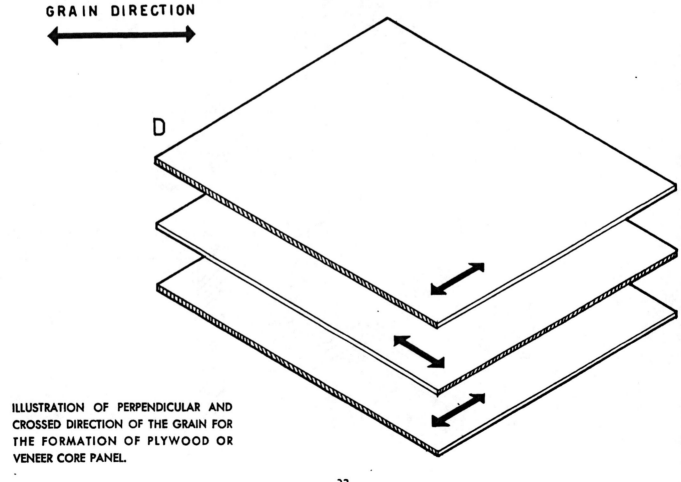

D

ILLUSTRATION OF PERPENDICULAR AND CROSSED DIRECTION OF THE GRAIN FOR THE FORMATION OF PLYWOOD OR VENEER CORE PANEL.

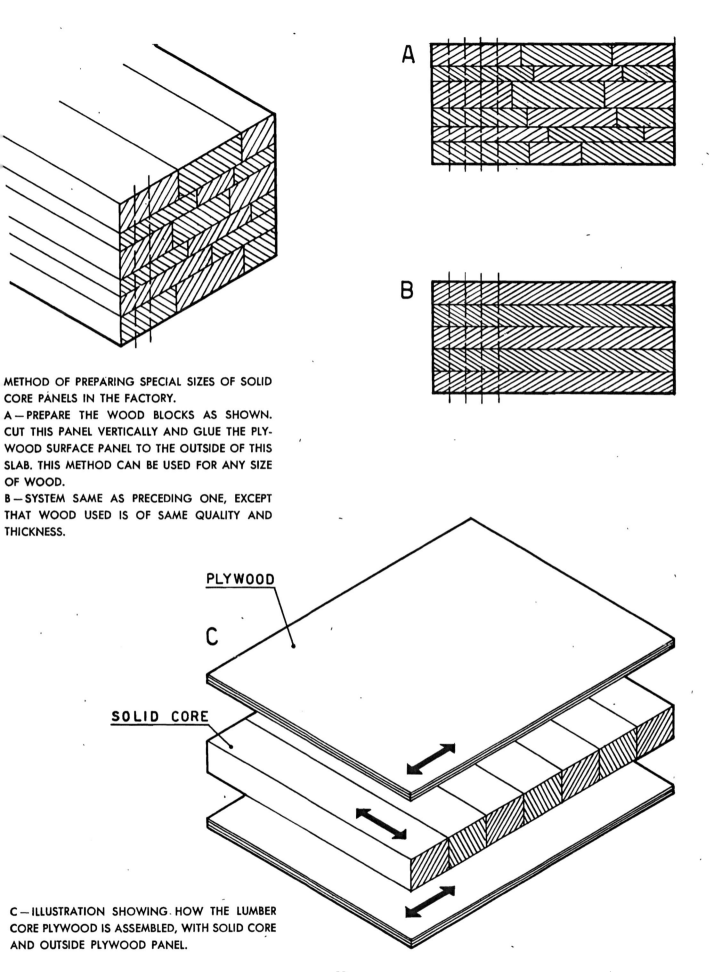

METHOD OF PREPARING SPECIAL SIZES OF SOLID CORE PANELS IN THE FACTORY.

A — PREPARE THE WOOD BLOCKS AS SHOWN. CUT THIS PANEL VERTICALLY AND GLUE THE PLYWOOD SURFACE PANEL TO THE OUTSIDE OF THIS SLAB. THIS METHOD CAN BE USED FOR ANY SIZE OF WOOD.

B — SYSTEM SAME AS PRECEDING ONE, EXCEPT THAT WOOD USED IS OF SAME QUALITY AND THICKNESS.

PLYWOOD

SOLID CORE

C

C — ILLUSTRATION SHOWING HOW THE LUMBER CORE PLYWOOD IS ASSEMBLED, WITH SOLID CORE AND OUTSIDE PLYWOOD PANEL.

THICK LUMBER CORE PLYWOOD. FOR BEST RE-
SULTS IT IS NECESSARY TO MAKE A CROSS
SAW KERF TO TAKE CARE OF ANY MOVEMENT
IN THE GRAIN.

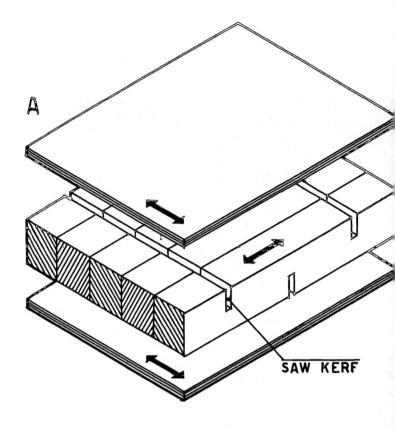

A

SAW KERF

CORRUGATED PANEL FORMED BY CELLULAR
CARDBOARD PLACED IN FRAME AND GLUED
BETWEEN TWO SHEETS OF PLYWOOD. THIS
TYPE OF CONSTRUCTION IS OFTEN USED IN
MAKING FLUSH PANEL DOORS.

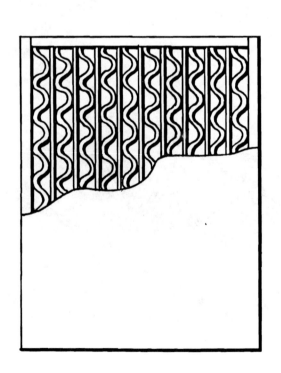

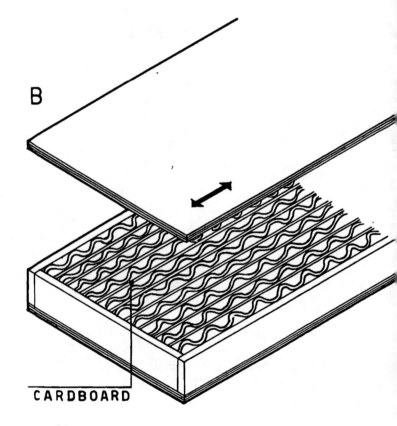

B

CARDBOARD

STANDARD THICKNESSES OF PLYWOOD AND LUMBER CORE PLYWOOD

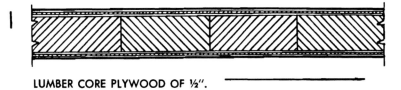

I

LUMBER CORE PLYWOOD OF ½".

A

/16" PLYWOOD FORMED BY THREE LAYERS OF WOOD.

B

/8" PLYWOOD FORMED BY THREE LAYERS.

C

/16" PLYWOOD FORMED BY THREE LAYERS.

D

¼" PLYWOOD FORMED BY THREE LAYERS.

E

⅜" PLWOOD FORMED BY THREE LAYERS.

F

/8" PLYWOOD FORMED BY FIVE LAYERS.

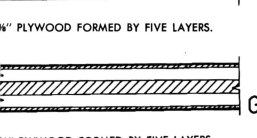

G

½" PLYWOOD FORMED BY FIVE LAYERS.

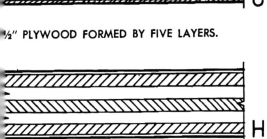

H

¾" PLYWOOD FORMED BY FIVE LAYERS.

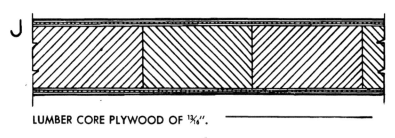

J

LUMBER CORE PLYWOOD OF 13/16".

SPECIAL PLYWOOD AND LUMBER CORE PLYWOOD

FOR SPECIAL WORK REQUIRING WOOD OF GREAT STRENGTH IT IS OFTEN ADVISABLE TO USE THIS METHOD OF FORMING PANELS OF PLYWOOD. LAYERS OF WOOD OF UNIFORM THICKNESS WITH THE GRAIN RUNNING IN CROSS DIRECTION WILL PROVIDE A STRONG BOARD.

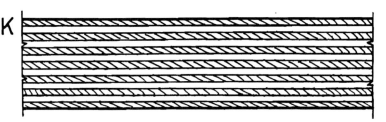

K

FORMATION OF SPECIAL PANEL OF PLYWOOD BY USE OF 13 LAYERS OF WOOD OF SAME THICKNESS PLACED ONE ON TOP OF THE OTHER WITH THE GRAINS RUNNING PERPENDICULAR.

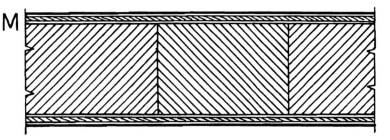

M

LUMBER CORE PLYWOOD WITH EXTRA THICKNESS. ITS FORMATION IS INDICATED ON PAGE 33, FIG. A-B.

PLYWOOD HOLLOW FRAME

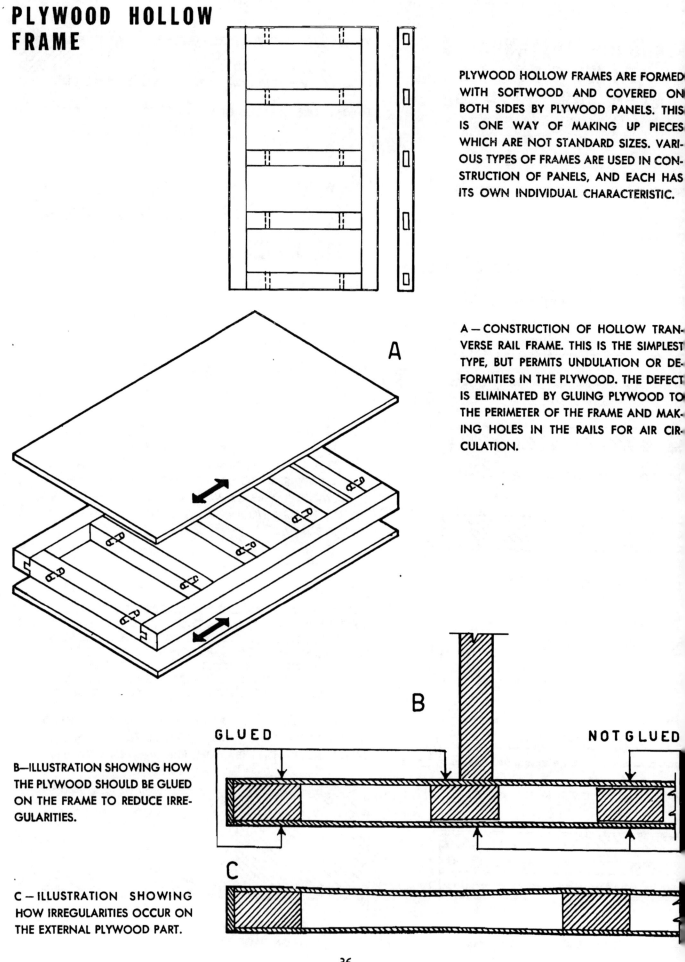

PLYWOOD HOLLOW FRAMES ARE FORMED WITH SOFTWOOD AND COVERED ON BOTH SIDES BY PLYWOOD PANELS. THIS IS ONE WAY OF MAKING UP PIECES WHICH ARE NOT STANDARD SIZES. VARIOUS TYPES OF FRAMES ARE USED IN CONSTRUCTION OF PANELS, AND EACH HAS ITS OWN INDIVIDUAL CHARACTERISTIC.

A — CONSTRUCTION OF HOLLOW TRANVERSE RAIL FRAME. THIS IS THE SIMPLEST TYPE, BUT PERMITS UNDULATION OR DEFORMITIES IN THE PLYWOOD. THE DEFECT IS ELIMINATED BY GLUING PLYWOOD TO THE PERIMETER OF THE FRAME AND MAKING HOLES IN THE RAILS FOR AIR CIRCULATION.

A

B

GLUED   NOT GLUED

B—ILLUSTRATION SHOWING HOW THE PLYWOOD SHOULD BE GLUED ON THE FRAME TO REDUCE IRREGULARITIES.

C

C — ILLUSTRATION SHOWING HOW IRREGULARITIES OCCUR ON THE EXTERNAL PLYWOOD PART.

36

CROSS RAIL FRAME. WITH THIS METHOD YOU CAN OBTAIN GOOD CONSTRUCTION OF THE FRAME WITH LIMITED DEFORMITIES IN THE PLYWOOD.

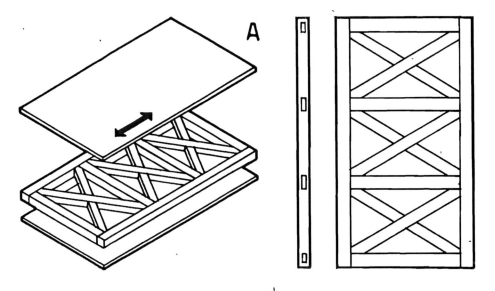

A

DIAGONAL RAIL FRAME USED IN GOOD CONSTRUCTION.

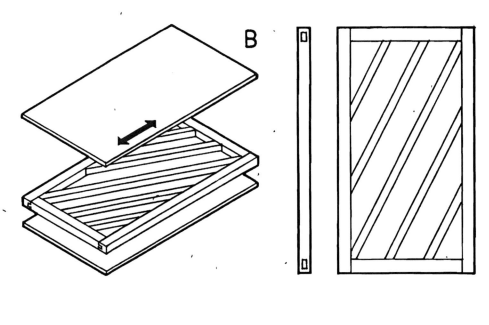

B

THE LOOSE CELLULAR FRAME IS THE TYPE BEST SUITED TO PLYWOOD.

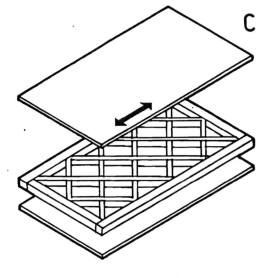
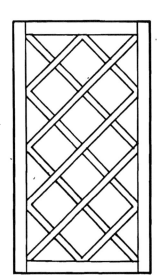

C

37

VENEER

VENEER IS FORMED BY STRIPPING A CONTINUOUS SHEET FROM THE LOG. THIS SHEET IS APPLIED WITH GLUE TO OTHER WOODS TO CREATE A RICH SURFACE EFFECT. THE APPLICATION IS MADE DURING THE PROCESS OF CONSTRUCTION.

VENEER MUST BE APPLIED ACROSS THE GRAIN.

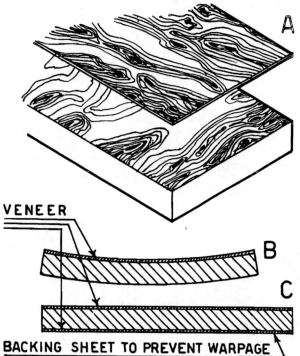

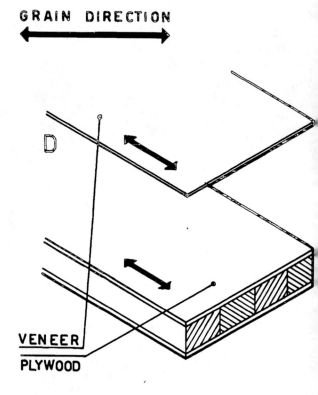

APPLYING VENEER TO OTHER PIECES SO THAT THE GRAINS RUN PARALLEL MAY CAUSE SMALL CRACKS IN TIME.

BACKING SHEET TO PREVENT WARPAGE

IF VENEER IS APPLIED TO ONE SIDE OF THE WOOD IT WILL BEND THE WOOD. TO OBTAIN A STRAIGHT PANEL APPLY VENEER TO BOTH SIDES.

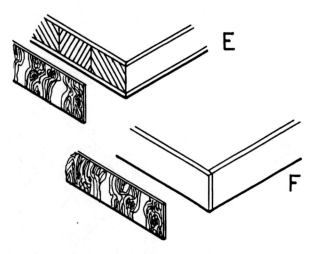

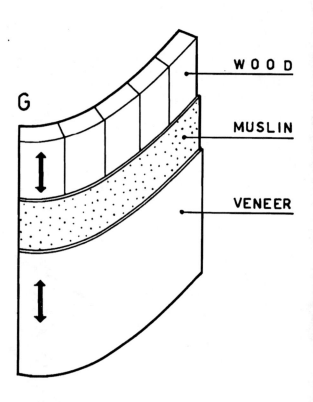

VENEER APPLIED TO BORDERS OF PLYWOOD PANELS WILL TEND TO SHOW JOINT MARKS. TO OBTAIN THE BEST WORK IT IS ADVISABLE TO BORDER THE PANEL WITH HARDWOOD.

CURVED PANEL MADE WITH VENEER-COVERED SEGMENT. TO AVOID MARKS IT IS BEST TO PLACE MUSLIN BETWEEN THE VENEER AND THE WOOD.

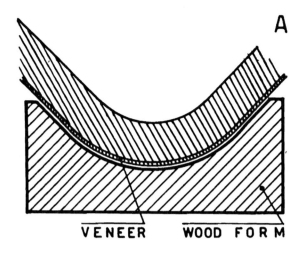

A

VENEER   WOOD FORM

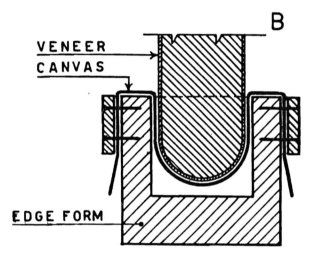

B

VENEER
CANVAS

EDGE FORM

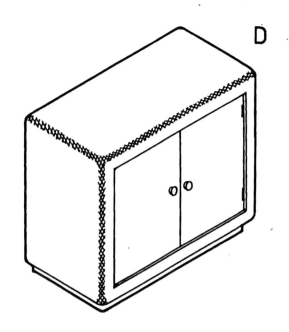

D

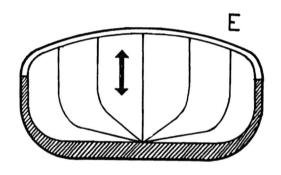

E

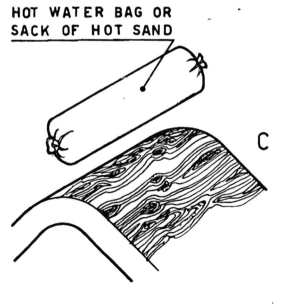

HOT WATER BAG OR
SACK OF HOT SAND

C

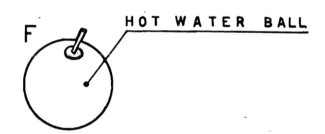

F

HOT WATER BALL

G

SMALL SACK OF HOT SAND

THREE DIFFERENT SYSTEMS TO KEEP VENEER BENT UNTIL THE GLUE HAS DRIED. SHOULD THE VENEER BE APPLIED TO SPECIFIC SURFACES, EITHER CONCAVE OR CONVEX, IT IS BEST TO USE A HOT WATER BALL, OR A SMALL SACK OF HOT SAND TO MAKE THE VENEER ADHERE TIGHTLY TO THE WOOD.

GRAIN DIRECTION IN CURVED PIECES

VARIOUS TYPES OF CURVES APPEAR IN FURNITURE DE-
SIGN. ONE FINDS BOTH INTERNAL AND EXTERNAL
ANGLES, AND COMPLETE CURVATURE IN CYLINDRICAL
SHAPES IS OBTAINED BY PRESSING MORE THAN ONE
LAYER OF WOOD TOGETHER.

THERE ARE MANY WAYS OF CONSTRUCTING THESE
CURVES. I SHALL EXPLAIN THE PROPERTIES OF THE
DIFFERENT CURVES, DESCRIBE SEVERAL WAYS TO BUILD
THEM, AND RECOMMEND THE BEST ONES TO USE IN
SPECIFIC TYPES OF WORK.

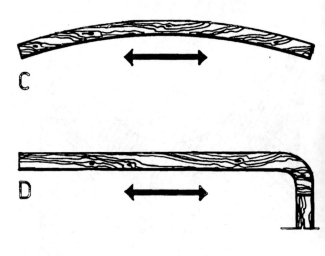

GRAIN DIRECTION

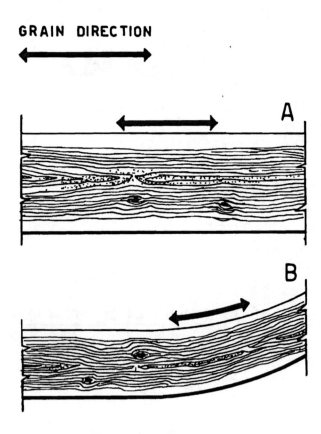

IN "A" THE NATURAL DIRECTION OF THE GRAIN IS
STRAIGHT, WHILE THE GRAIN IN "B" IS NATURALLY
CURVED.

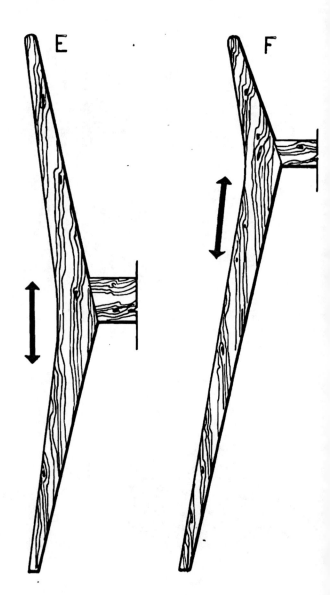

FOUR DIFFERENT EXAMPLES OF GRAIN DIRECTION IN
CURVED PIECES. NOTE THAT THE FUNDAMENTAL BASE
OF THE GRAIN RUNS IN THE DIRECTION IT MUST SUP-
PORT. THIS IS DONE TO KEEP THE WOOD FROM
CRACKING.

FEATHER JOINT. THIS IS A COM-
MON METHOD OF JOINING
CURVED PIECES.

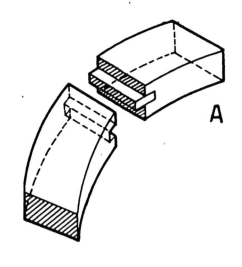 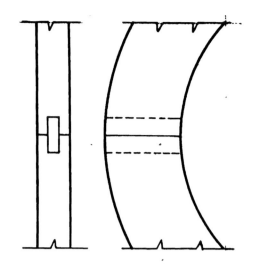

A

DOWEL JOINT. EASILY MADE AND
USED BY THE AMATEUR CRAFTS-
MAN.

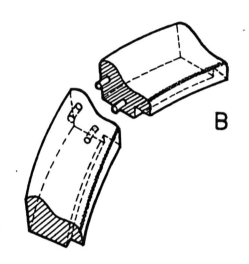 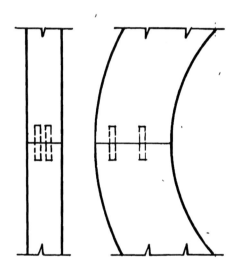

B

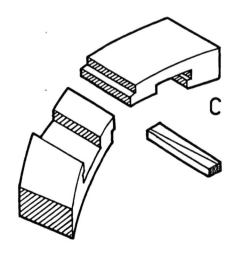 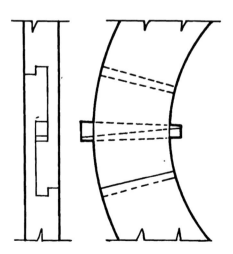

C

SCARF JOINT WITH WEDGES.
USED IN CARPENTRY WORK.

FRAME WITH ROUND CURVE.
COMMON TYPE AND USED EX-
TENSIVELY.

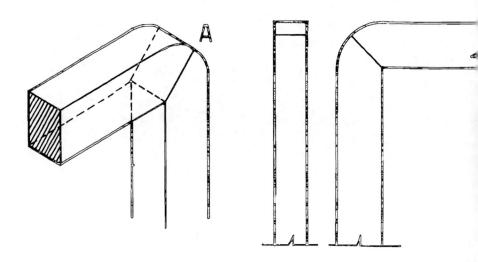

ROUND CORNER FRAME REIN-
FORCED WITH BLOCK. USED
WHEN CURVE HAS WEAKENED
THE JOINT OF THE TWO RAILS.

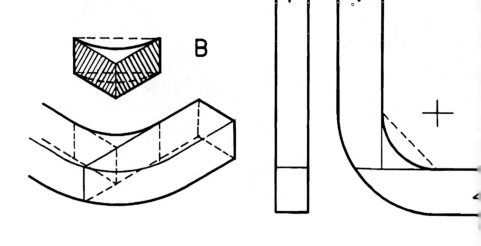

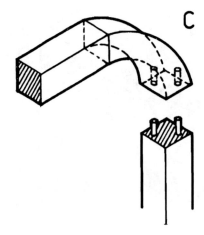
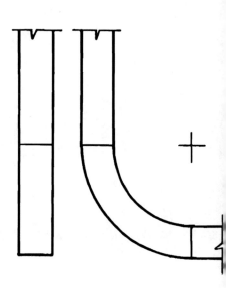

ROUND CORNER WITH DOWEL.
USED WHEN THERE IS A LARGE
CURVE.

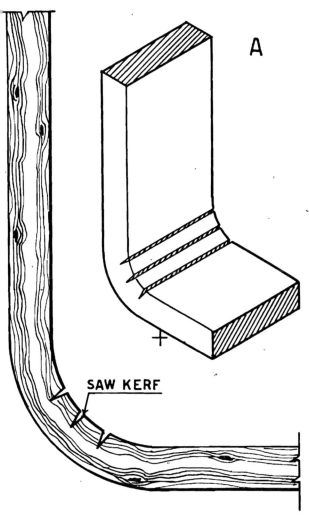

A

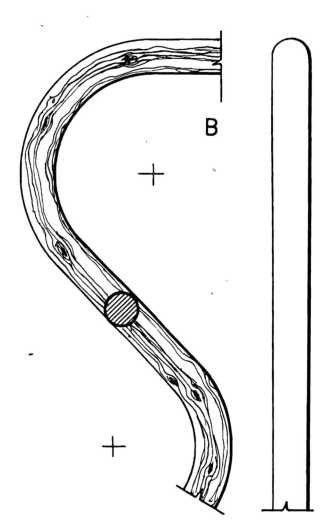

B

SAW KERF

A — CURVE IN A NORMAL TRANSVERSE TO ACHIEVE DESIRED RESULTS A SERIES OF SAW KERFS SHOULD BE MADE IN THE WOOD.

B — CURVE OF A WOOD DOWEL. ALMOST ANY TYPE OF A CURVE CAN BE MADE WITH A DOWEL.

C — CURVE OF A CLOSED BAND WITH A THIN BATTEN.

C

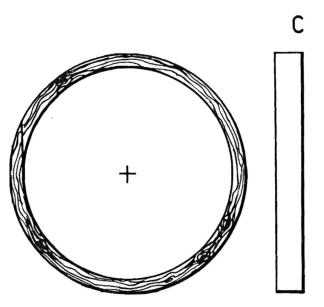

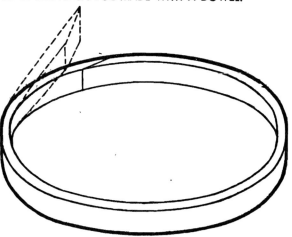

STEAM BENDING. WOOD WHICH IS CURVED WITH STEAM GIVES EXCELLENT RESULTS IN SOME TYPES OF WOOD SUCH AS THE HARD WOODS, OAK, ASH, AND WALNUT. IT IS OF ABSOLUTELY NO USE IN OTHER TYPES.

THE EXAMPLES SHOWN PRESENT THE BASIC TYPES OF CURVES WHICH MAY BE CONSTRUCTED BY THIS METHOD.

GRAIN BANDING ON A PLY-
WOOD BOARD. THIS IS USED IN
STANDARD PRODUCTION.

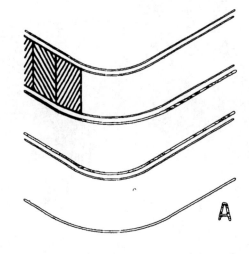
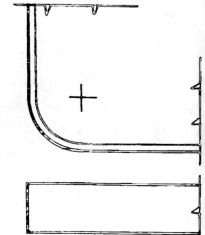

A

ROUND CORNER EDGE AS AP-
PLIED IN GOOD TYPES OF CON-
STRUCTION.

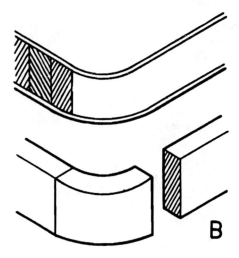
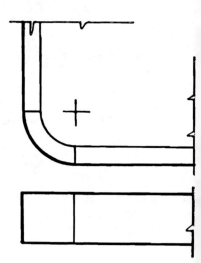

B

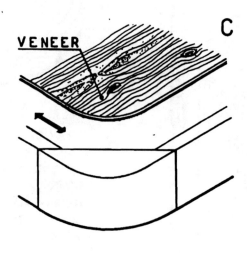

C

VENEER

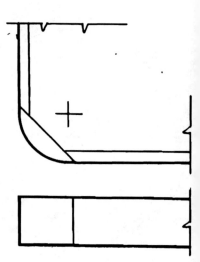

CORNER BLOCK, USED WHEN THE
PANEL IS COVERED WITH VENEER. —

44

JOINING TWO FRAMES WITH
CURVED CORNER BLOCK. THIS
TYPE OF CONSTRUCTION IS USED
IN SMALL CURVED PIECES.

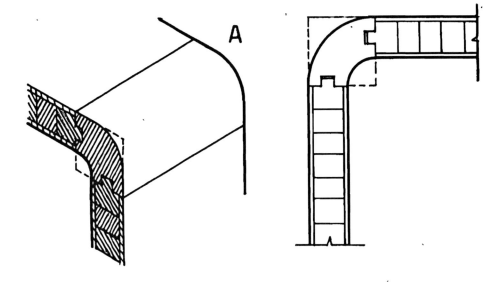

A

VENEER
MUSLIN

FRAME JOINT USING CURVED
SEGMENT. THIS METHOD GIVES
MAXIMUM STABILITY TO A CURVE.

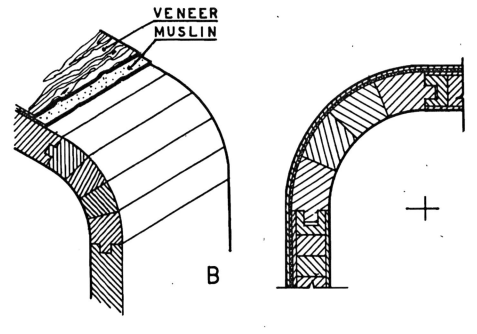

B

C

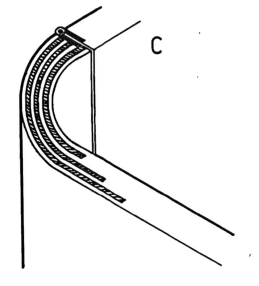
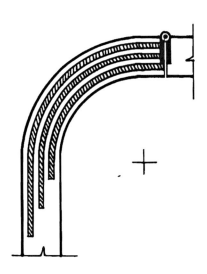

LAMINATED CURVE IN THE COR-
NER FRAME. THIS MAKES A GOOD
STRONG CURVE. IT IS OFTEN
USED IN DOOR CONSTRUCTION.

45

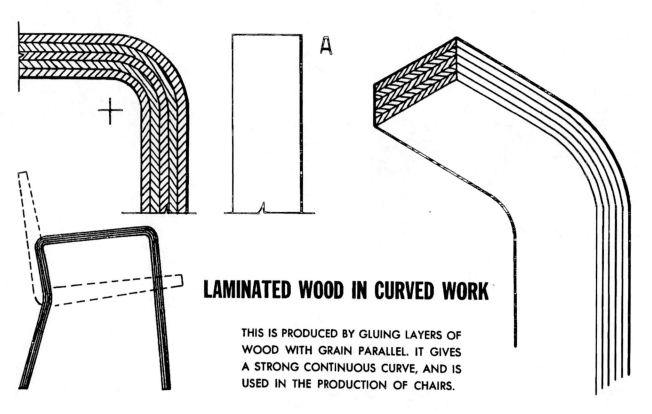

LAMINATED WOOD IN CURVED WORK

THIS IS PRODUCED BY GLUING LAYERS OF
WOOD WITH GRAIN PARALLEL. IT GIVES
A STRONG CONTINUOUS CURVE, AND IS
USED IN THE PRODUCTION OF CHAIRS.

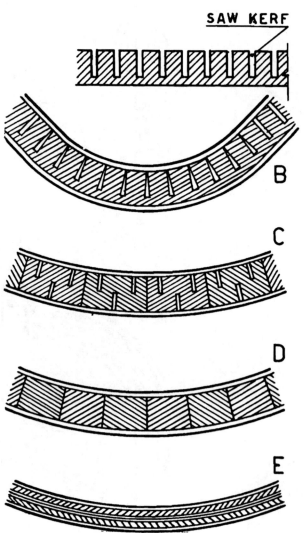

SAW KERF

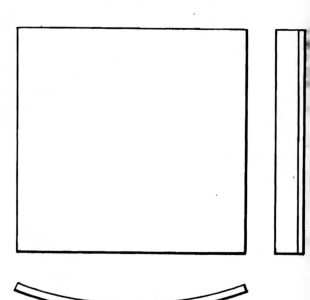

B — LUMBER CORE PLYWOOD: SAW KERFING SHOULD
BE DONE ON ONE SIDE OF THE SOLID CORE, THEN
GLUED INTO THE FRAME WITH TWO PANELS OF PLY-
WOOD ON EACH SIDE. THIS MAKES A GOOD PANEL.
C — D — HERE ARE TWO OTHER METHODS.

E — TWO PLYWOOD PANELS ARE GLUED TOGETHER
IN A FORM TO OBTAIN ONE PANEL WITH DESIRED
CURVATURE.

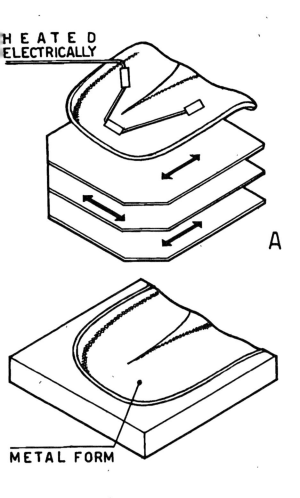

A

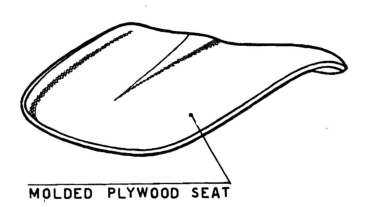

MOLDED PLYWOOD SEAT

METAL FORM

MOLDED PLYWOOD

LIGHT MOLDED PLYWOOD IS OBTAINED
BY GLUING LAYERS OF WOOD INTO
FORMS OF METAL (MALE AND FEMALE).
THE MOLD IS PRESSED TOGETHER WITH
CLAMPS. THIS METHOD IS IN WIDE USE
IN THE PRODUCTION OF CHAIR SEATS
AND BACKS.

B

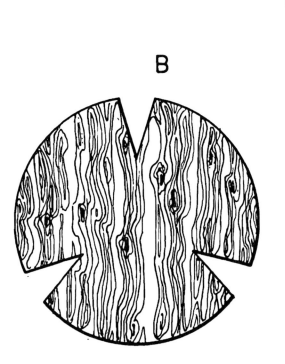

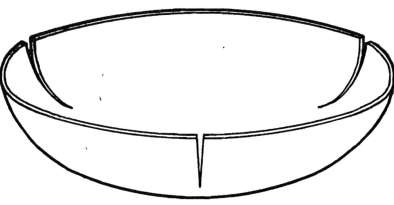

HEAVY MOLDED PLYWOOD. THE WOOD
IS DIFFICULT TO MOLD IN A FORM. ITS
STRENGTH MAKES IT VERY DIFFICULT TO
SHAPE IN OTHER THAN NORMAL CURVES.
IF ONE DESIRES TO MAKE OTHER CURVES
IT IS NECESSARY TO CUT OR REMOVE
SECTORS OF THE WOOD SO THAT THE
CURVING WILL FILL IN THE OPEN SEC-
TORS. WITH THIS METHOD YOU CAN
MAKE LARGE CURVED SHAPES SUITABLE
FOR CHAIRS, ARMCHAIRS, ETC.

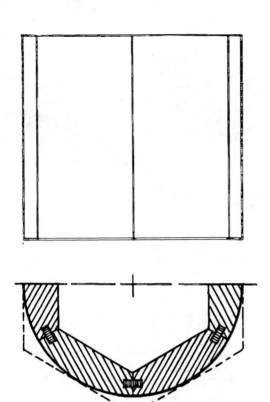

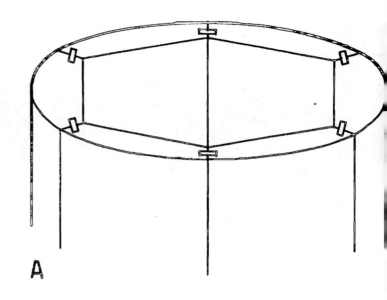

A

CYLINDER WITH FEATHER.

B

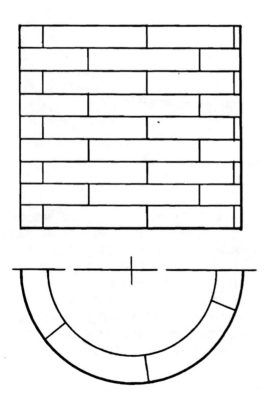

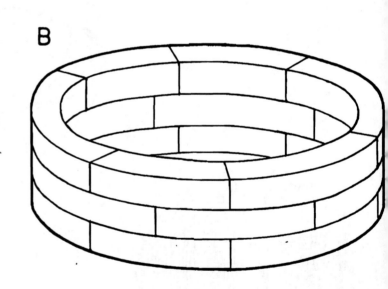

CYLINDER WITH LAP BUTT JOINT.
A STRONG TYPE OF JOINT EX-
CEPT THAT THE GRAIN RUNNING
PARALLEL TO THE LENGTH HAS A
TENDENCY TO SHRINK.

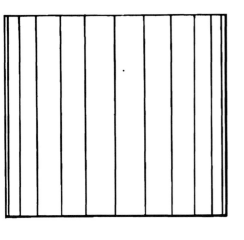

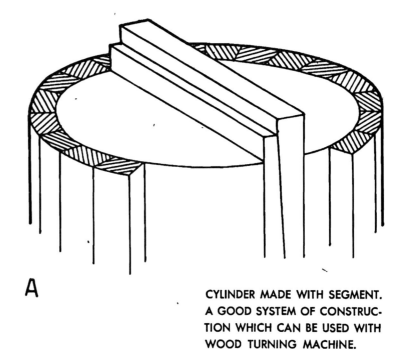

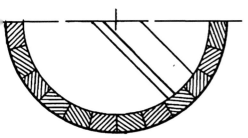

A

CYLINDER MADE WITH SEGMENT.
A GOOD SYSTEM OF CONSTRUC-
TION WHICH CAN BE USED WITH
WOOD TURNING MACHINE.

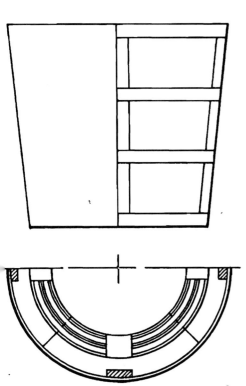

B

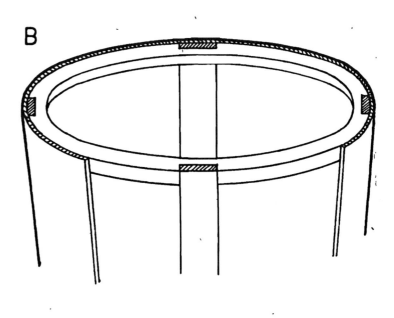

CONE WITH EXTERIOR PLYWOOD,
IF USED IN CABINET WORK, AND
WITH CARDBOARD IF USED IN
UPHOLSTERY WORK.

EDGE TREATMENT

IN ORDER TO KEEP THE LAMINATES IN PLYWOOD OR EDGE OF A LUMBER CORE PANEL FROM VIEW THE LAYER SURFACES MUST BE COVERED WITH HARDWOOD EDGES. THE METHODS USED ARE ILLUSTRATED AS FOLLOWS:

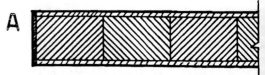

A

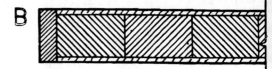

B

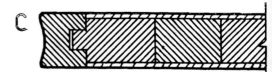

C

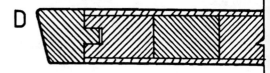

D

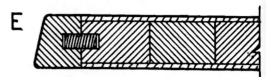

E

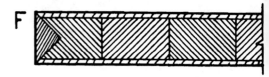

F

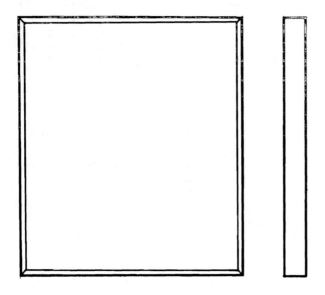

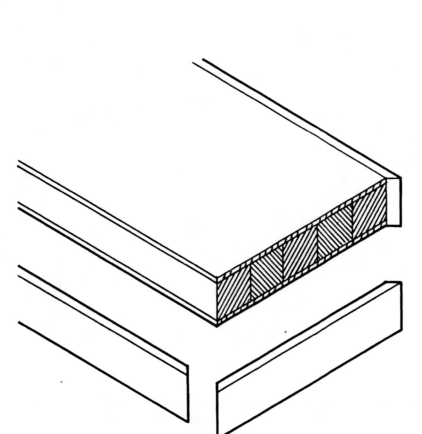

A — VENEER BANDING USED IN STANDARD WORK.

B — WITH SOLID EDGE.

C — TONGUE, FRAME, AND GROOVE EDGE.

D — TONGUE EDGE AND GROOVE FRAME.

E — WITH FEATHER.

F — WITH MITER JOINT USED IN FINE WORK.

FIXED FABRIC ON BOARD

THERE ARE VARIOUS TECHNIQUES WHEREBY THE FABRIC MAY BE ATTACHED TO A PANEL.

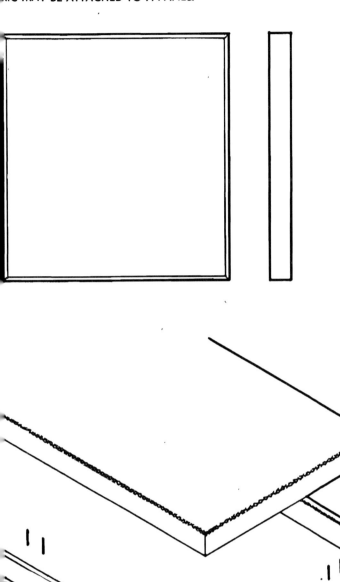

SOLID EDGE

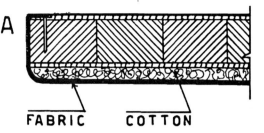

A

FABRIC   COTTON

B

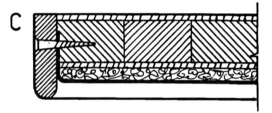

C

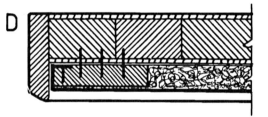

D

A — FABRIC APPLIED IN THE BACK WITH TACKS.

B — WITH STRIP IN BACK.

C — WITH THE SOLID BOARD EDGE.

D — SOLID EDGE IN THE BOARD OF AN INDEPENDENT PANEL FRONT. EACH OF THESE TYPES GIVES EXCELLENT RESULTS.

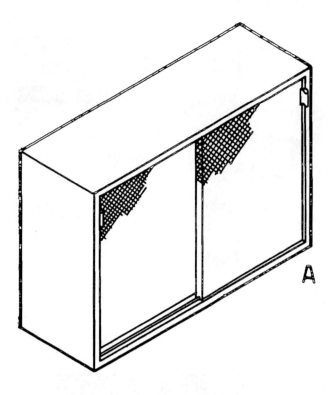

A — PANDANUS APPLICATION IN A SLIDING DOOR
WITH FEATHER EDGE.

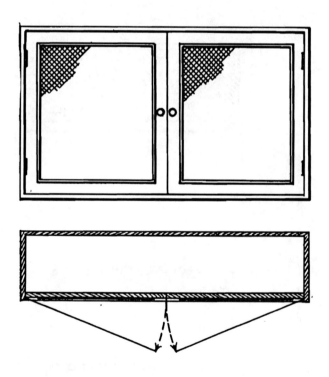

B — PANDANUS APPLICATION ON THE FRONT DOORS.
C, D — TWO DIFFERENT APPLICATIONS OF PANDANUS
PANEL ON THE FRAME.

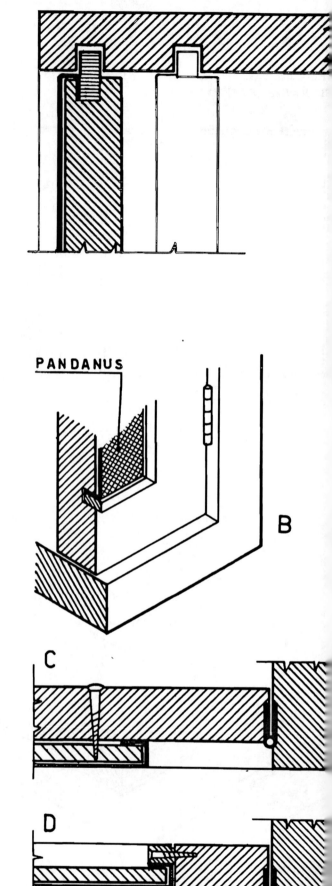

PANDANUS

B

C

D

DOOR STOPS

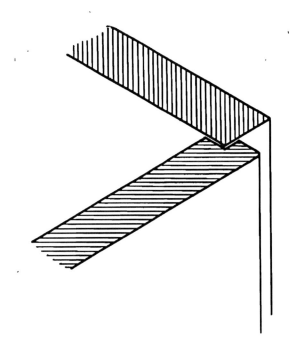

THE BASIC USES OF THE SINGLE OR DOUBLE DOOR STOPS ARE MAINLY TO SEAL THE FURNITURE PIECE AND TO PROTECT ITS CONTENTS FROM DUST AND OTHER DETRIMENTAL OBJECTS. THEY ALSO HELP TO AVOID ANY SHRINKING WHICH WOULD TAKE PLACE IN THE WOOD. IN MASS PRODUCTION THESE PRINCIPLES ARE NOT FOLLOWED. IN ORDER TO EXPEDITE THE WORK A STRAIGHT BOARD IS USUALLY USED.

THE TYPES PRESENTED GIVE YOU VARIOUS SOLUTIONS ... STRAIGHT BOARD, RABBET, TONGUE AND GROOVE. THIS LAST ONE IS USED WHEN DOORS ARE UPRIGHT WITH SIMULTANEOUS OPENING.

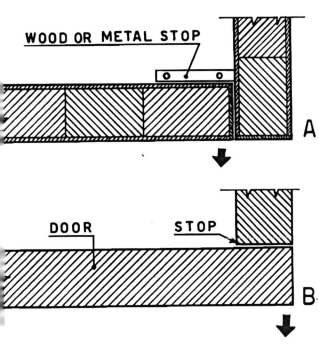

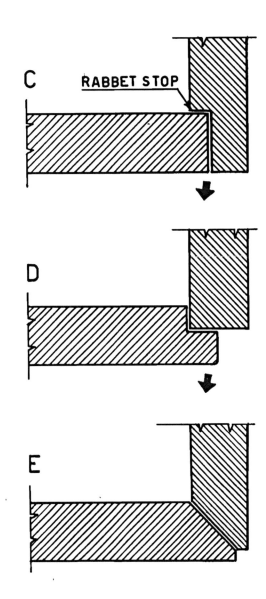

A — STRAIGHT BOARD DOOR WITH WOOD OR METAL STOPS. NORMAL METHOD USED IN STANDARD PRODUCTION.

B — STRAIGHT STOP BOARD. USED FOR SPECIAL SOLUTION.

C — RABBET STOP ON SIDE.

D — RABBET STOP ON DOOR. VERY GOOD METHOD.

E — MITER STOP USED IN SPECIAL WORK.

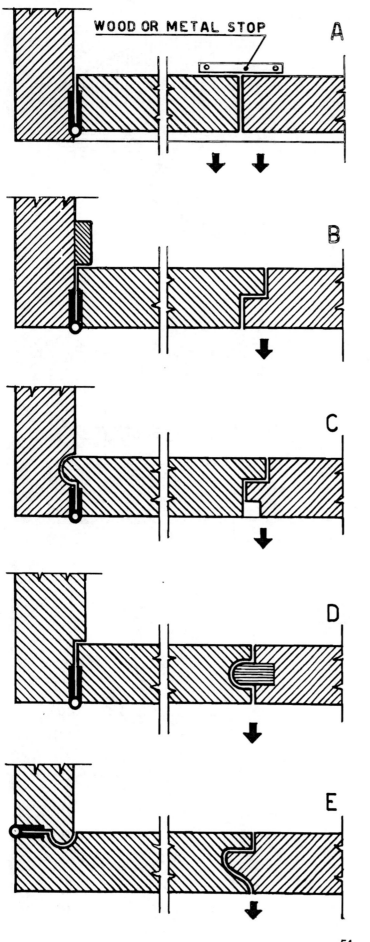

WOOD OR METAL STOP

A

B

C

D

E

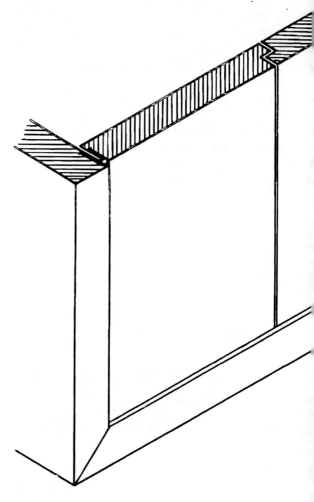

A — STRAIGHT BOARD WITH WOOD OF
METAL STOP AS USED IN MASS PRO-
DUCTION.

B — WITH RABBET STOP ON THE BOARD

C — RABBET STOP SAME AS PRECEDING
THE SCORE IN THE FRONT HIDES ES-
SENTIAL MOVEMENTS OR SHRINKING OF
DOORS.

D — WITH TONGUE AND GROOVE. THIS
METHOD ALLOWS SIMULTANEOUS OPEN-
ING OF THE DOORS.

E — VARIATION OF THE PRECEDING TYPE

54

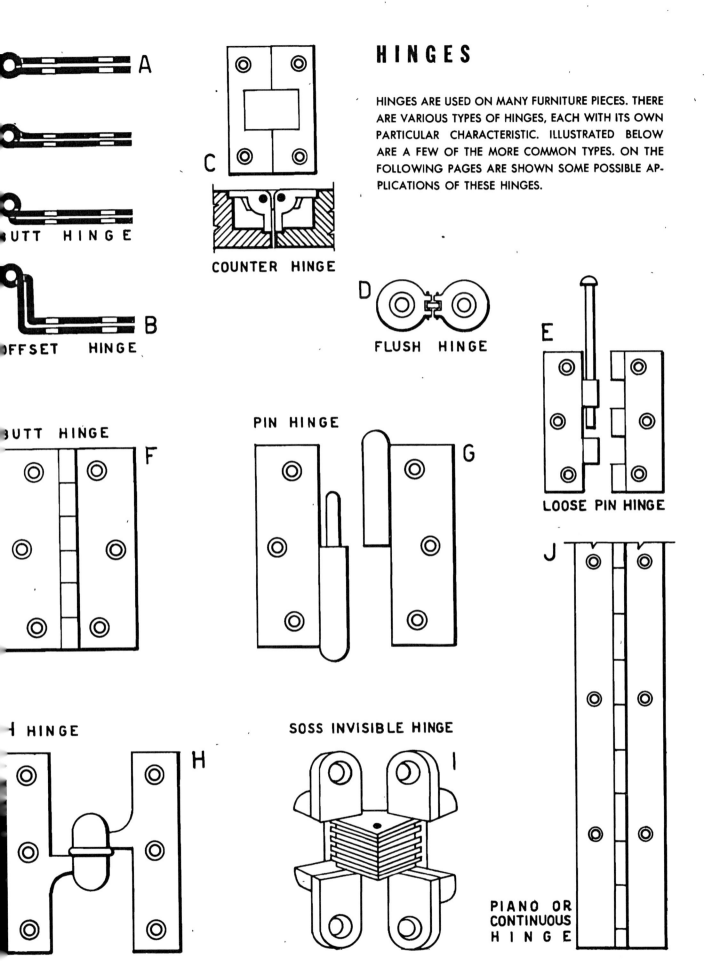

A

B

ᴮUTT HINGE

ᴼFFSET HINGE

C

COUNTER HINGE

HINGES

HINGES ARE USED ON MANY FURNITURE PIECES. THERE ARE VARIOUS TYPES OF HINGES, EACH WITH ITS OWN PARTICULAR CHARACTERISTIC. ILLUSTRATED BELOW ARE A FEW OF THE MORE COMMON TYPES. ON THE FOLLOWING PAGES ARE SHOWN SOME POSSIBLE APPLICATIONS OF THESE HINGES.

D

FLUSH HINGE

E

LOOSE PIN HINGE

ᴮUTT HINGE

F

PIN HINGE

G

J

ᴴ HINGE

H

SOSS INVISIBLE HINGE

I

PIANO OR CONTINUOUS HINGE

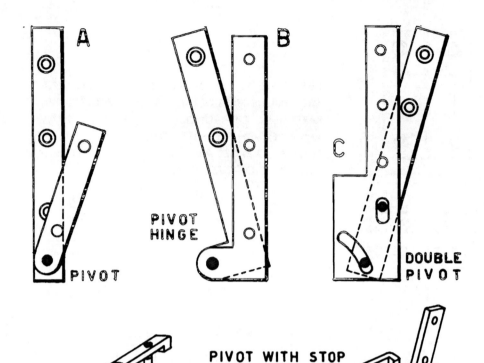

A

B

C

PIVOT HINGE

DOUBLE PIVOT

PIVOT

PIVOT HINGES

LIKE THE HINGE, THE PIVOT IS A
NECESSARY ACCESSORY IN TH
CONSTRUCTION OF FURNITUR
THE ILLUSTRATIONS SHOW TH
PRINCIPAL TYPES, WITH METHOD
OF APPLICATION.

PIVOT WITH STOP

D

E

SUPPORTS

ALTHOUGH SUPPORTS ARE NO
SO PRACTICAL AS THE HINGE
OR PIVOT, THEY PLAY AN IMPORT
ANT PART IN THE CONSTRUCTIO
OF THE FURNITURE PIECES. HER
ARE VARIOUS TYPES WITH THE
METHODS OF APPLICATION.

SUPPORTS

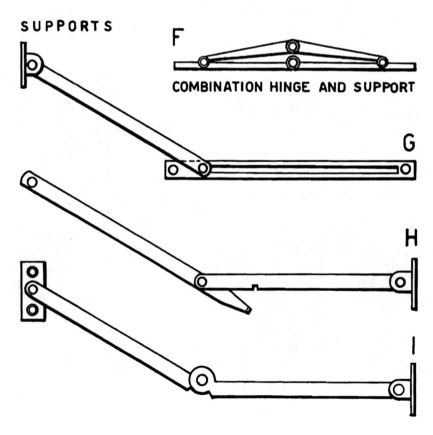

F

COMBINATION HINGE AND SUPPORT

G

H

I

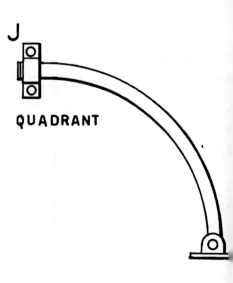

J

QUADRANT

56

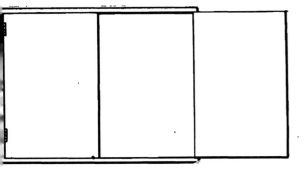

APPLICATION OF DOORS TO FURNITURE

THE APPLICATION OF NORMAL DOORS TO FURNITURE PIECES MAY BE DONE BY VARIOUS METHODS ACCORDING TO THE TYPE OF HINGE USED. SYSTEMS OF APPLICATION MAY VARY. GENERALLY THESE HINGES ARE APPLIED BY MEANS OF SCREWS.
PIANO HINGES MAY ALSO BE USED.

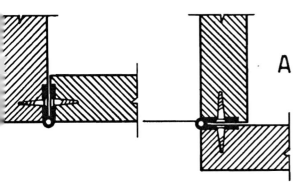

A

UTT HINGES ARE USED IN MASS PRODUCTION.

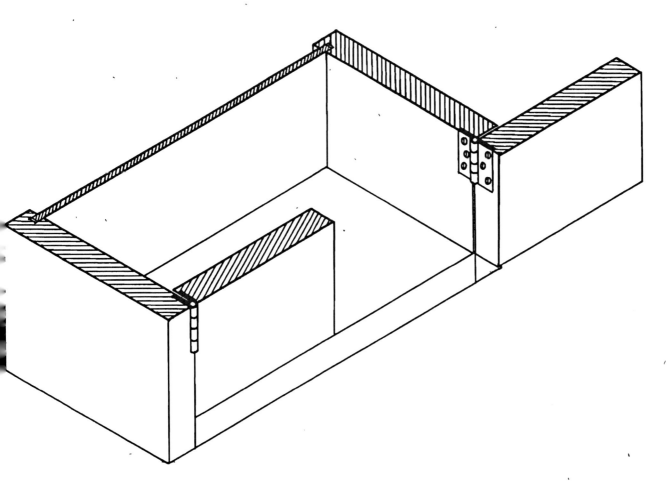

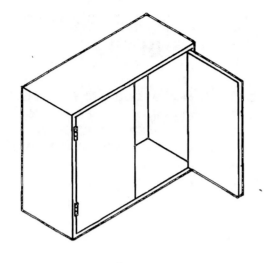

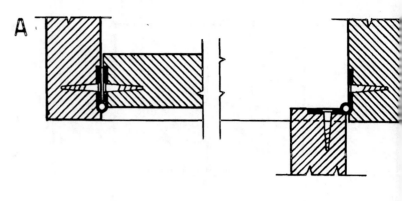

A

RECESS DOORS WITH BUTT HINGES. NOTE THAT SIDE PANEL ACTS AS DOOR STOP.

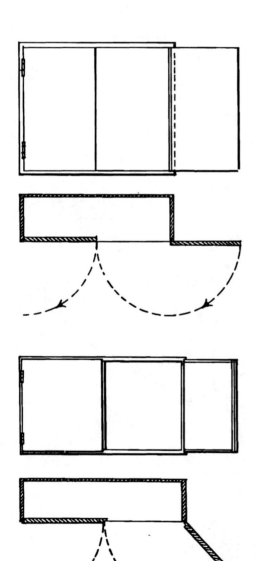

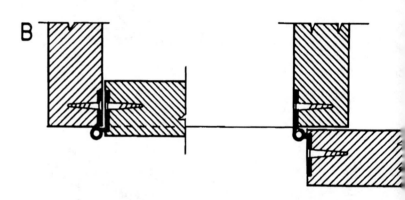

B

EXTERNAL DOORS WITH BUTT HINGES. DOORS USING THIS TYPE OF HINGE OPEN ALL THE WAY.

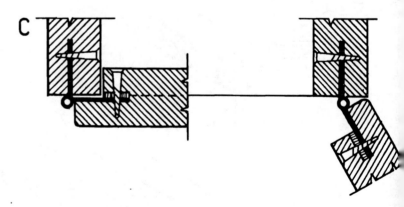

C

RABBET DOORS WITH BUTT HINGES. ALL THESE METHODS ARE USED IN GOOD WORK.

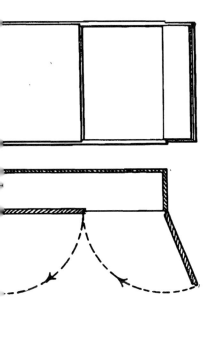

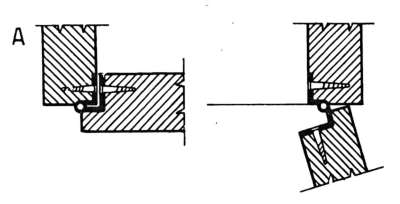

A

RABBET DOORS WITH OFFSET HINGES.

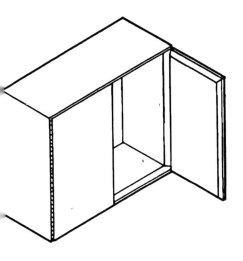

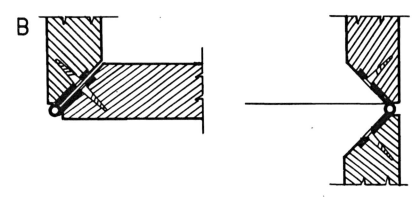

B

MITER DOORS WITH BUTT HINGES USED FOR SPECIAL WORK.

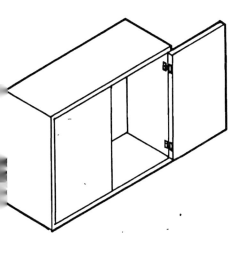

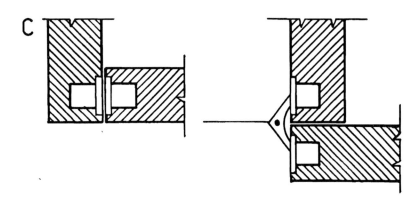

C

DOOR APPLICATION WITH SOSS INVISIBLE HINGES USED IN FINE FURNITURE.

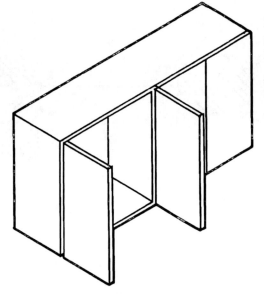

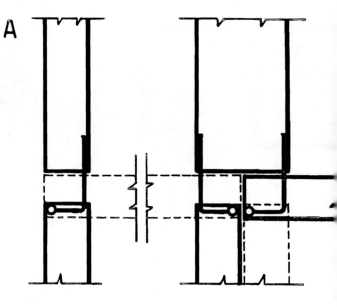

METAL KITCHEN CABINET DOORS OFTEN USE THIS TYPE OF SPECIAL HINGE, WHICH IS BOLTED OR WELDED TO THE SIDE PANEL.

OPEN

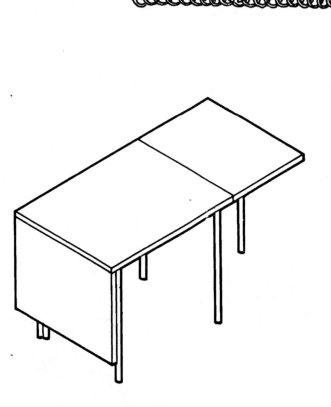

CLOSED

SLIDING

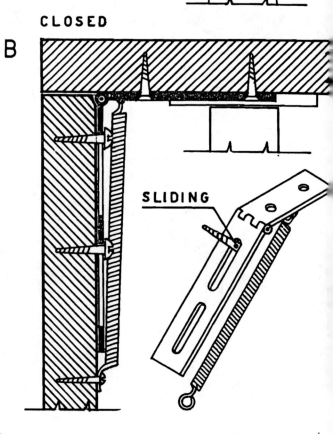

THIS LOOSE SPRING HINGE IS OFTEN USED IN EXTENSION TABLES AND DESKS. IT IS FAIRLY EASY TO ATTACH.

A

B

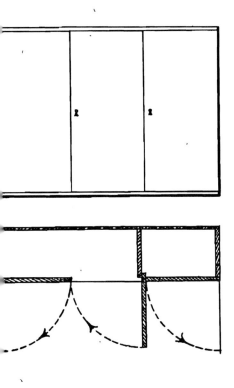

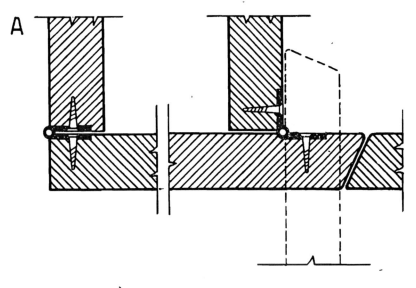

A CABINET WITH THREE DOORS PRESENTS SPECIAL PROBLEMS. HERE IS ONE SOLUTION.

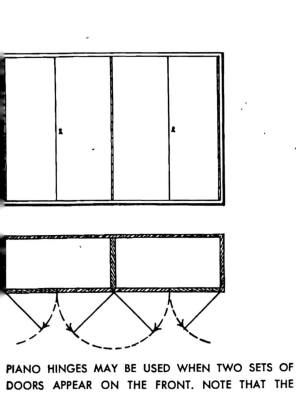

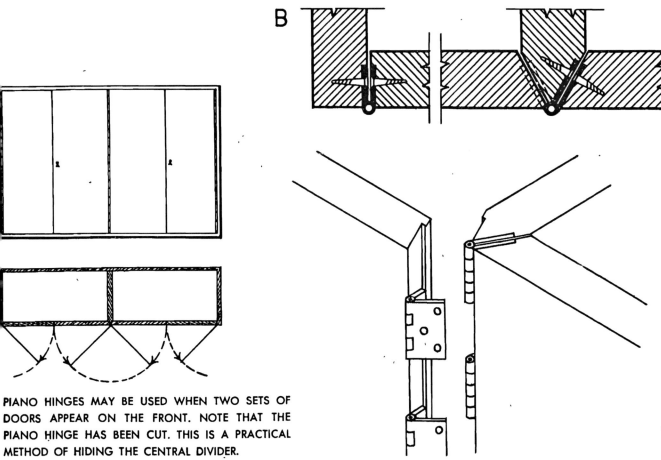

PIANO HINGES MAY BE USED WHEN TWO SETS OF DOORS APPEAR ON THE FRONT. NOTE THAT THE PIANO HINGE HAS BEEN CUT. THIS IS A PRACTICAL METHOD OF HIDING THE CENTRAL DIVIDER.

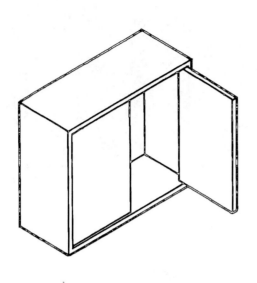

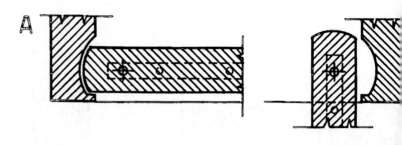

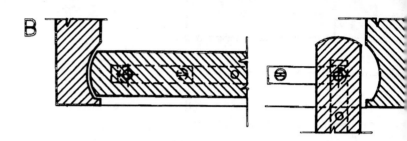

THESE DOORS USE INTERNAL PIVOTS AT THE TOP AND BOTTOM. NOTE THAT "B" USES A STOP PIVOT. (SEE PAGE 56, FIG. D).

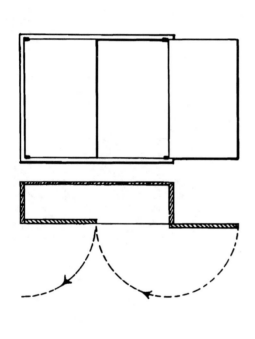

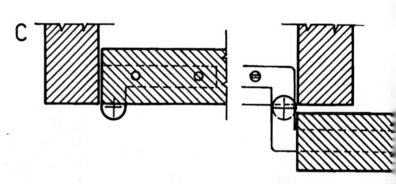

THIS SET OF DOORS USES AN EDGE OR EXTERNAL TYPE OF PIVOT HINGE.

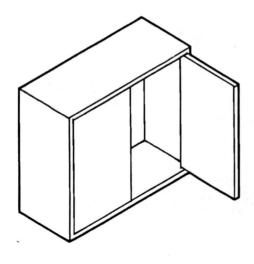

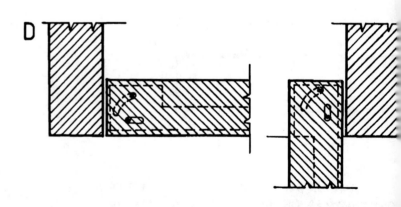

A DOUBLE PIVOT HINGE HAS BEEN USED ON THESE DOORS. NOTE HOW THE SIDE PANEL ACTS AS THE DOOR STOP (SEE PAGE 56.

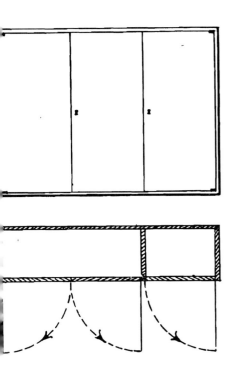

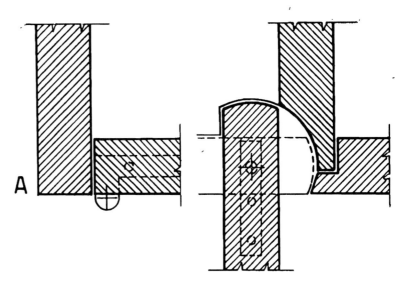

THIS THREE-DOOR PROBLEM HAS BEEN SOLVED BY USING AN EXTERNAL PIVOT HINGE ON TWO DOORS AND AN INTERNAL ONE ON THE MIDDLE PANEL.

A COMMON PIVOT HINGE ON A FOUR-DOOR CABINET ALLOWS HIDING OF THE CENTER DIVIDER.

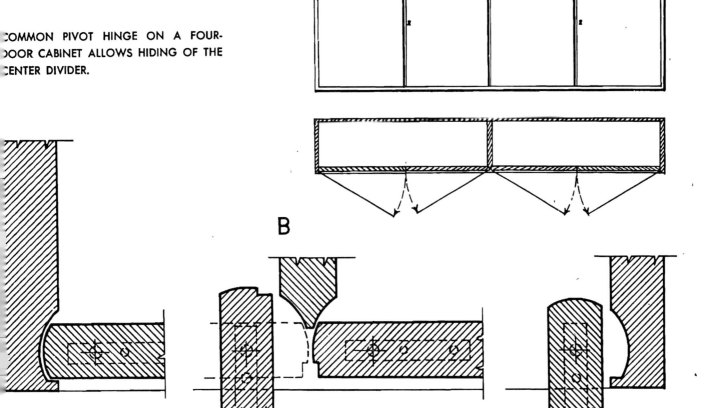

DROP DOORS

A DROP DOOR MAY USE ALMOST ANY TYPE OF HINGE ALONG ITS BOTTOM EDGE. A CHARACTERISTIC OF THIS TYPE OF DOOR IS THAT IT CAN BE USED IN A NUMBER OF WAYS. WHEN OPEN, THE DOOR MAY ACT AS A DESK OR SUPPORT. IT IS THEREFORE ESSENTIAL TO HAVE THE DOOR HELD IN A RIGID POSITION. THIS CAN BE DONE BY USING METAL SUPPORTS ALONG THE OUTER EDGE.

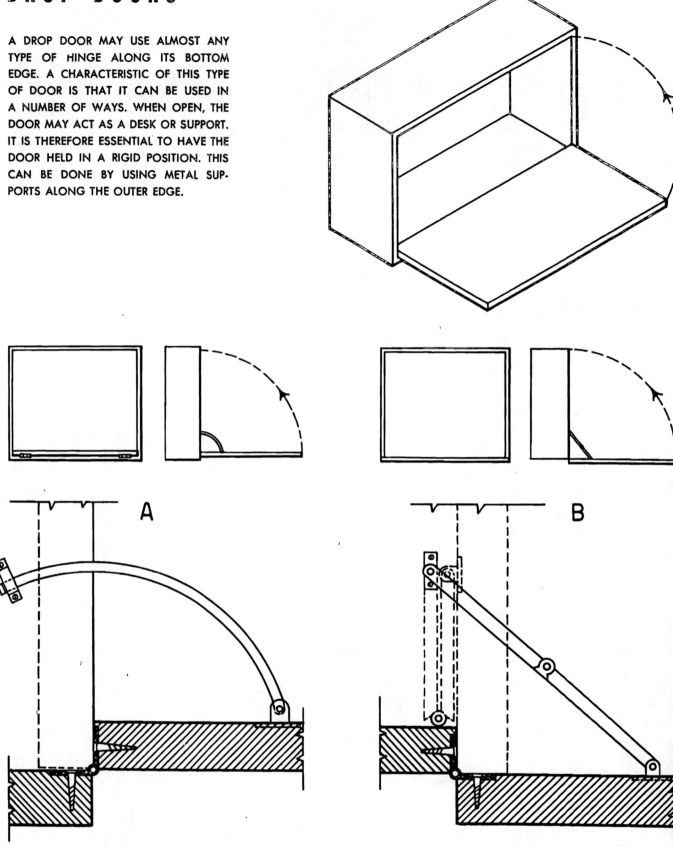

A

B

TWO WAYS OF USING A BUTT HINGE. BOTH TYPES OF SUPPORTS ARE VERY PRACTICAL.

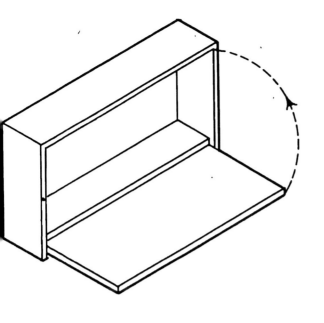

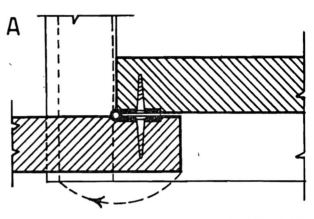

A

THIS SIMPLE METHOD USES A BUTT HINGE. THE DOOR OVERHANG ACTS AS ITS OWN STOP.

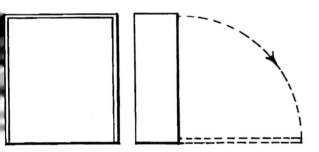

A COMBINATION HINGE AND SUPPORT IS USED WITH THIS DROP DOOR. IT IS A SATISFACTORY METHOD SO LONG AS THE DOOR IS SMALL.

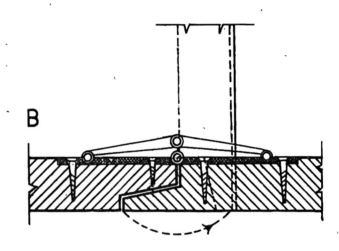

B

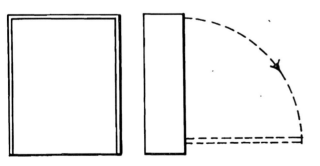

OFFSET HINGES ARE USED IN THIS SCHEME.

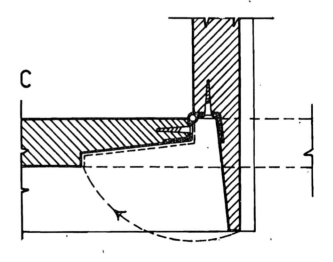

C

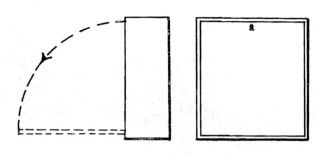

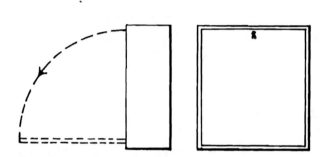

A, C — THESE TWO DOORS USE A COMMON PIVOT.
NOTE THE METHODS OF STOPPING THE DOOR.
B — THIS DOOR USES A SPECIAL STOP PIVOT (SEE
PAGE 56, FIG. E).

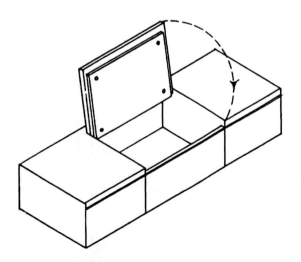

D — PIVOT DROP DOOR SUITABLE FOR VANITIES.
VERTICAL AND HORIZONTAL METHOD OF HINGING
FOLDED DOORS.

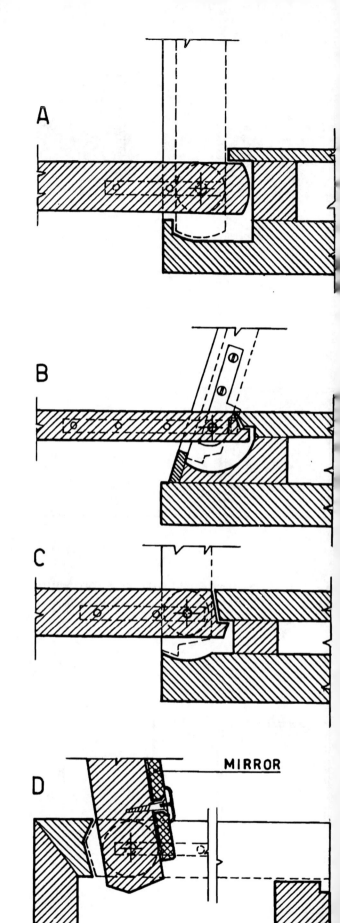

A

B

C

D

MIRROR

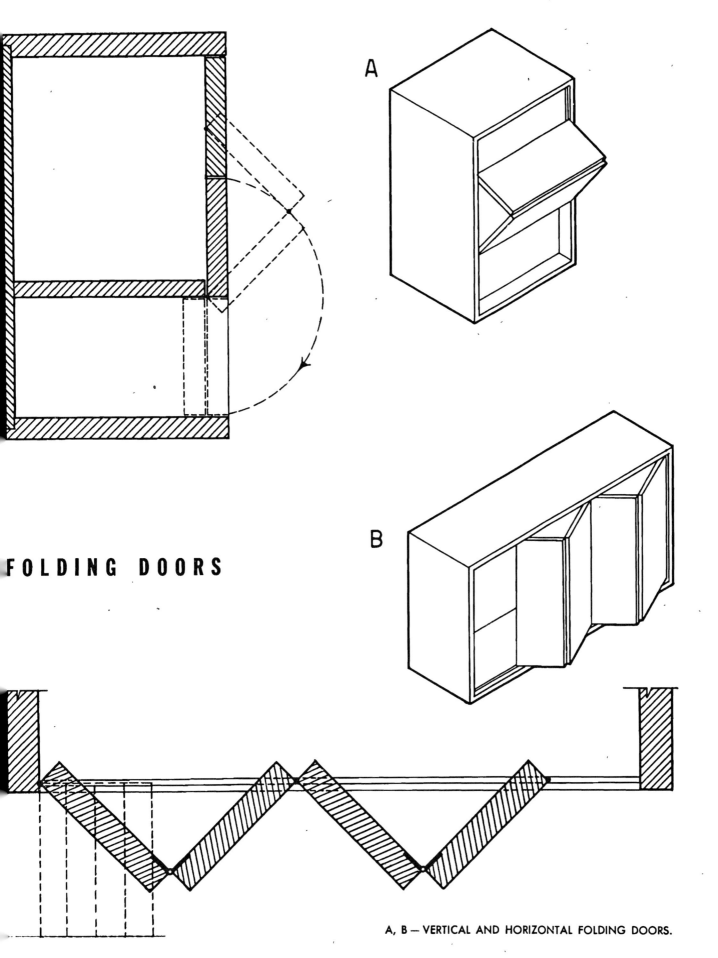

FOLDING DOORS

A, B — VERTICAL AND HORIZONTAL FOLDING DOORS.

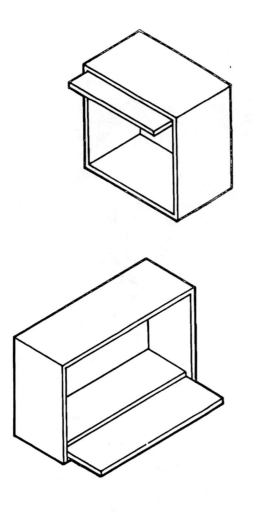

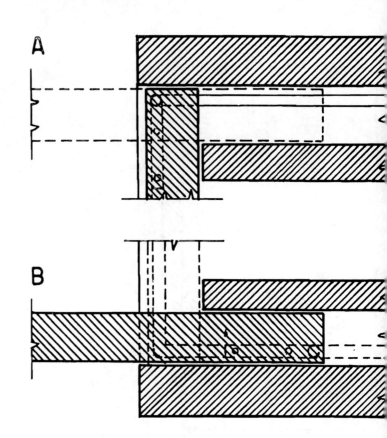

A

B

COMBINATION DROP AND SLIDING DOOR SHOWN HERE USES A
COMMON PIVOT AND ROUTED TRACK TO PERFORM ITS FUNCTION

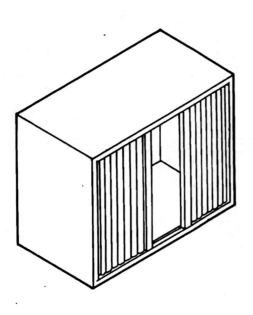

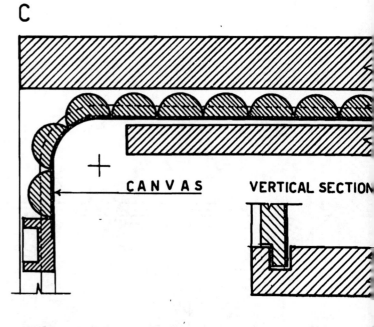

C

CANVAS   VERTICAL SECTION

TAMBOUR DOOR AS USED IN OFFICE FURNITURE. THIS IS NOT
DIFFICULT TO MAKE.

68

LIDING DOORS

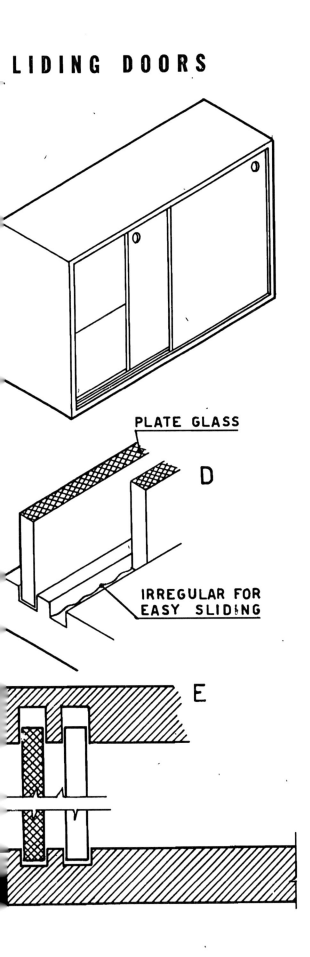

PLATE GLASS

D

IRREGULAR FOR
EASY SLIDING

E

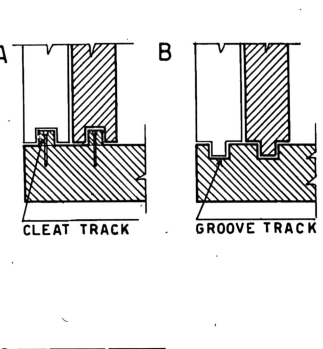

A

CLEAT TRACK

B

GROOVE TRACK

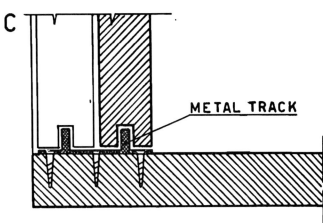

C

METAL TRACK

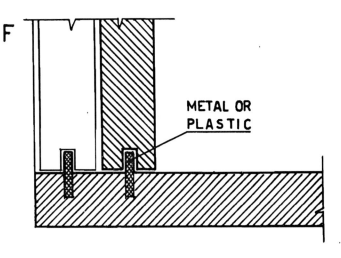

F

METAL OR
PLASTIC

DOORS MAY BE MADE TO SLIDE IN A NUMBER OF
DIFFERENT WAYS. HERE ARE SEVERAL METHODS.

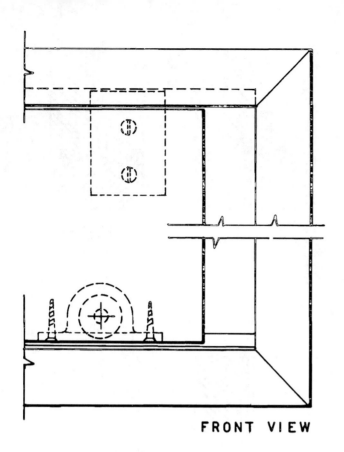

FRONT VIEW

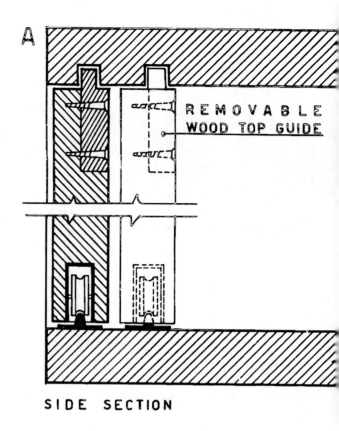

A

REMOVABLE
WOOD TOP GUIDE

SIDE SECTION

DOORS WILL MOVE MORE EASILY IF WHEELS ARE
USED. THESE TWO METHODS WILL GIVE VERY SATIS-
FACTORY RESULTS.

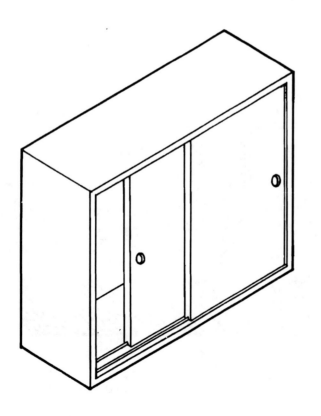

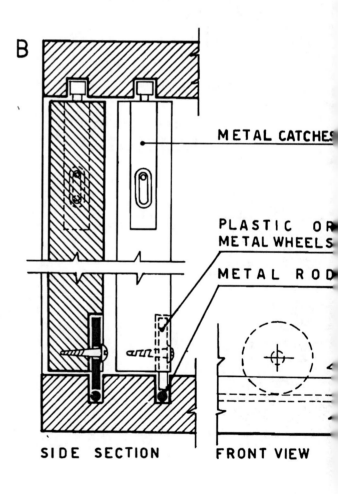

B

METAL CATCHES

PLASTIC OR
METAL WHEELS

METAL ROD

SIDE SECTION   FRONT VIEW

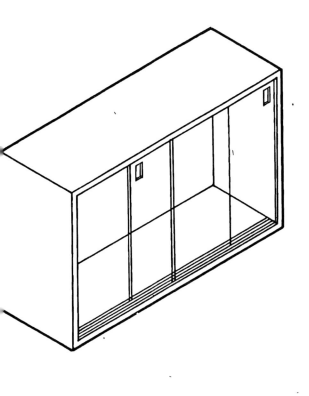

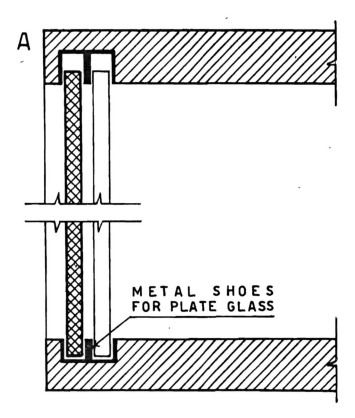

A

METAL SHOES
FOR PLATE GLASS

B

SPACE TO REMOVE THE DOOR

GROOVE TRACK

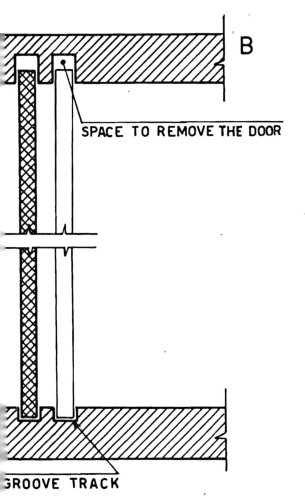

C

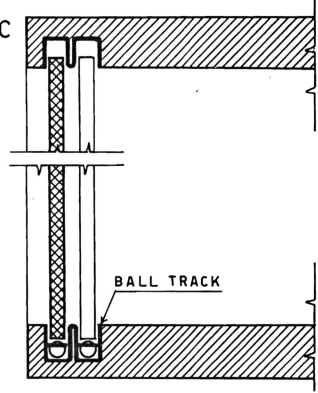

BALL TRACK

SLIDING DOORS OF PLATE GLASS MAY USE ANY OF
THESE THREE METHODS. "C" WOULD PROBABLY GIVE
THE BEST RESULTS.

CATCHES AND LOCKS FOR DOORS

DOOR HOLDING DEVICES ARE DIVDED INTO TWO GROUPS: CATCHES AND LOCKS THE CATCH IS INTENDED O HOLD THE DOOR IN CLOSED POSITION. IT IS COMMONLY USED IN FURNITURE.

DOOR LOCKS DFFER FROM CATCHE IN THAT THEY REQUIRE KEYS IN THIS SECTION I HAVE LLUSTRATED A FEW COMMON TYPES OF LOCKS AND CATCHES.

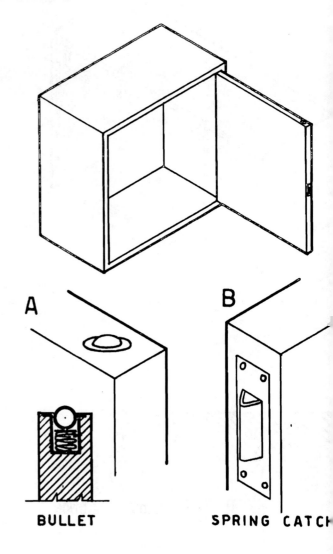

A

B

BULLET

SPRING CATCH

VARIOUS TYPES OF CATCHES.

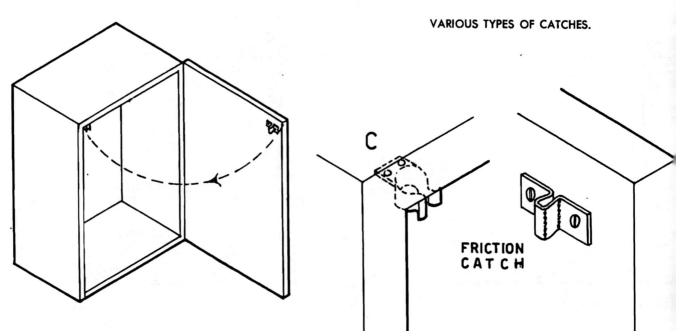

C

FRICTION CATCH

DOOR KNOB

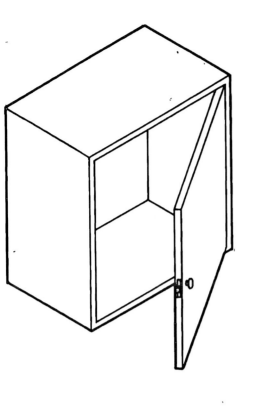

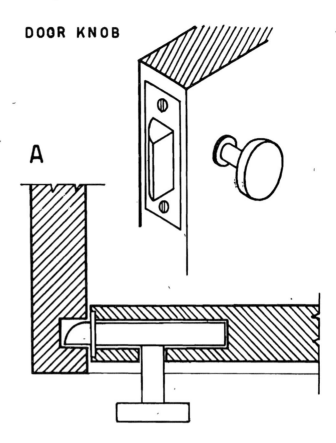

A

CATCH WITH HANDLE.

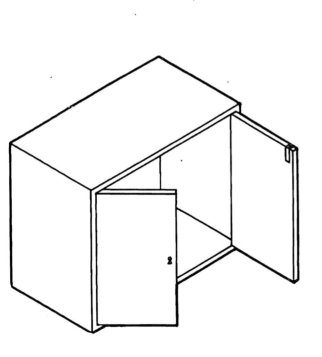

APPLICATION OF FLUSH AND NECK BOLTS
TO DOOR BACK.

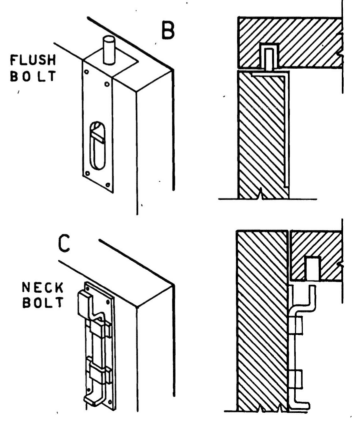

B

FLUSH
BOLT

C

NECK
BOLT

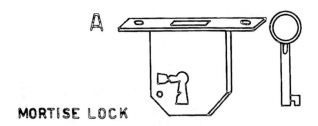

MORTISE LOCK

A — MORTISE LOCK IS A COMMON TYPE FOUND IN FURNITURE WORK. IT CAN BE USED WITH SINGLE OR DOUBLE DOORS AND WITH DRAWERS.

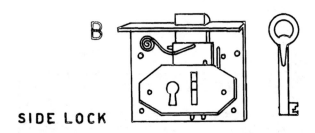

SIDE LOCK

SIDE LOCK, WHICH IS SELDOM USED TODAY.

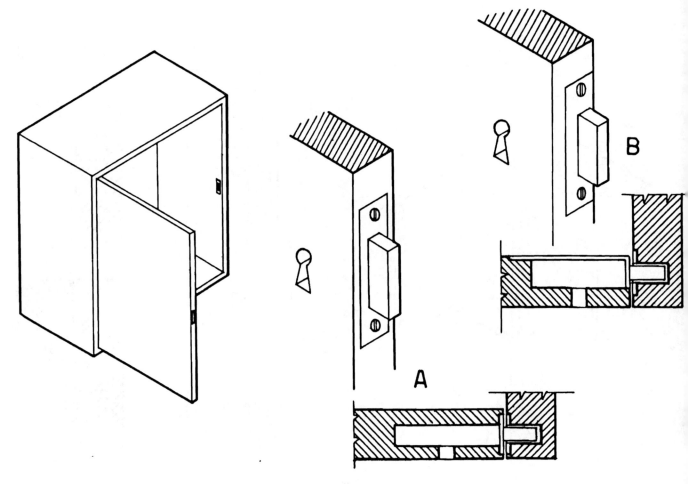

A

B

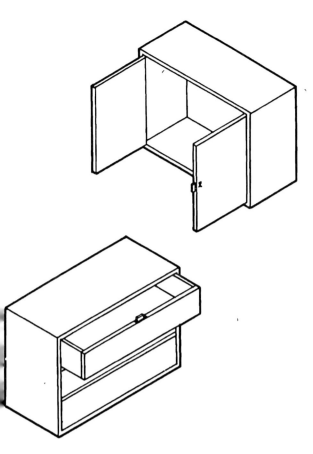

MORTISE AND SIDE LOCK THAT MAY BE APPLIED TO EITHER DOORS OR DRAWERS.

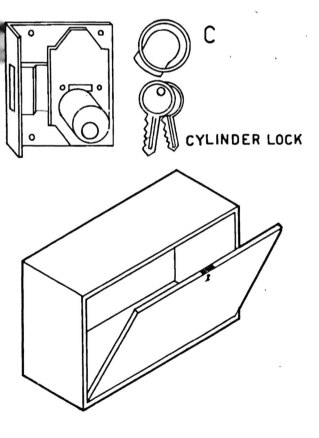

CYLINDER LOCK

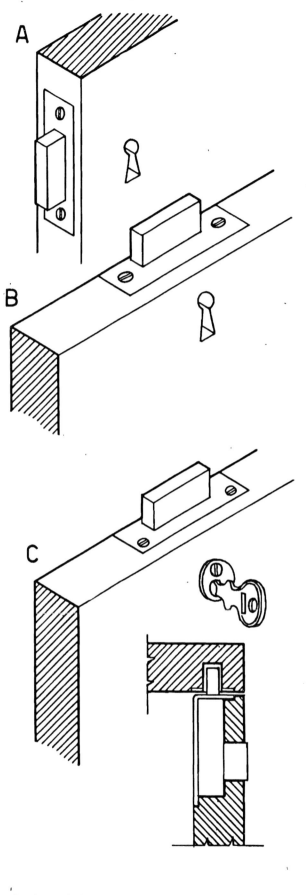

CYLINDER TYPE LOCK WHICH MAY BE USED ON ANY TYPE OF DOOR.

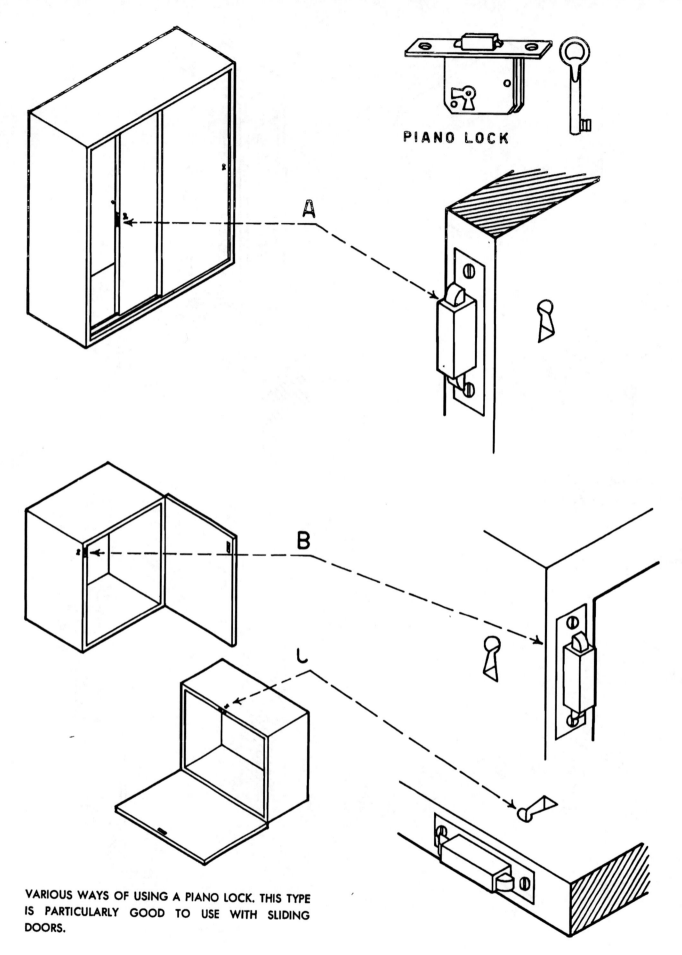

PIANO LOCK

A

B

L

VARIOUS WAYS OF USING A PIANO LOCK. THIS TYPE IS PARTICULARLY GOOD TO USE WITH SLIDING DOORS.

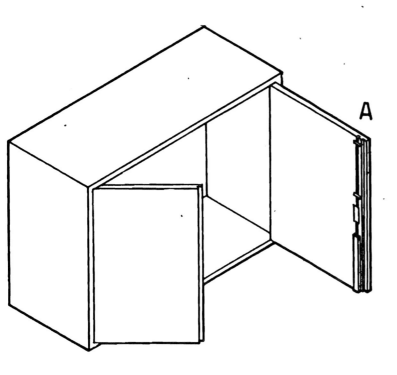

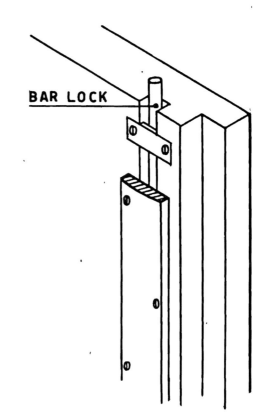

BAR LOCK

THIS BAR LOCK METHOD CLOSES BOTH DOORS AT
THE SAME TIME.

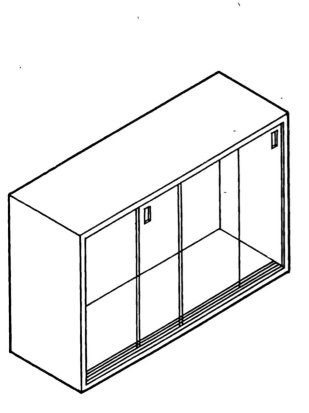

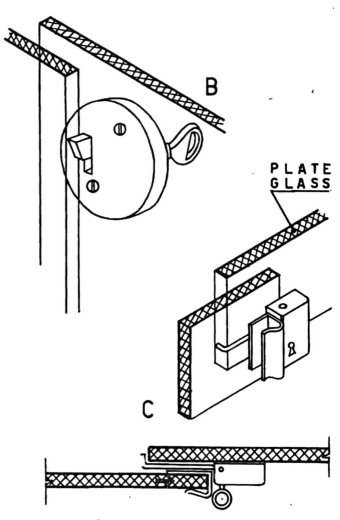

B

PLATE
GLASS

C

PLATE GLASS LOCKING DEVICES WHICH ARE PAR-
TICULARLY USEFUL. "B" IS SECURED WITH SCREWS;
"C" IS APPLIED TO THE BASE OF THE PLATE GLASS.

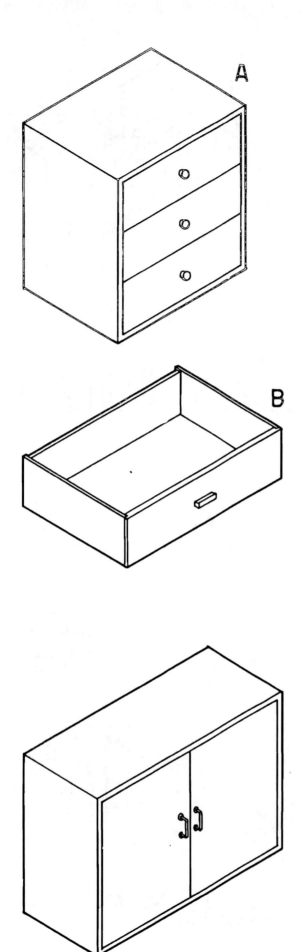

PULLS

THERE ARE MANY TYPES OF PULLS OR KNOBS MADE OF WOOD OR METAL. THESE MAY BE APPLIED TO THE FURNITURE OR BUILT INTO THE ACTUAL DESIGN. IN SOME CASES THE PULLS ARE USED DECORATIVELY, BUT IT IS USUALLY BEST TO BUILD THEM INTO THE ACTUAL FURNITURE AS SHOWN ON PAGE 79.

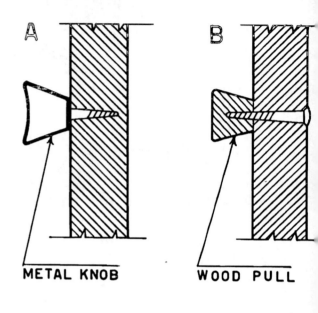

METAL KNOB   WOOD PULL

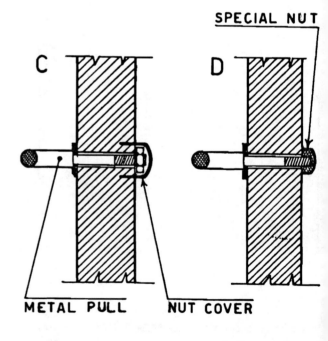

METAL PULL   NUT COVER

VARIOUS TYPES OF KNOBS AND PULLS WHICH ARE ATTACHED TO THE DOORS OR DRAWERS.

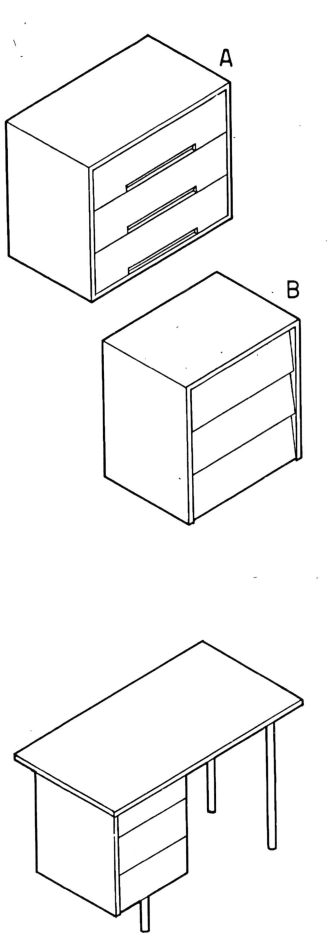

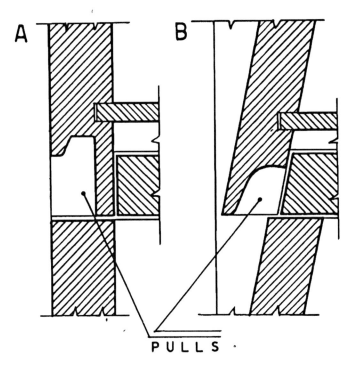

A   B

PULLS

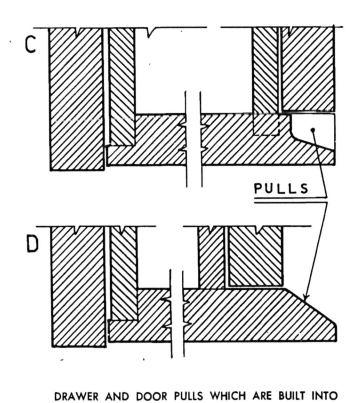

C

PULLS

D

DRAWER AND DOOR PULLS WHICH ARE BUILT INTO
THE FURNITURE.

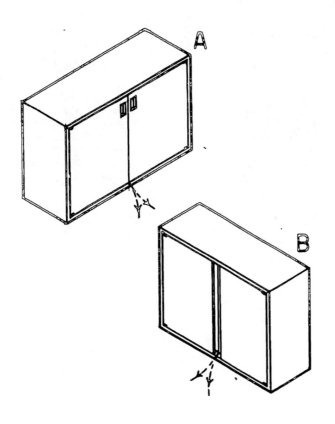

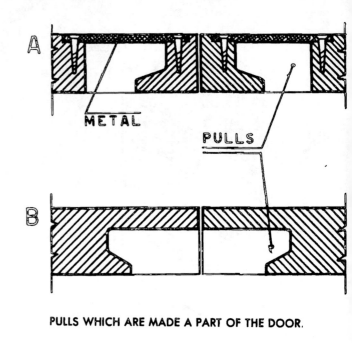

PULLS WHICH ARE MADE A PART OF THE DOOR.

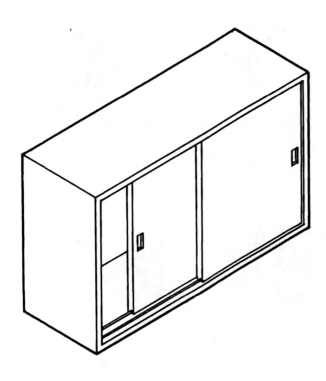

SLIDING DOOR PULLS CUT INTO THE WOOD OR PLATE GLASS.

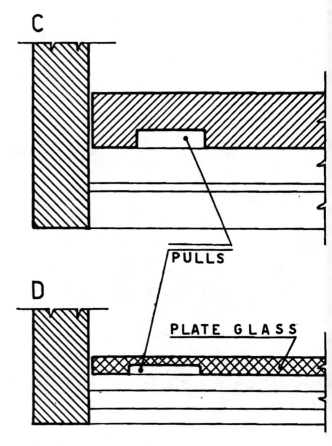

ADJUSTABLE SHELVES

AN ADJUSTABLE SHELF HAS SEVERAL ADVANTAGES. CHIEF OF THESE IS THAT THE SPACING OF THE SHELVES MAY BE VARIED IN ACCORDANCE WITH THE OBJECT TO BE DISPLAYED. THESE SHELVES ARE OFTEN USED IN BOOK STORES, EQUIPMENT, KITCHEN CABINETS AND OTHER FURNITURE. HERE ARE SEVERAL TYPES.

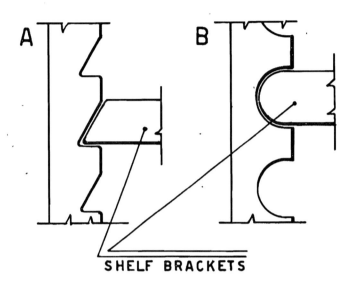

A

B

SHELF BRACKETS

ADJUSTABLE SHELF PINS

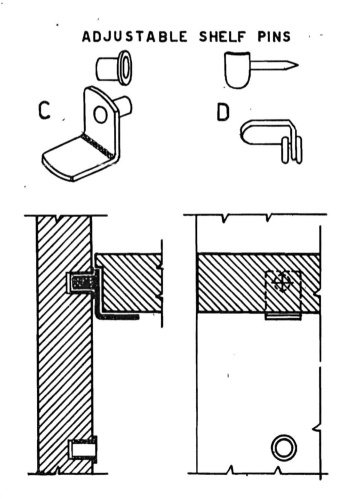

C

D

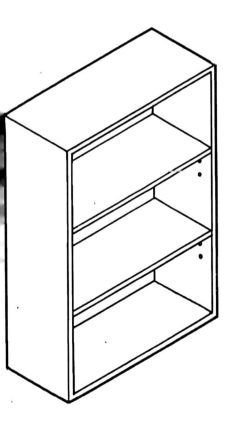

VARIOUS EXAMPLES OF ADJUSTABLE SHELVES. TYPE "C" IS ONE OF THE BEST ARRANGEMENTS.

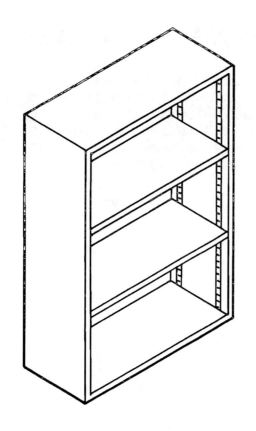

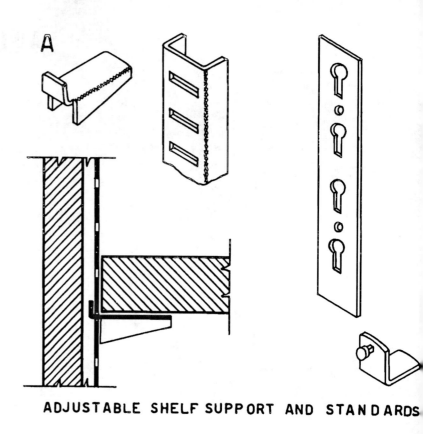

ADJUSTABLE SHELF SUPPORT AND STANDARDS

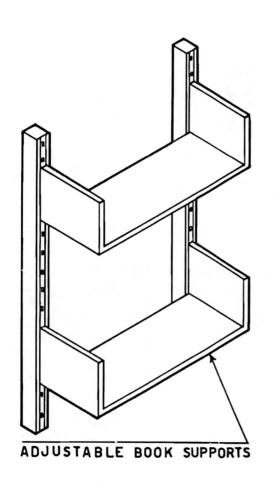

ADJUSTABLE BOOK SUPPORTS

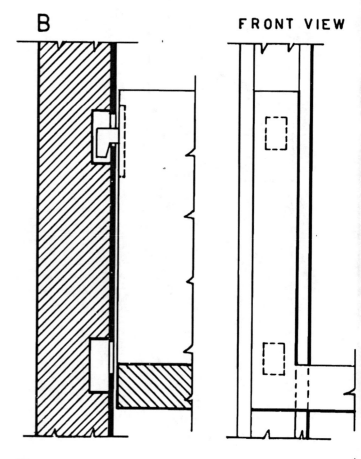

FRONT VIEW

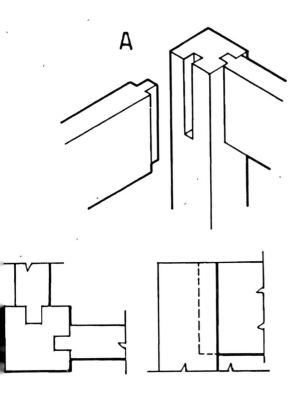

LEGS

THERE ARE MANY WAYS OF JOINING LEGS TO TRANSVERSE RAILS AND ATTACHING LEGS AND RAILS TO THE BODY OF THE PIECE OF FURNITURE. GREAT CARE SHOULD BE TAKEN IN THE SELECTION AND EXECUTION OF SUCH JOINTS SO THAT THEY WILL BE ABLE TO WITHSTAND THE STRAIN WHICH MAY BE PUT UPON THEM. IN ADDITION TO THESE JOINTS, THE BUILDER MUST CONSIDER HOW THE LEG IS TO BE PROTECTED WHERE IT IS IN CONTACT WITH THE FLOOR.

OPEN MORTISE AND TENON JOINT.

JOINING RAILS TO LEGS

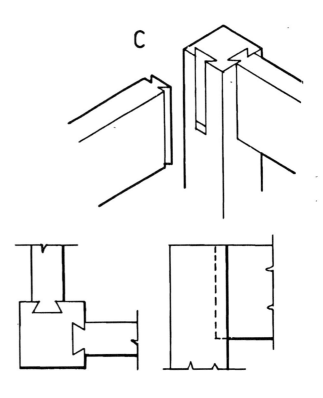

DOWEL JOINT THAT MIGHT BE USED BY THE AMATEUR CRAFTSMAN.

DOVETAIL JOINT: A VERY STRONG METHOD OF JOINING THE PIECES.

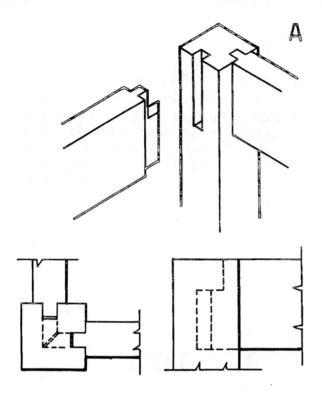

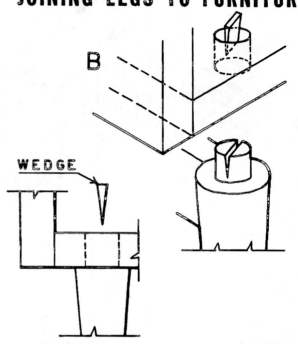

JOINING A LEG TO A RAIL WITH A RABBET MORTISE AND TENON IS AN EXCELLENT METHOD.

WEDGE AND DOWEL JOINT THAT MAY BE USED. AFTER INSTALLATION THE WEDGE IS CUT FLUSH WITH THE TOP.

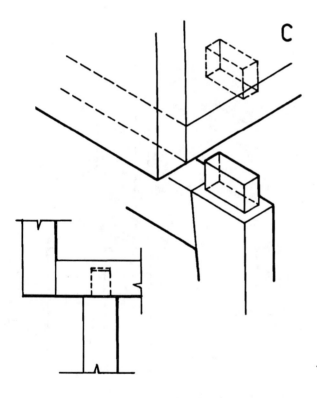

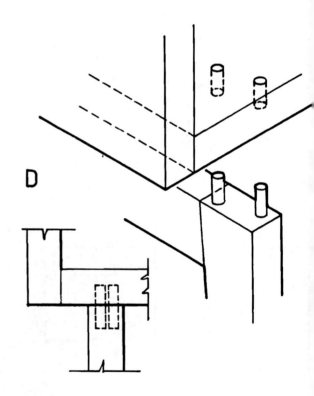

STUB MORTISE AND TENON JOINT WHICH IS GLUED TO THE BODY PIECE.

DOWEL JOINT THAT IS IDEAL FOR HOME CRAFTSMEN.

WEDGE IN STUB DOWEL.
NOTE THAT HOLE DOES NOT
RUN THROUGH.

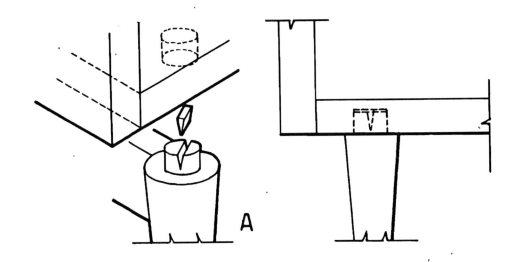

A

SCREW JOINT THAT IS EASY
TO MAKE.

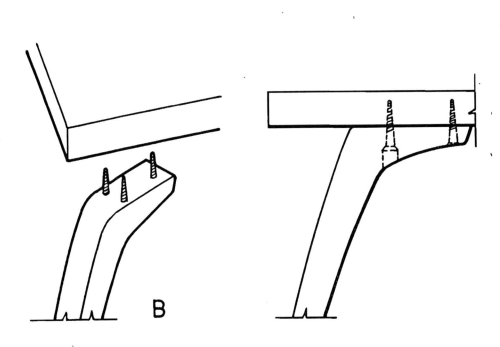

B

METAL CORNER

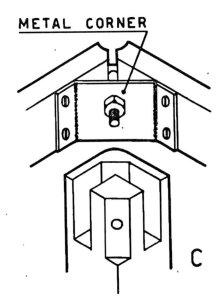

C

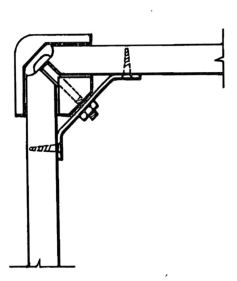

DEMOUNTABLE LEG WITH
METAL CORNER. THIS METHOD
IS OFTEN USED ON KITCHEN
TABLES.

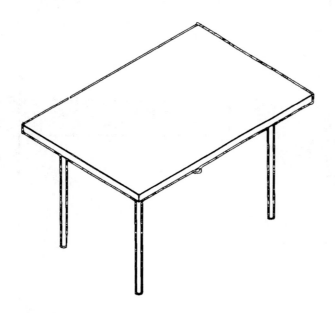

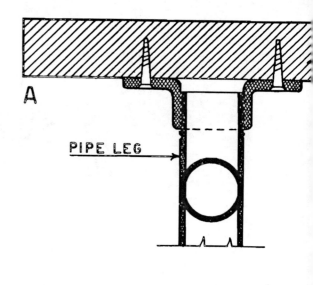

A

PIPE LEG

JOINING METAL LEGS TO WOOD TOP

VARIOUS METHODS OF JOINING METAL LEGS TO A WOOD TOP. EACH EXAMPLE ASSURES GOOD RESULTS. "A" USES A METAL PIPE SCREWED TO A PLATE, "B" IS MADE WITH A WOOD STUB TO WHICH A METAL TUBE IS SCREWED. "C" USES A METAL STUB INSTEAD OF A WOODEN ONE. "D" IS SCREWED DIRECTLY TO THE TABLE TOP.

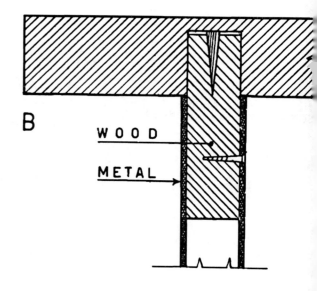

B

WOOD

METAL

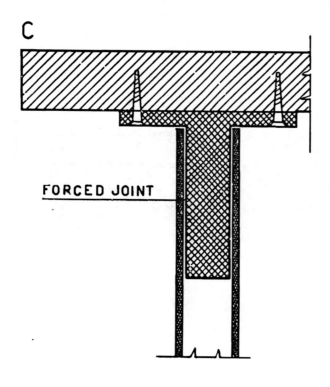

C

FORCED JOINT

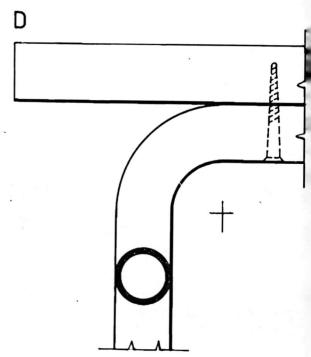

D

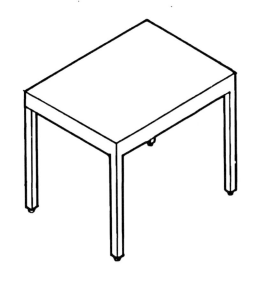

LEG END FITTINGS

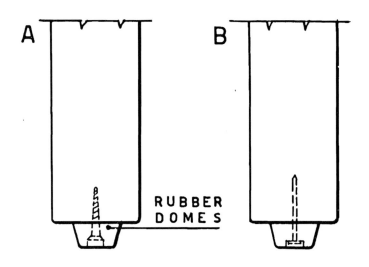

A

B

RUBBER DOMES

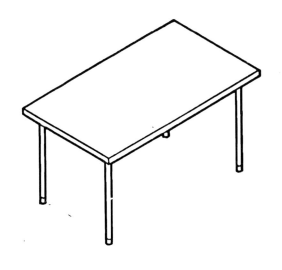

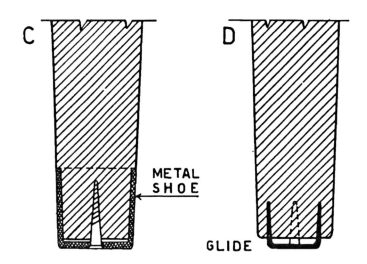

C

D

METAL SHOE

GLIDE

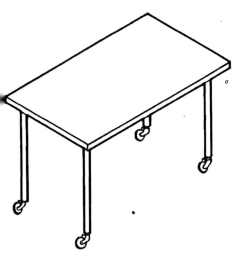

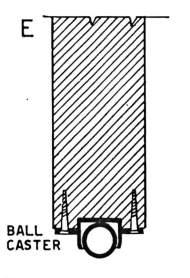

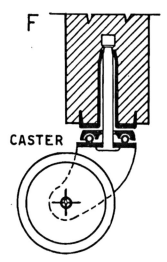

E

F

BALL CASTER

CASTER

DIFFERENT WAYS OF PROTECTING THE BOTTOM OF THE WOODEN LEG.

87

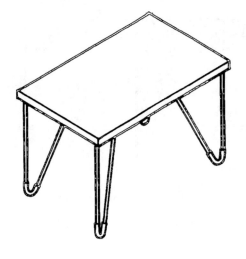

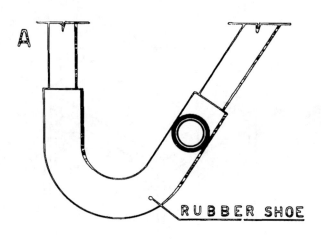

A

RUBBER SHOE

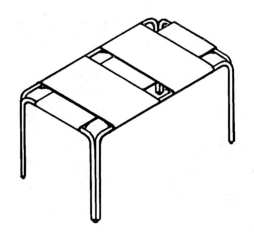

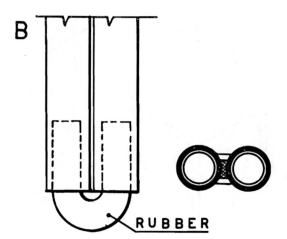

B

RUBBER

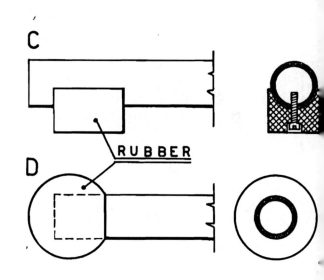

C

RUBBER

D

VARIOUS METHODS OF PROTECTING METAL LEGS BY
USING RUBBER.

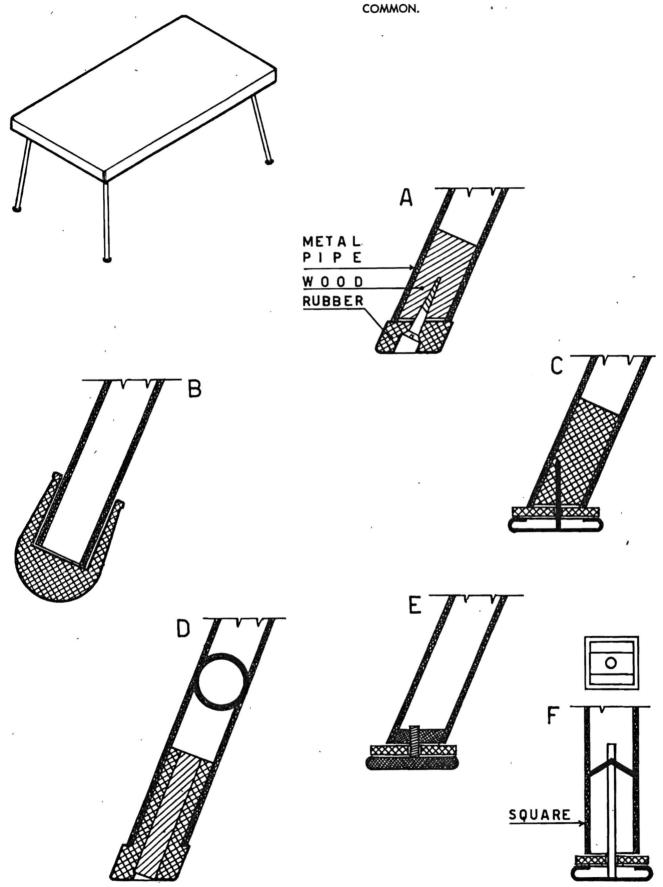

RUBBER CAPS AND GLIDES WHICH MAY BE USED WITH METAL LEGS. ALL METHODS SHOWN ARE FAIRLY COMMON.

A

METAL PIPE
WOOD
RUBBER

B

C

D

E

F

SQUARE

DRAWERS

A DRAWER IS ONE OF THE MOST USEFUL AND IM-
PORTANT PARTS OF FURNITURE CONSTRUCTION. THE
SMOOTH OPERATION OF THE DRAWER DEPENDS UPON
THE PERFECT ASSEMBLY AND DESIGN OF THE FUR-
NITURE PIECE.

DRAWERS MAY BE HIDDEN BY DOORS OR THEY MAY
BE EXPOSED. MANY SOLUTIONS ARE POSSIBLE UNDER
EITHER CONDITION. THE TYPES SHOWN IN THIS SEC-
TION GIVE A CLEAR IDEA OF THEIR CONSTRUCTION
AND APPLICATION.

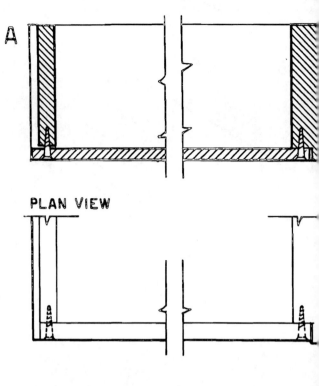

A

PLAN VIEW

RABBET JOINT USING SCREWS: AN EASY METHO
FOR AMATEUR CRAFTSMEN.

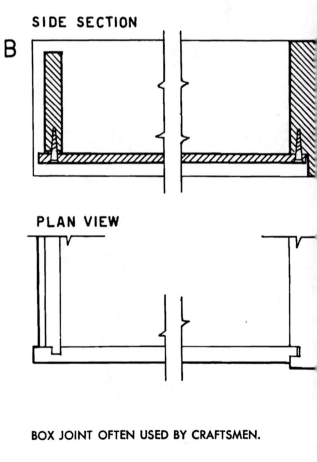

SIDE SECTION

B

PLAN VIEW

BOX JOINT OFTEN USED BY CRAFTSMEN.

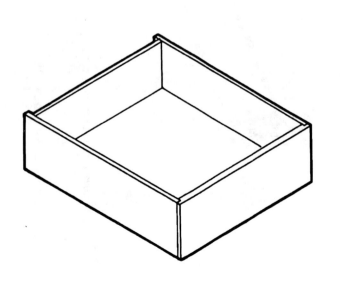

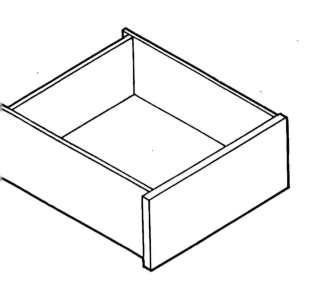

DOVETAIL JOINT WHICH MAY BE USED IN ALL TYPES OF WORK.

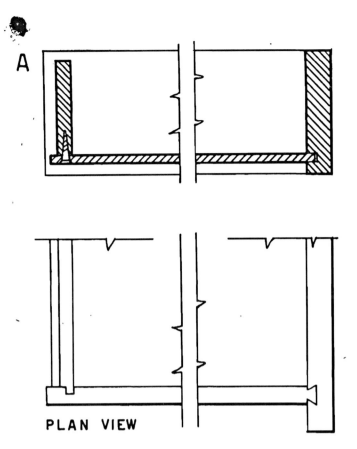

A

PLAN VIEW

SIDE

B

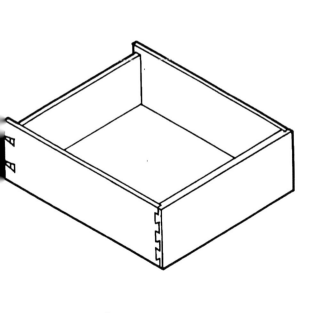

HALF BLIND DOVETAIL OFTEN USED IN FINE WORK.

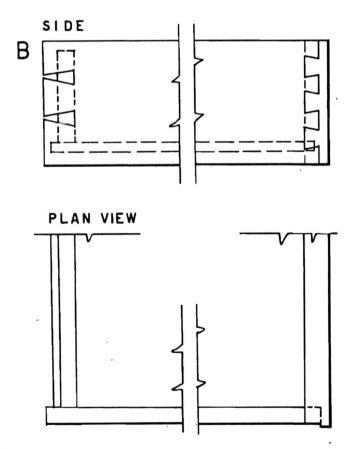

PLAN VIEW

91

TYPES OF DRAWERS

DUST PANEL USED BETWEEN DRAWERS.

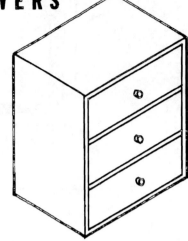

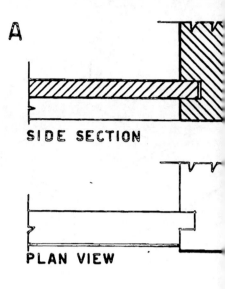

A

SIDE SECTION

PLAN VIEW

INVISIBLE DUST PANEL BETWEEN DRAWERS.

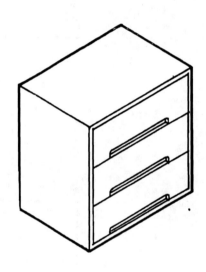

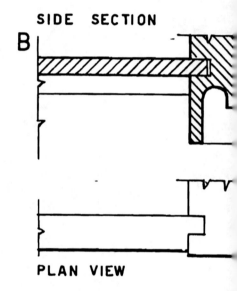

SIDE SECTION

B

PLAN VIEW

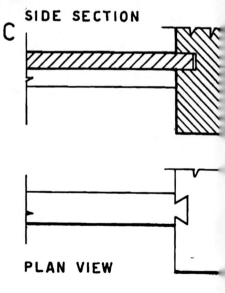

SIDE SECTION

C

PLAN VIEW

DRAWERS WITH INVISIBLE EDGE.

92

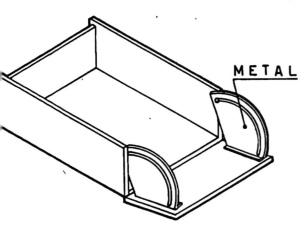

METAL

DRAWER WITH DROP FRONT. THIS TYPE IS OFTEN USED
N OFFICE FURNITURE.

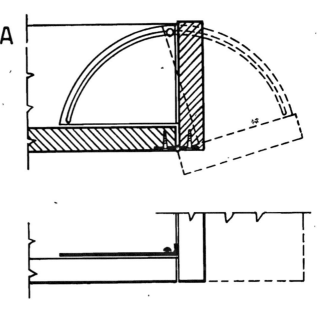

A

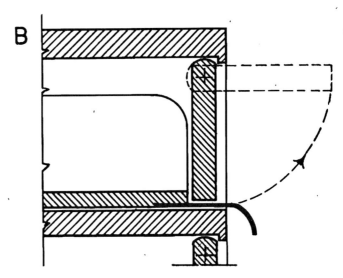

B

DISAPPEARING DRAWER FRONT. NOTE THE APPLICA-
TION OF THE PIVOT HINGE.

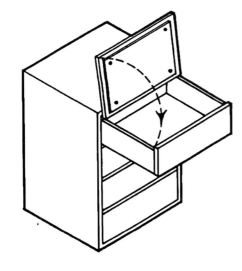

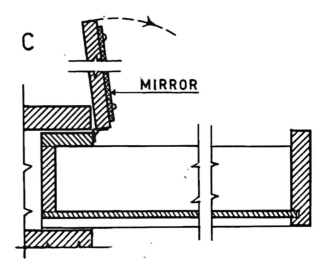

C

MIRROR

DROP TOP MIRROR USED INSIDE A CHEST DRAWER.

93

TO TAKE THE STRIP.

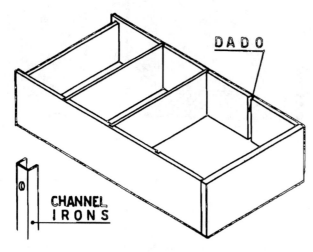

CHANNEL IRONS

DADO

DRAWER WITH REMOVABLE DIVISION STRIPS. THIS
METHOD USES A DADO OR A CHANNEL IRON IN THE
SIDE OF THE DRAWER.

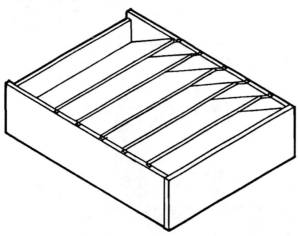

DRAWER WITH OBLIQUE AND REMOVABLE DIVISION
STRIPS.

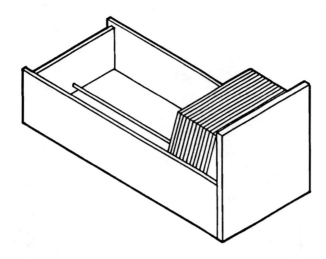

DRAWER FOR FILE INDEX. THESE THREE SYSTEMS ARE
USED MAINLY IN OFFICE FURNITURE.

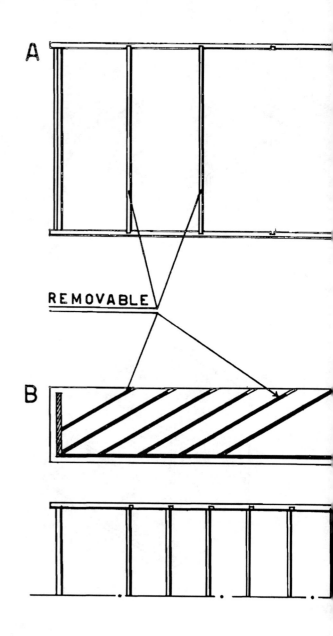

A

REMOVABLE

B

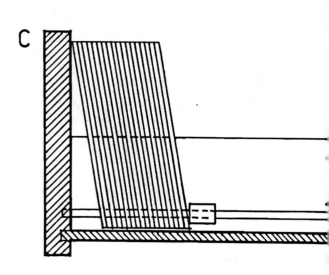

C

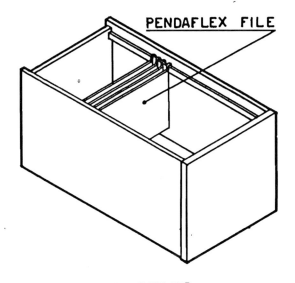

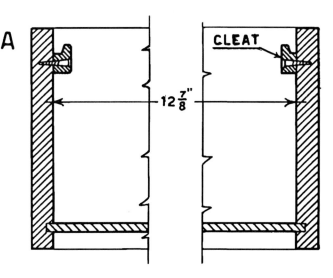

DRAWER FOR CORRESPONDENCE FILE.

A

CLEAT

$12\frac{7}{8}''$

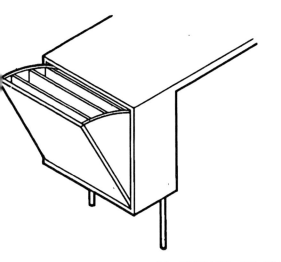

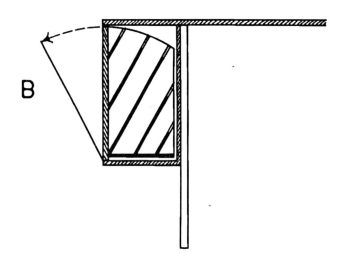

FOLDING DRAWER USED FOR STORAGE OR STA-
TIONERY.

B

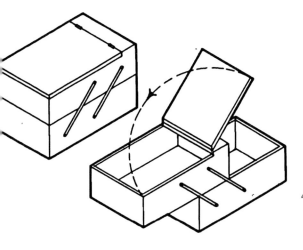

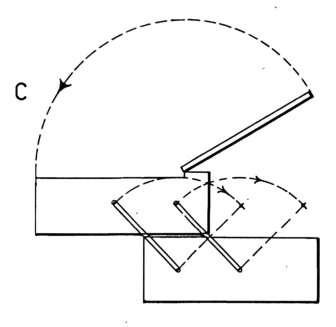

FOLDING DRAWERS USING METAL FLAT STRIPS ON
SIDES.

C

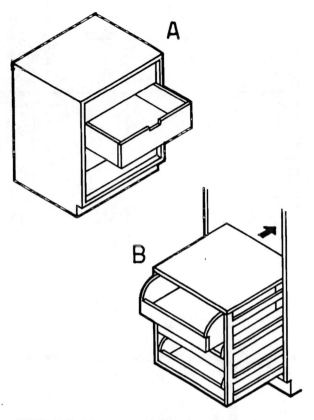

CHEST AND BOX DRAWER FOR WARDROBE.

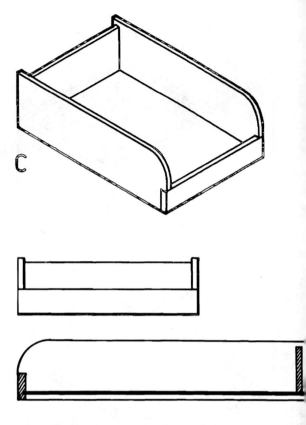

INTERIOR DRAWERS FOR WARDROBE OR CABINE

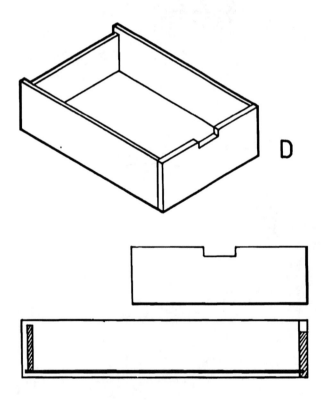

OTHER TYPES OF SIMPLE DRAWERS.

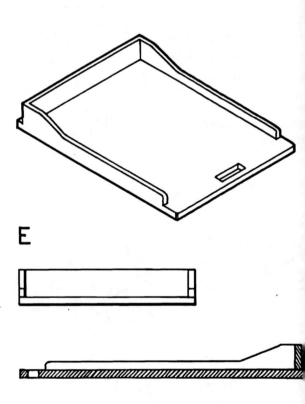

SHIRT DRAWER.

96

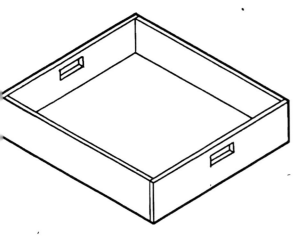

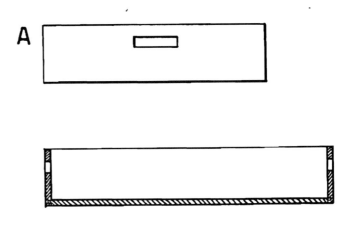
A

DRAWER WITH PULLS FOR TRAY.

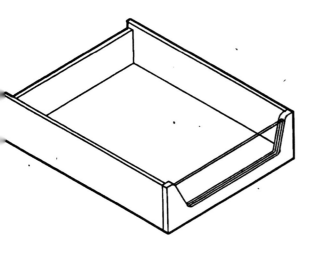

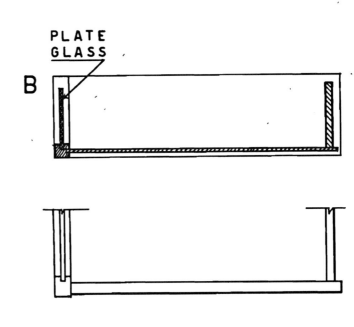
B

PLATE
GLASS

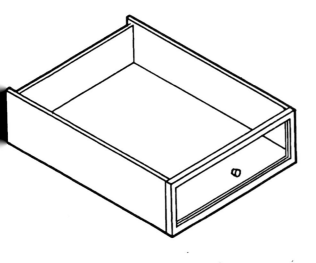

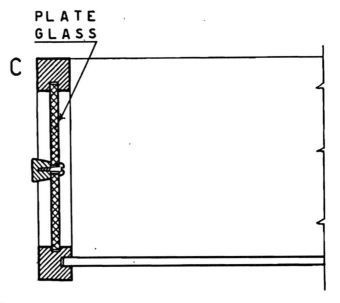
C

PLATE
GLASS

TWO TYPES OF DRAWERS WITH PLATE GLASS FRONT.

SLIDING DRAWER SYSTEMS

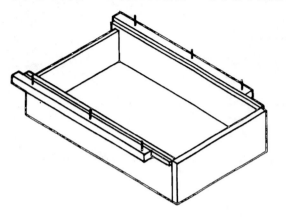

DRAWER WITH SCREWED CLEAT.

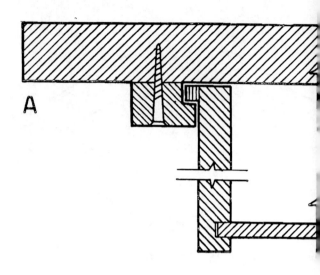

A

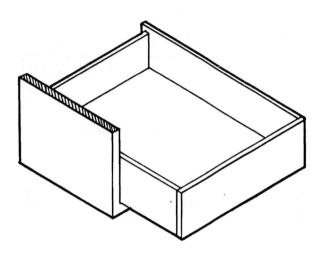

DRAWER WITH BOTTOM RAIL.

B

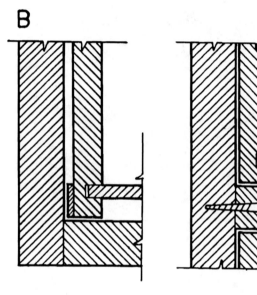

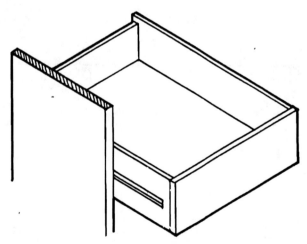

DRAWER WITH RAIL ON THE SIDE. THIS IS AN EASY
AND PRACTICAL SYSTEM WHICH IS USED IN ALL TYPES
OF WORK.

C

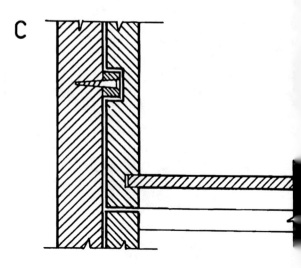

98

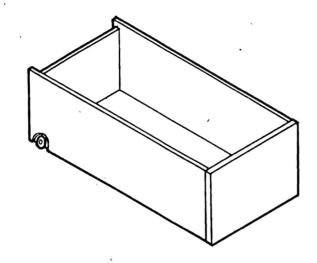

ROLLERS ARE USED WITH HEAVY DRAWERS.

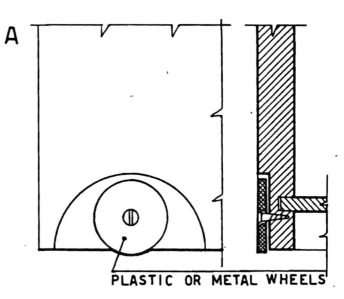

A

PLASTIC OR METAL WHEELS

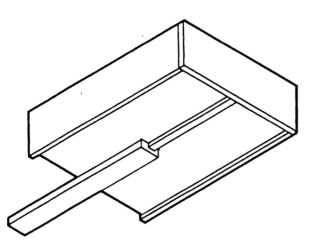

DRAWER WITH CENTER GUIDE. THE GUIDE IS ADVIS-
ABLE AS IT FACILITATES THE MOVEMENT OF THE
DRAWER. IT IS A TYPE USED EXTENSIVELY IN STANDARD
PRODUCTION.

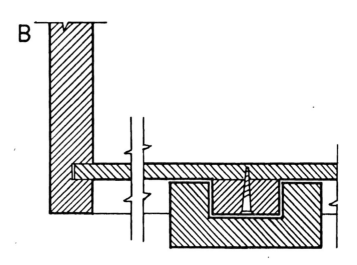

B

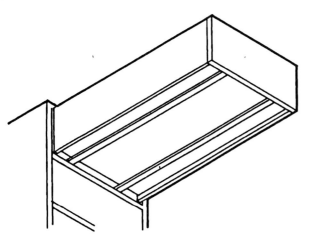

SLIDE DOVETAIL AND SUPPORT. USED WHEN DRAWERS
ARE TAKEN OUT THROUGH THE BACK.

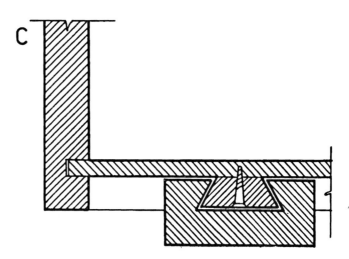

C

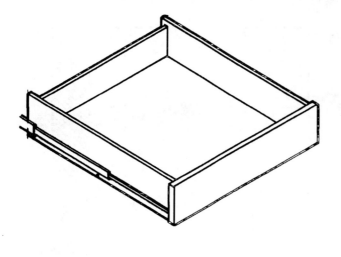

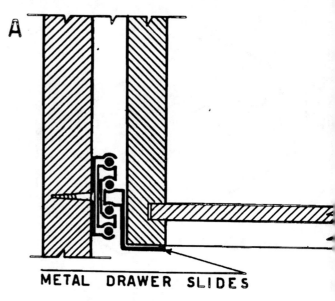

METAL DRAWER SLIDES

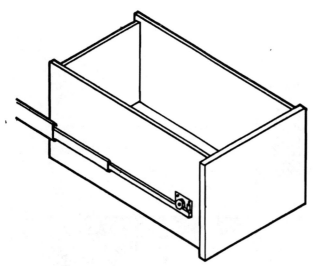

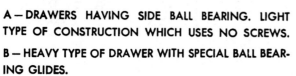

A — DRAWERS HAVING SIDE BALL BEARING. LIGHT TYPE OF CONSTRUCTION WHICH USES NO SCREWS.

B — HEAVY TYPE OF DRAWER WITH SPECIAL BALL BEARING GLIDES.

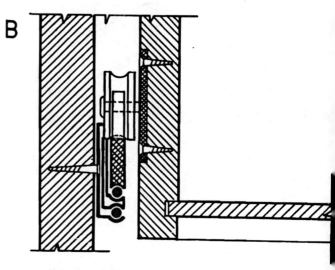

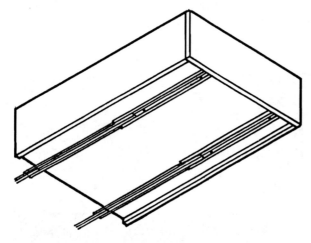

C — BALL BEARING IN BOTTOM OF DRAWER. EACH OF THESE SYSTEMS WILL PRODUCE AN EASILY-GLIDING DRAWER.

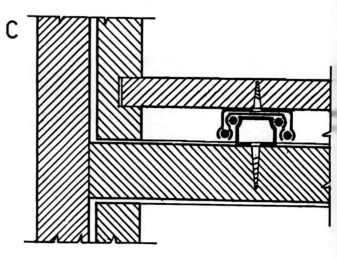

DRAWER STOPS

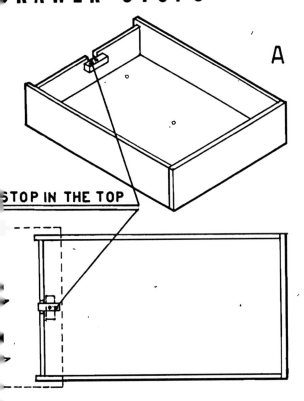

STOP IN THE TOP

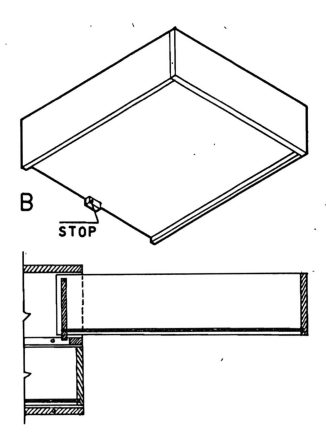

STOP

TWO DIFFERENT SOLUTIONS OF STOPS FOR SINGLE DRAWERS.

WOOD LOCK IN OPEN POSITION

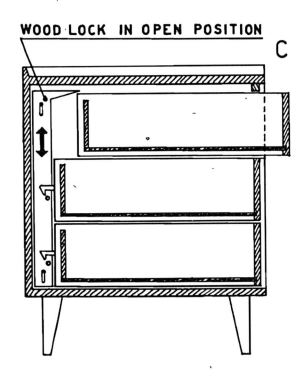

LOCK INSTALLED IN SINGLE PEDESTAL DESK.

METAL STOP

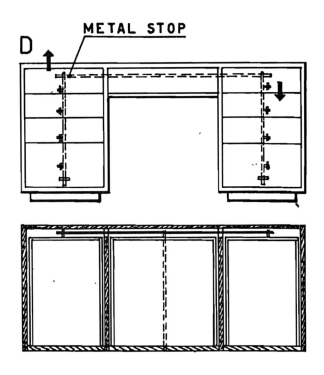

LOCK INSTALLED IN DOUBLE PEDESTAL DESK.

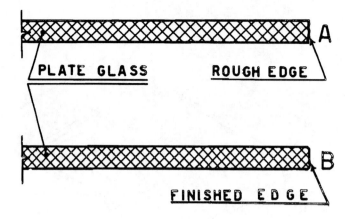

PLATE GLASS   ROUGH EDGE

A

FINISHED EDGE

B

JOINING WOOD AND GLAS

THE APPLICATION OF GLASS, PLATE GLASS OR MIRRO
TO THE WOOD IS CONSIDERED ONE OF THE MOS
DELICATE TYPES OF WORK IN THE FURNITURE FIEL
THE POSSIBILITY OF BREAKING THE GLASS DURIN
THE WORKING PROCESS MAKES IT IMPERATIVE THA
GREAT CARE BE TAKEN.

PLATE GLASS OR A MIRROR MAY BE ATTACHED T
THE WOOD IN A HORIZONTAL, VERTICAL OR OBLIQU
POSITION. IT MAY ALSO BE WELDED TO WOOD WIT
GLUE OR CEMENT.

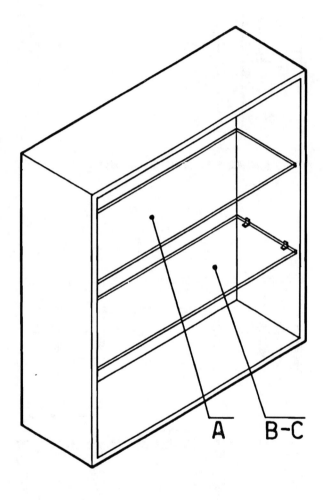

A   B-C

APPLICATION OF PLATE GLASS SHELF "A" SHOWS
ROUGH EDGE; "B" AND "C" SHOW METHOD WITH
FINISHED EDGE.

A   PLATE GLAS

B

C

A — APPLICATION OF GLASS IN-
SIDE A PICTURE FRAME.

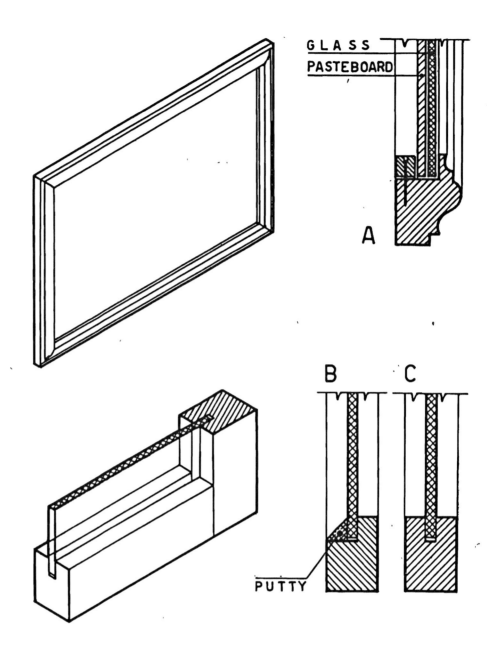

GLASS

PASTEBOARD

A

B — RABBET FRAME SHOWING
PLATE GLASS HELD IN PLACE WITH
PUTTY.
C — PLATE GLASS IN A GROOVE.

B   C

PUTTY

D

D — SLIDING PLATE GLASS IN A
GROOVED TRACK.

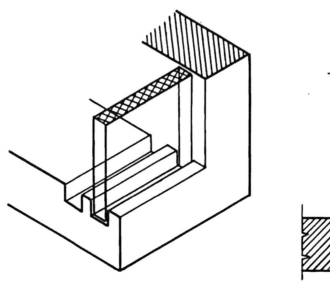

103

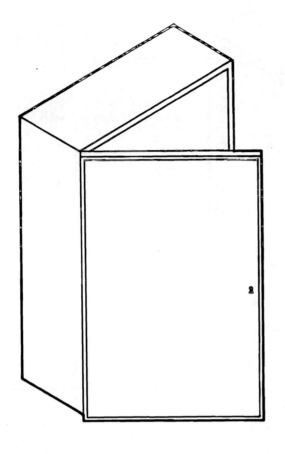

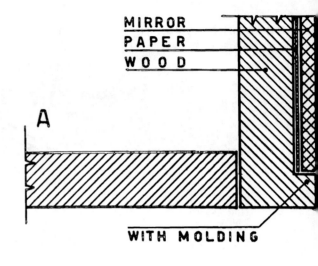

A

WITH MOLDING

MIRROR
PAPER
WOOD

MIRROR FLUSH WITH DOOR

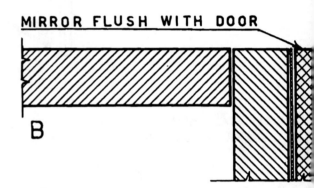

B

THERE ARE SEVERAL WAYS OF ATTACHING GLASS TO
WOOD SURFACES. THE TWO EXAMPLES ABOVE USE
PAPER BETWEEN THE MIRROR AND WOOD SURFACE.
GLUE IS USED IN BOTH CASES. LARGE GLASS AREAS
SHOULD HAVE A MOLDING AROUND THE EDGE. GLASS
MAY BE ATTACHED TO WOOD WITH CEMENT WITH-
OUT USING A PAPER BACKING.

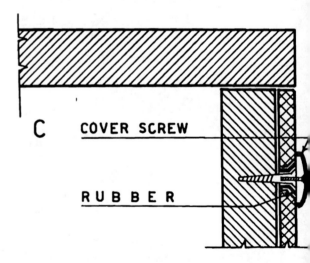

C

COVER SCREW

RUBBER

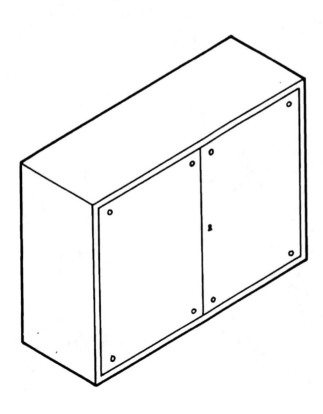

SCREWS ARE USED TO ATTACH THE MIRROR TO THE
WOOD IN THIS CASE.

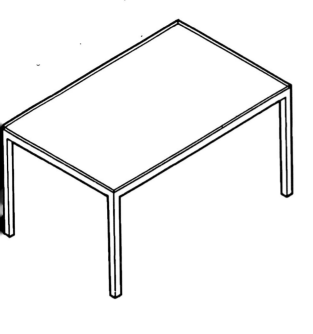

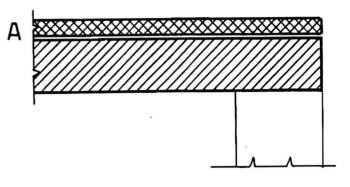

A

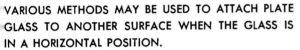

PLATE
GLASS

B

RECESS FOR CLEARANCE

VARIOUS METHODS MAY BE USED TO ATTACH PLATE
GLASS TO ANOTHER SURFACE WHEN THE GLASS IS
IN A HORIZONTAL POSITION.

A — PLATE GLASS WITHOUT FASTENERS IS ADVISABLE
ONLY FOR LARGE TOPS.

B — GLASS WITH MOLDING AND RECESS BENEATH.

C — GLASS OVER SPECIAL LEGS. NOTE RUBBER PRO-
TECTOR.

D — SAME ARRANGEMENT AS ABOVE EXCEPT THAT A
SCREW IS ALSO USED.

PLATE
GLASS

C

RUBBER

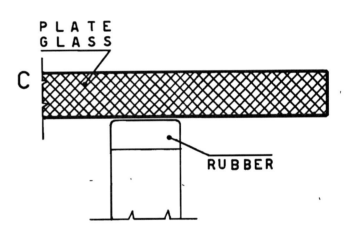

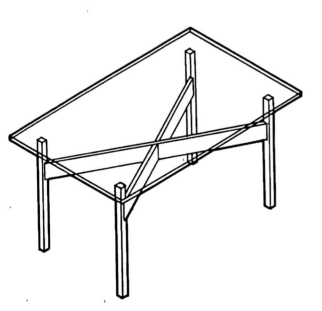

COVER SCREWS

D

RUBBER

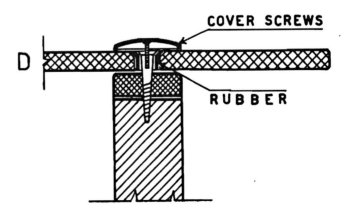

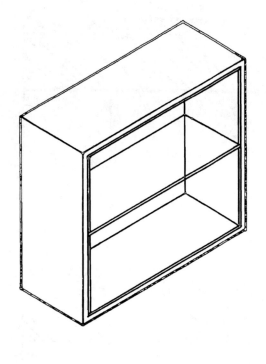

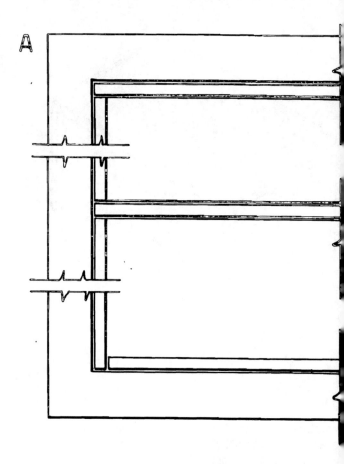

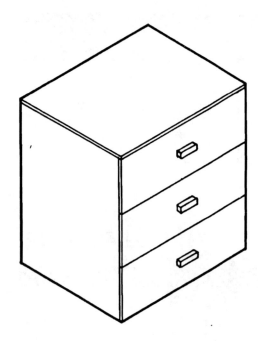

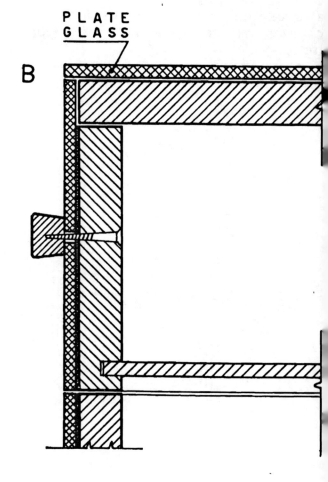

PLATE GLASS

A

B

VARIOUS METHODS OF ATTACHING MIRRORS TO THE
INTERIOR AND EXTERIOR OF FURNITURE PIECES.

106

JOINING METAL AND WOOD

IN THE CONSTRUCTION OF FURNITURE PIECES IT IS OFTEN NECESSARY TO JOIN WOOD AND METAL PARTS. WHILE IT IS CUSTOMARY TO JOIN THESE MATERIALS WITH BOLTS OR SCREWS, SPECIAL ADHESIVES MAY BE USED INSTEAD. BY MEANS OF GLUE, METAL SHEETS CAN BE WELDED TO CELLULAR CORES TO FORM LARGE WATERPROOF PANELS.

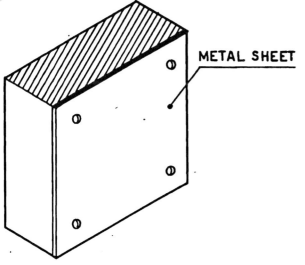

METAL SHEET

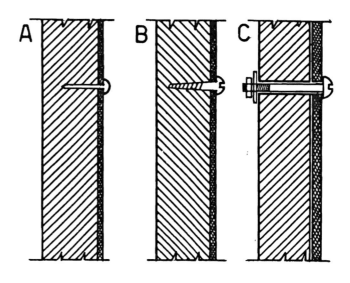

THREE DIFFERENT METHODS OF JOINING METAL SHEETS TO WOOD PANELS.

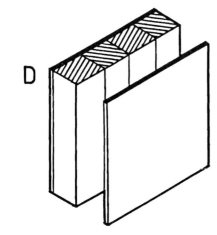

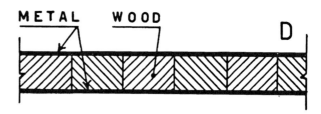

TWO METAL SHEETS HAVE BEEN WELDED TO A WOOD CORE WITH SPECIAL GLUES.

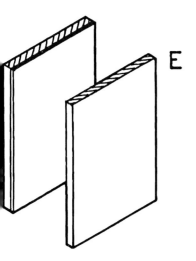

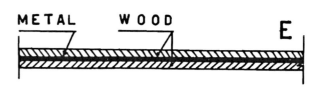

LIGHT METAL SHEET WELDED BETWEEN TWO LAYERS OF WOOD. THIS SHEET WOULD BE WATERPROOF.

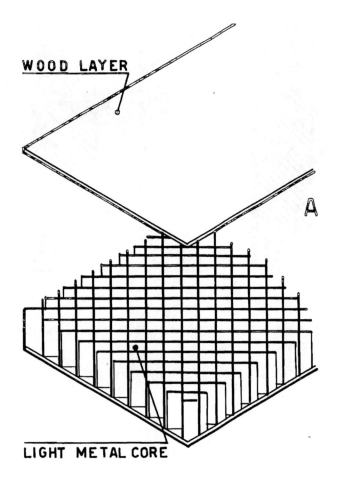

WOOD LAYER

LIGHT METAL CORE

A

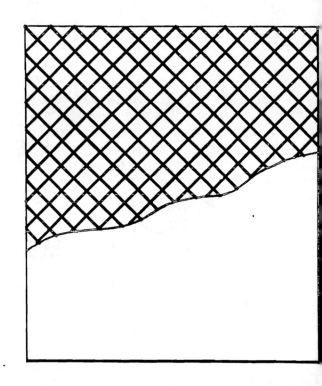

LIGHT METAL HONEYCOMB WELDED BETWEEN TWO WOOD SHEETS. A SPECIAL GLUE MAKES THIS WATERPROOF.

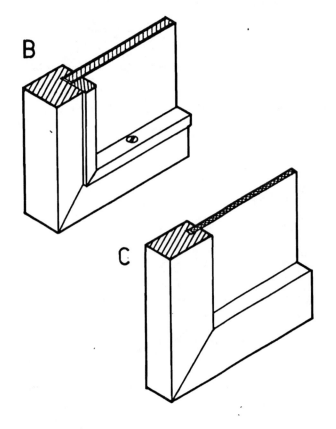

B

C

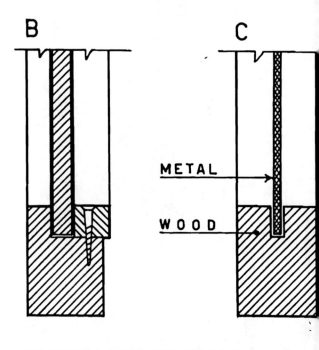

B

C

METAL

WOOD

"B" SHOWS A WOOD AND METAL PANEL IN A RABBET FRAME WITH MOLDING. "C" IS A METAL SHEET IN A GROOVED FRAME.

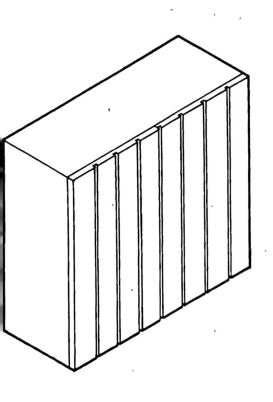

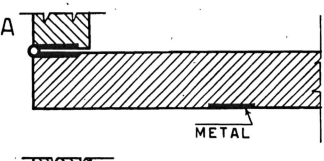

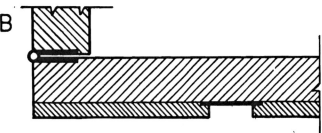

TWO DIFFERENT WAYS OF ATTACHING FLAT METAL
TO WOOD SURFACES. TYPE "A" IS EASY TO APPLY
BUT HAS A TENDENCY TO PULL OUT IN TIME. TYPE
"B" ARRANGEMENT IS PREFERABLE.

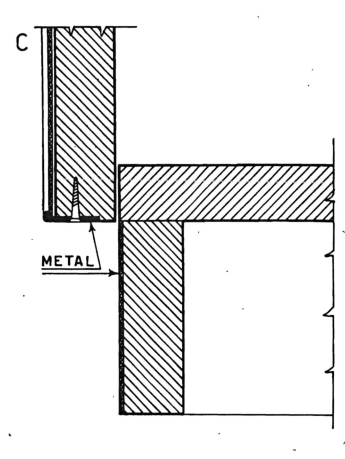

POSSIBLE METHOD OF ATTACHING METAL MOLDING
AND A METAL KICK PLATE.

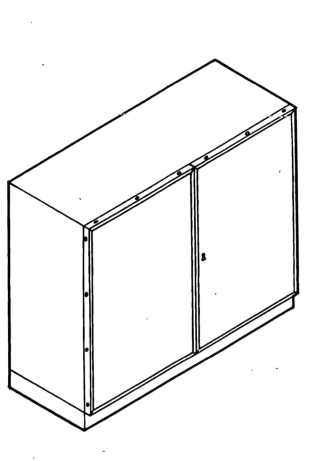

109

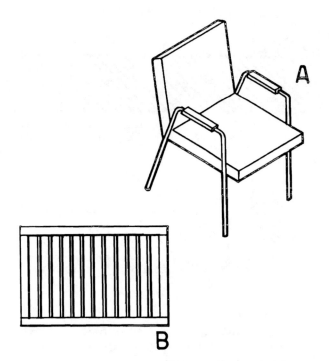

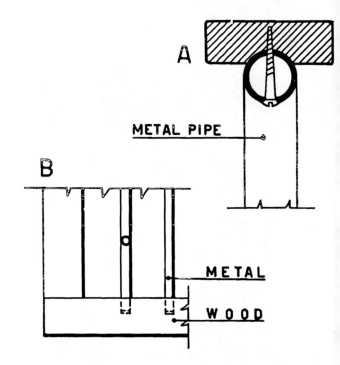

A, B — TWO COMMON WAYS OF JOINING METAL AND WOOD PARTS.

METAL PIPE

METAL

WOOD

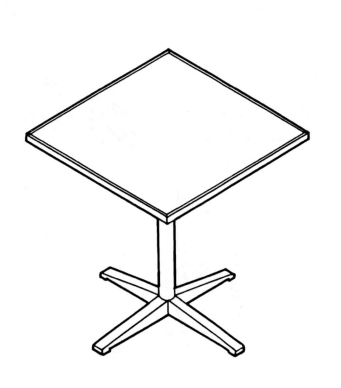

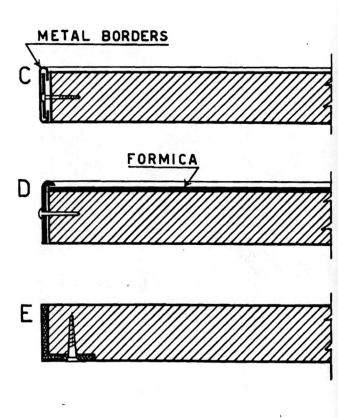

METAL BORDERS

FORMICA

C, D, E — THREE DIFFERENT METHODS OF APPLYING METAL BORDERS.

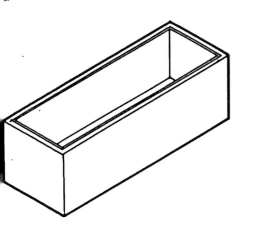

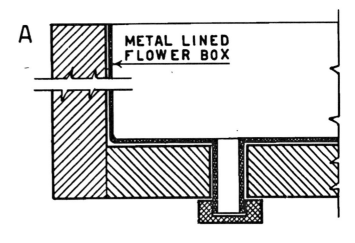

A

METAL LINED
FLOWER BOX

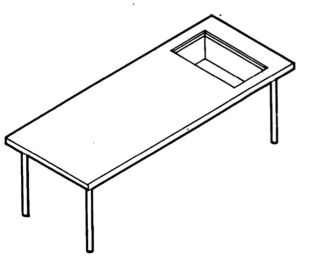

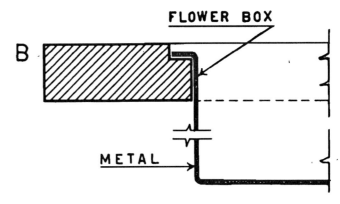

B

FLOWER BOX

METAL

SEVERAL METHODS OF JOINING METAL PANS AND
TRAYS TO WOOD. THE METAL DRAWER ARRANGEMENT
IS PARTICULARLY SUITABLE FOR KITCHEN CABINET
WORK.

PERFORATED METAL DRAWER

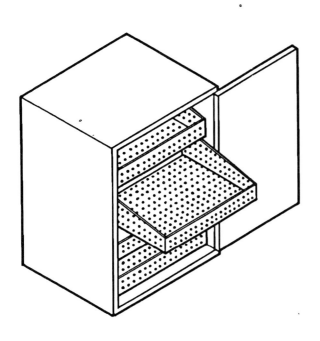

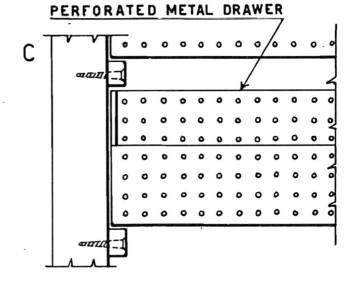

C

JOINING MARBLE AND WOOD

MARBLE AND WOOD MAY BE JOINED IN A NUMBER OF WAYS. BASICALLY, THE METHODS ARE THE SAME USED WITH GLASS. SHOWN ON THIS PAGE ARE THE USUAL METHODS. SCREWS AND BOLTS MAY BE USED.

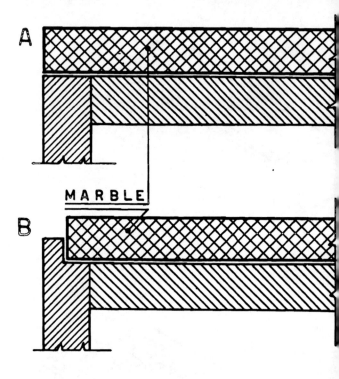

A

B

MARBLE

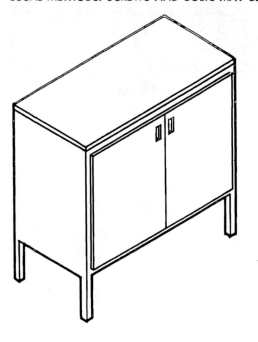

THE TWO EXAMPLES SHOWN ABOVE ARE SIMPLE METHODS. THE EXAMPLE BELOW USES A STUB TENON WITH A MORTISE IN THE MARBLE.

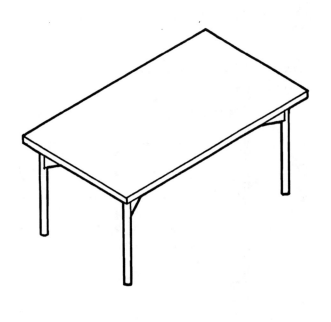

MARBLE

C

WOOD

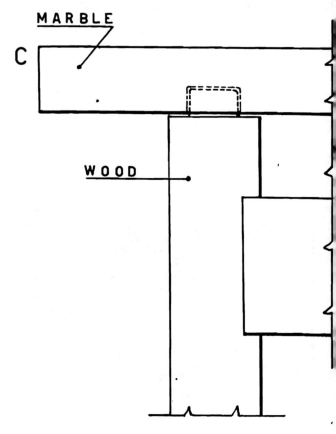

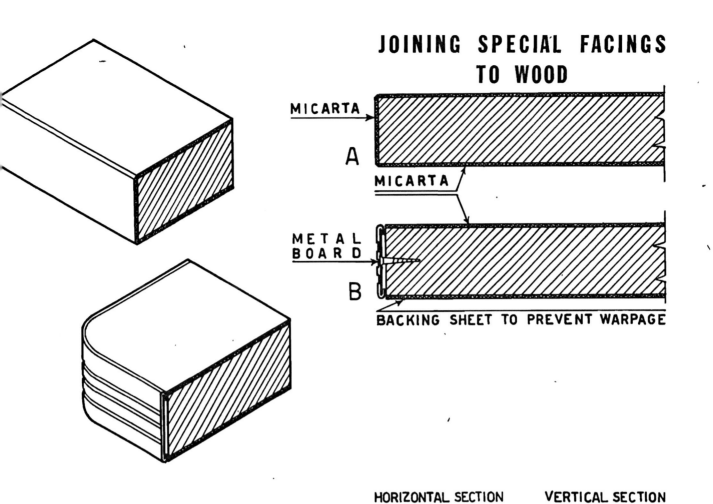

JOINING SPECIAL FACINGS TO WOOD

MICARTA

A

MICARTA

METAL BOARD

B

BACKING SHEET TO PREVENT WARPAGE

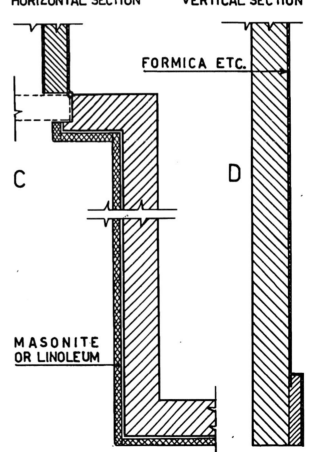

HORIZONTAL SECTION   VERTICAL SECTION

FORMICA ETC.

C

D

MASONITE OR LINOLEUM

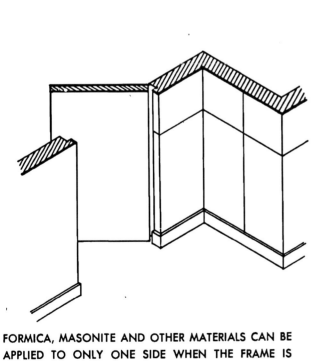

FORMICA, MASONITE AND OTHER MATERIALS CAN BE APPLIED TO ONLY ONE SIDE WHEN THE FRAME IS TOTALLY ENCLOSED.

JOINING RUBBER TO WOOD

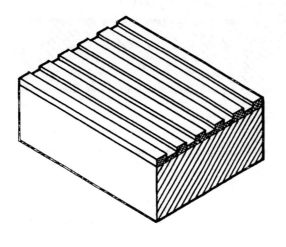

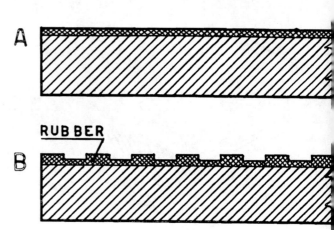

A

RUBBER

B

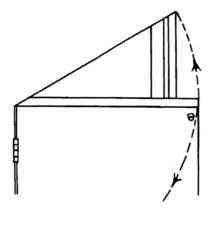

DOOR

C

RUBBER DOMES

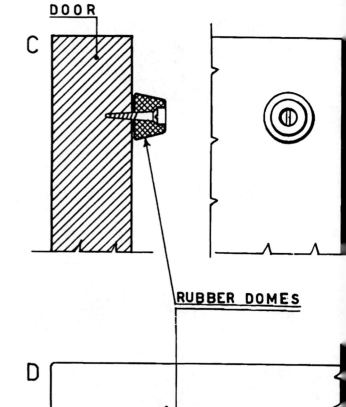

D

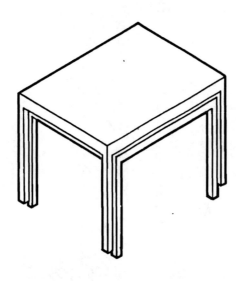

RUBBER IS A GOOD MATERIAL TO USE IN PROTECTING
FURNITURE. HERE ARE SOME WAYS IT MAY BE USED.

PERFORATED TRANSITE JOINED TO WOOD

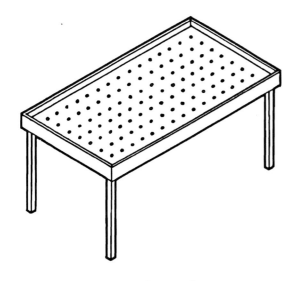

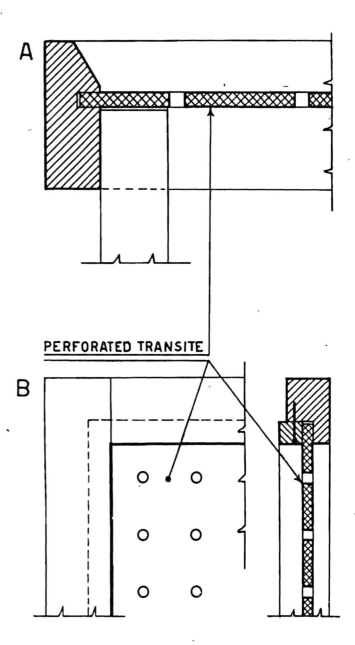

PERFORATED TRANSITE

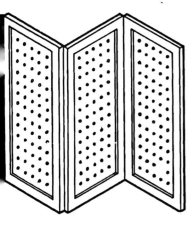

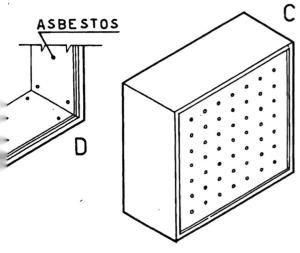

ASBESTOS

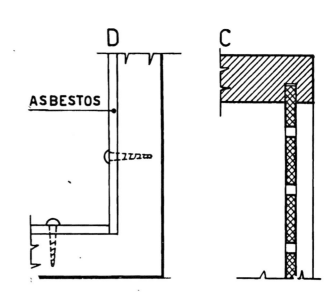

PERFORATED TRANSITE MAY BE ATTACHED IN THE VARIOUS WAYS SHOWN ABOVE. "D" USES ASBESTOS FOR FIRE PROTECTION.

115

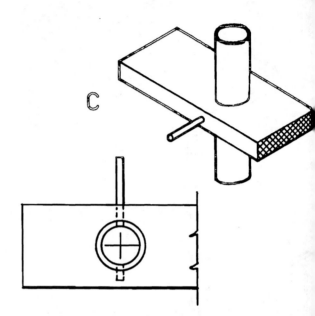

COMMON METAL JOINTS

HERE ARE SEVERAL COMMON METAL JOINTS. METAL
MAY BE USED FOR COMPLETE FURNITURE PIECES OR
FOR PARTS OF FURNITURE.

SLIDING METAL JOINTS. NOTE THAT EITHER PIECE MAY
BE FIXED IN PLACE WITH SCREWS.

UNION OF PIPE AND METAL STRIP HELD IN PLACE
WITH A LOCKING PIN.

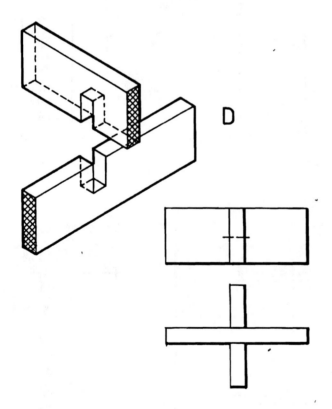

CROSS LAP JOINT USING TWO METAL STRIPS.

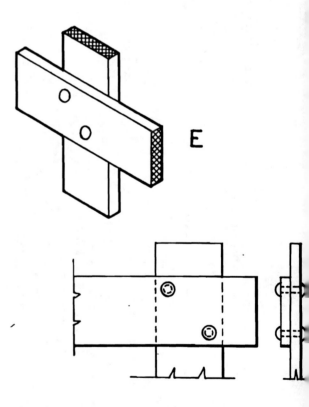

RIVETED JOINING OF TWO METAL STRIPS.

116

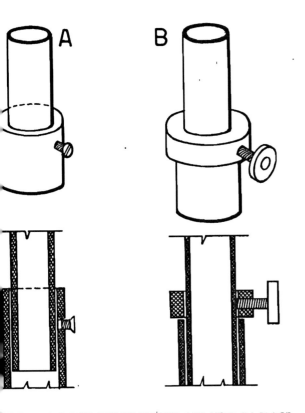

REMOVABLE PIPE JOINTS WHICH ARE HELD IN PLACE
WITH SCREWS.

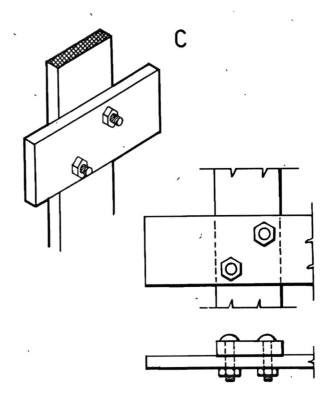

METAL STRIP JOINT HELD IN PLACE WITH BOLTS.

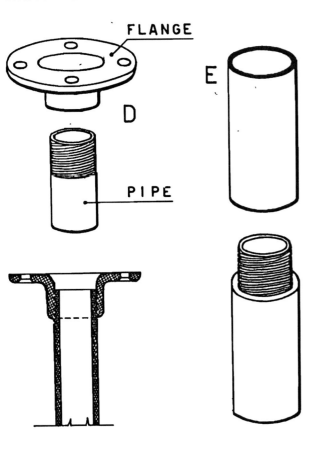

PIPE JOINTS USING SCREWED ENDS.

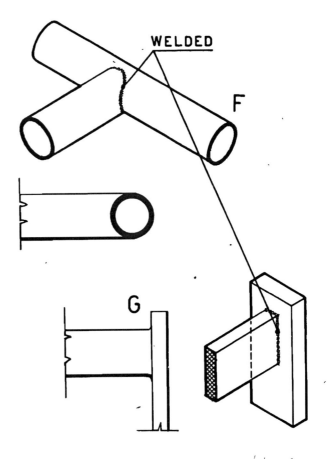

WELDED PIPE AND STRIP JOINTS.

117

JOINING PLATE GLASS TO METAL

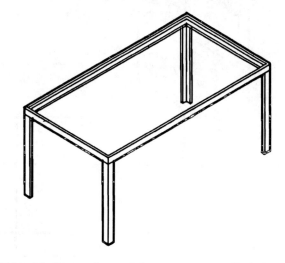

METHOD OF APPLYING PLATE GLASS TO METAL FRAME.

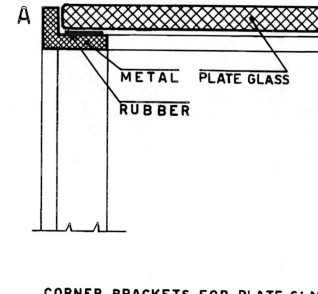

A

METAL   PLATE GLASS

RUBBER

CORNER BRACKETS FOR PLATE GLASS

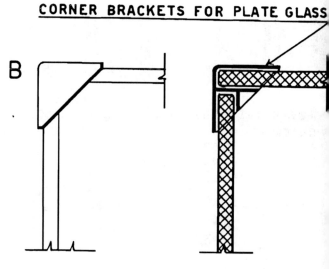

B

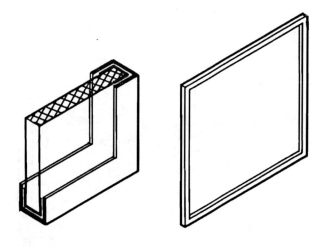

GLASS BOX WITH WOOD BASE USING METAL CORNERS.

VARIOUS WAYS OF ATTACHING METAL FRAMES TO GLASS.

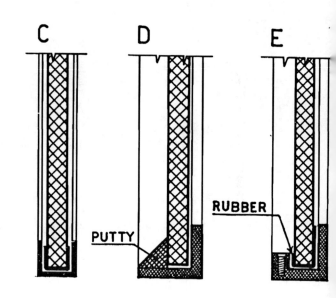

C   D   E

PUTTY   RUBBER

JOINING METAL TO RUBBER

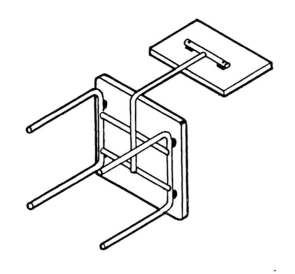

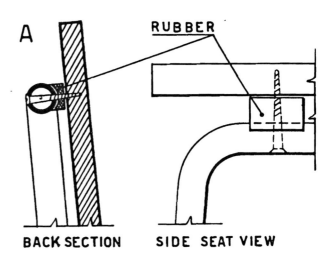

A

RUBBER

BACK SECTION   SIDE SEAT VIEW

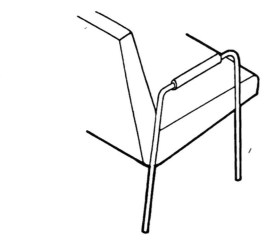

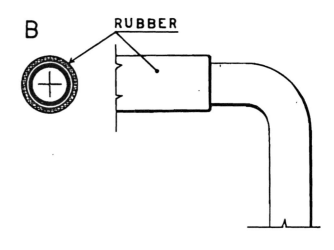

B   RUBBER

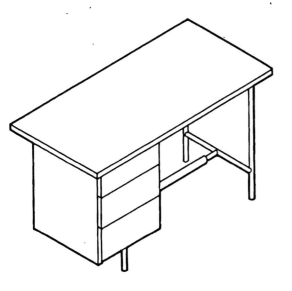

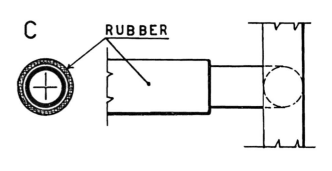

C   RUBBER

RUBBER AND METAL MAY BE JOINED IN ANY OF THE
WAYS SHOWN ABOVE.

MOLDED PLASTIC

WITHIN THEIR OWN DOMAIN, PLASTICS POSSESS AT LEAST AS BROAD A RANGE OF PROPERTIES AS METALS, AND ARE CAPABLE OF AT LEAST AS GREAT A DIVERSITY OF COMPOSITIONS. IN GENERAL, THEY HAVE THE ADVANTAGE THAT THEY CAN BE MOLDED IN FORMS. IT IS ONLY COMPARATIVELY RECENTLY THAT PLASTICS HAVE COME INTO COMMON USE IN THE FURNITURE FIELD. CONTINUOUS RESEARCH IS BEING CONDUCTED TO FURTHER DEVELOP THEIR MANY USES.

WE DO KNOW ENOUGH ABOUT THE CHARACTERISTICS OF PLASTICS TODAY SO THAT THEY MAY BE USED WITH THE ASSURANCE THAT THEY WILL STAND WEAR. HOWEVER, IT IS BEST TO CHECK THE SPECIFIC CHARACTERISTICS OF EACH PLASTIC BEFORE USING IT.

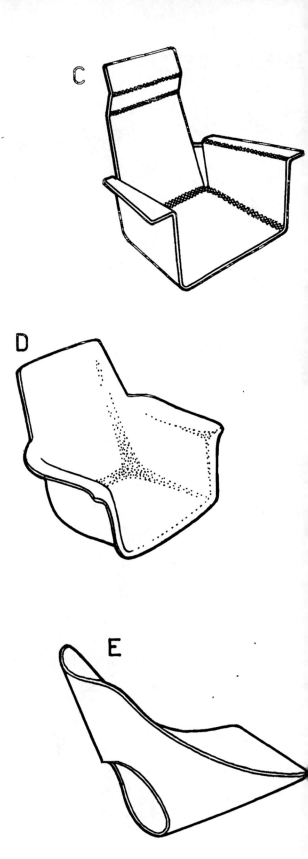

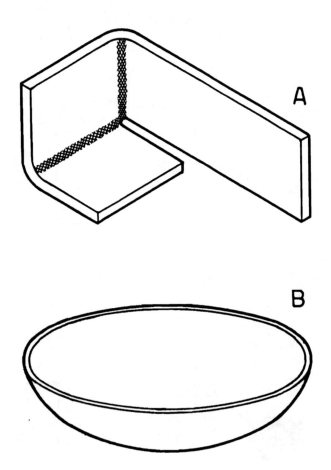

"A," ABOVE, USES HEAT-TREATED PLASTIC TO FORM A CURVE. "B" IS MADE WITH A MOLD. ALMOST ANY SHAPE MAY BE MADE IN THIS MANNER.

THREE PLASTIC CHAIRS

THE METHOD OF MAKING CHAIR "C" IS SIMILAR TO "A." "D" USES A MOLD. "E" IS ALSO MOLDED, BUT HAS A SECTION REMOVED TO TAKE UPHOLSTERING.

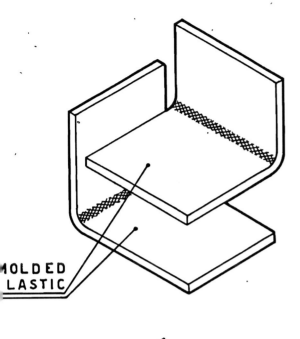

MOLDED PLASTIC

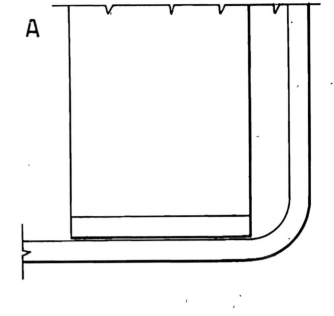

A

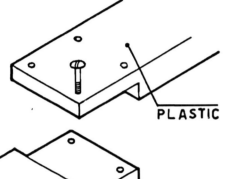

PLASTIC

WOOD

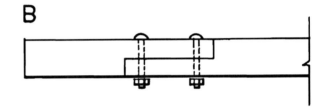

B

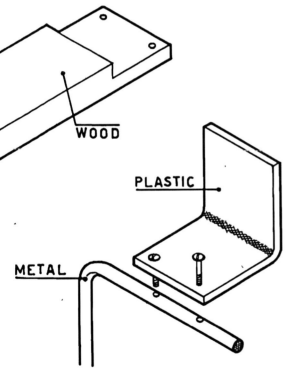

PLASTIC

METAL

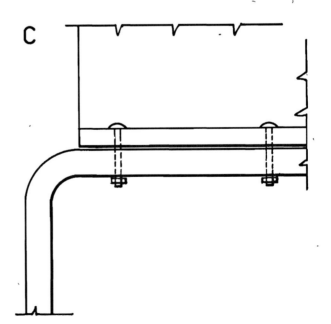

C

A — PLASTIC PIECES JOINED WITH ADHESIVE. SPECIFIC ADHESIVES HAVE BEEN DEVELOPED FOR USE WITH THE VARIOUS TYPES OF PLASTICS.

B — WOOD AND PLASTIC JOINED WITH GLUE AND BOLTS.

C — PLASTIC AND METAL JOINED WITH BOLTS.

UPHOLSTERY WORK

UPHOLSTERING IS AN ART IN ITSELF AND IT STILL RE-
MAINS A HANDCRAFT SYSTEM OF PRODUCTION.
WHILE OTHER PARTS OF FURNITURE CONSTRUCTION
ARE MOSTLY DONE BY MACHINE, THE UPHOLSTERY
WORK IS STILL DONE BY HAND. EXPERT WORKMEN
HAVE USUALLY SERVED A LONG APPRENTICESHIP BE-
FORE ACQUIRING THE SKILL NECESSARY FOR UP-
HOLSTERING A CHAIR OR DIVAN.

THERE ARE, HOWEVER, SEVERAL WAYS THAT UP-
HOLSTERY WORK CAN BE DONE BY APPRENTICES AND
AMATEURS. CHAIRS, STOOLS AND OTHER PIECES CAN
BE UPHOLSTERED BY SUBSTITUTING FOAM RUBBER FOR
THE MATERIALS USED IN NORMAL WORK.

I SHALL NOT GO INTO DETAIL ABOUT UPHOLSTERING,
BUT I HAVE ILLUSTRATED THE VARIOUS TYPES OF
FRAMES; MATERIALS AND METHODS OF APPLICATION.
I HAVE TRIED TO SIMPLIFY THE PRESENTATION TO EN-
ABLE EVEN THE UNSKILLED TO UNDERSTAND EACH
METHOD.

FRAME

THE FRAME, IN EITHER WOOD OR METAL, IS THE SKELE-
TON OF THE FURNITURE PIECE. UPON ITS CONSTRUC-
TION DEPENDS THE COMFORT AND STRENGTH OF
THE CHAIR.

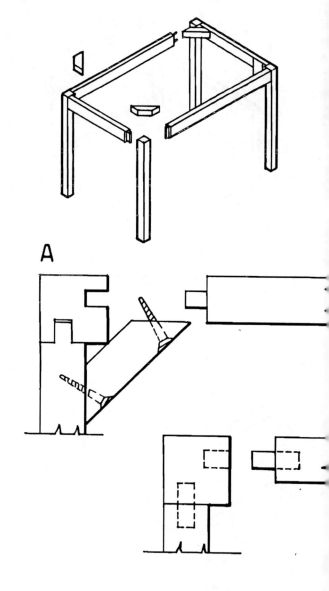

A

TWO DIFFERENT TYPES OF BENCH FRAMES.

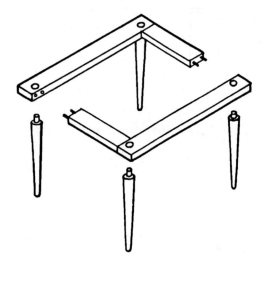

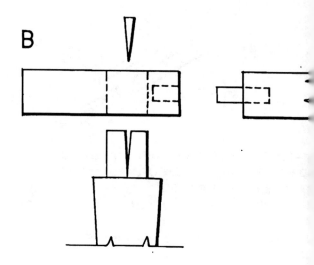

B

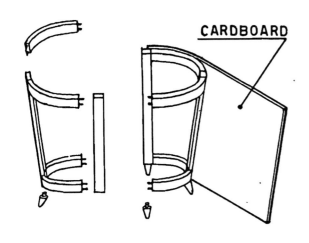

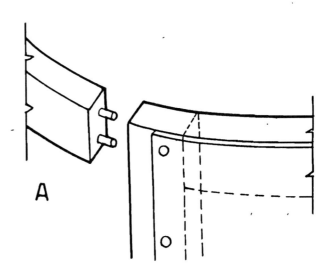

CARDBOARD

A

ROUND FRAME THAT IS COVERED WITH CARDBOARD.
THE UPHOLSTERING MATERIAL IS ADDED LATER.

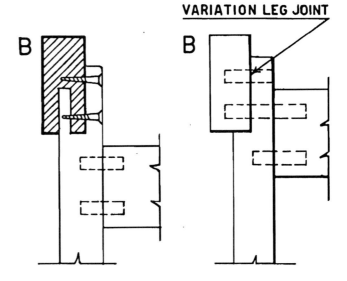

VARIATION LEG JOINT

B

B

FRAME FOR WEBBING SEAT.

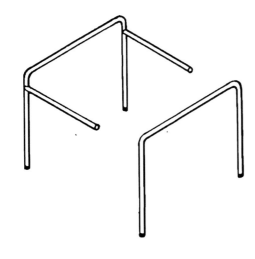

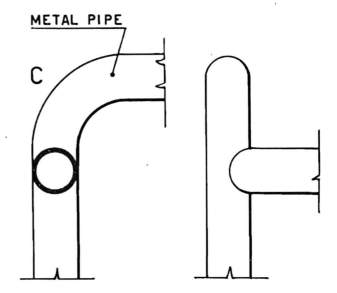

METAL PIPE

C

METAL FRAME STOOL FOR CORD OR CANVAS SEAT.

123

MASS PRODUCED WOODEN CHAIR. NOTE THE TWO
METHODS OF JOINING SEAT AND LEGS.

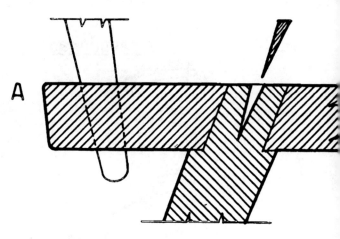

A

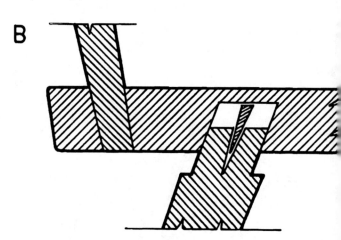

B

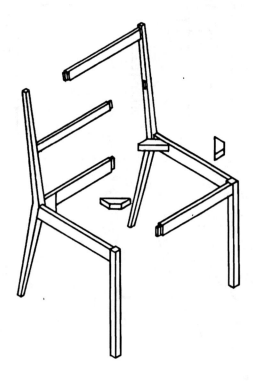

COMMON TYPE OF CHAIR FRAME THAT WILL TAKE AN
UPHOLSTERED SEAT.

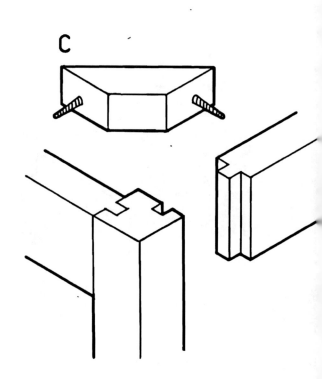

C

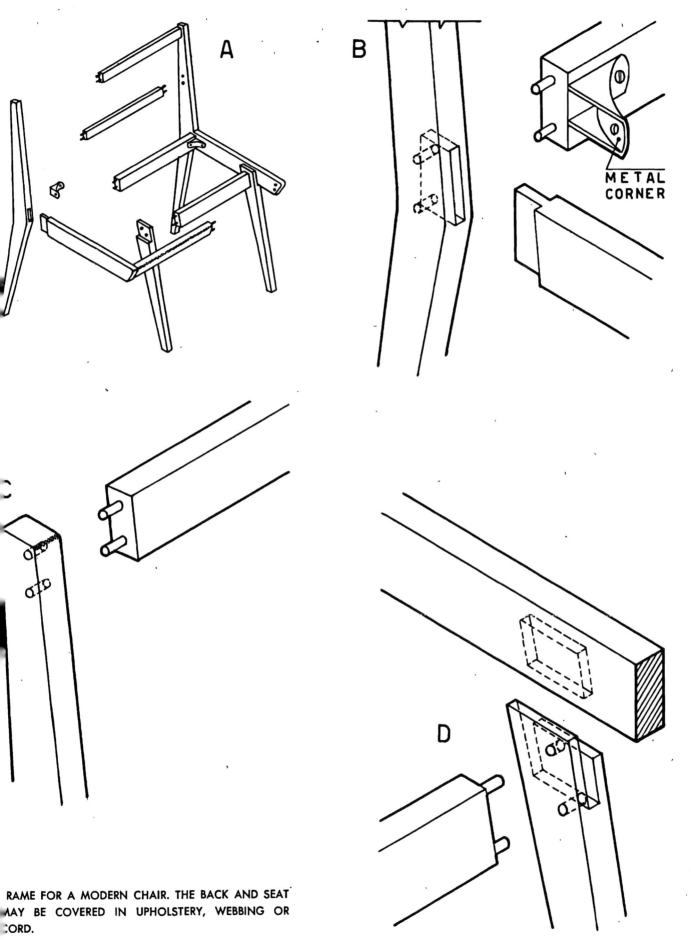

A

B

METAL
CORNER

C

D

RAME FOR A MODERN CHAIR. THE BACK AND SEAT
MAY BE COVERED IN UPHOLSTERY, WEBBING OR
CORD.

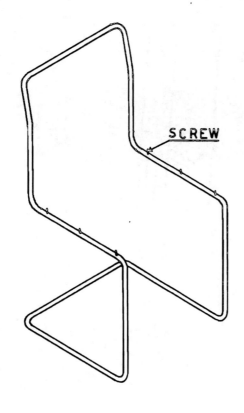

SCREW

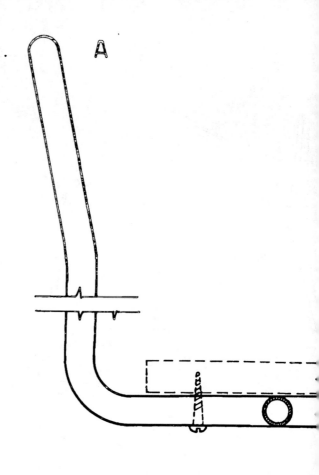

A

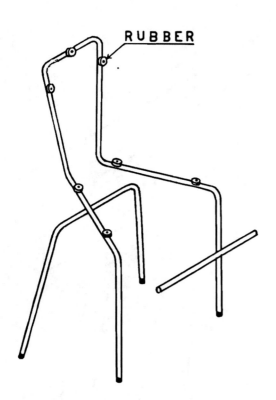

RUBBER

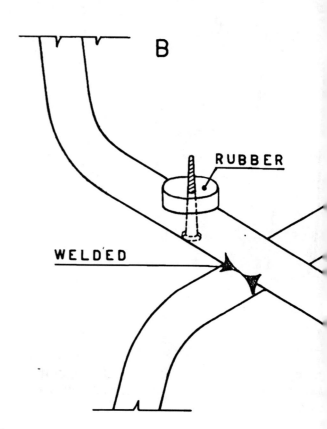

B

RUBBER

WELDED

TWO EXAMPLES OF A METAL FRAME CHAIR. THE RUB-
BER SUPPORTS BETWEEN THE SEAT AND BACK GIVE
ELASTICITY TO THE SEAT.

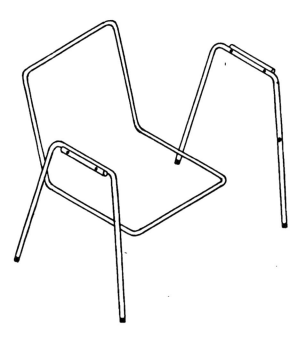

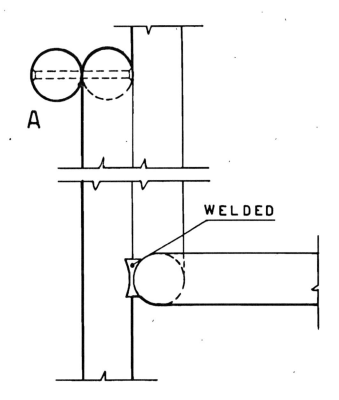

A

WELDED

METAL FRAME ARMCHAIR. THE SEAT AND BACK CAN
BE COVERED WITH CANVAS OR CORD.

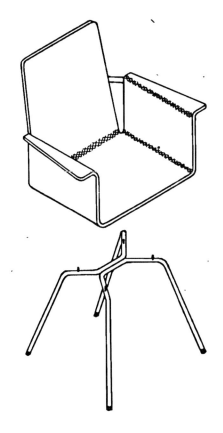

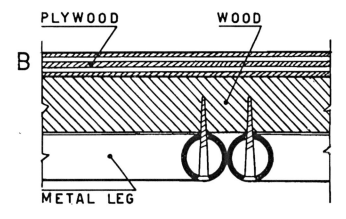

PLYWOOD   WOOD

B

METAL LEG

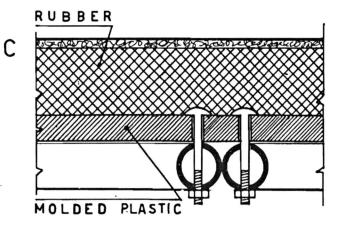

RUBBER

C

MOLDED PLASTIC

PLASTIC CHAIR THAT CAN BE UPHOLSTERED WITH RUB-
BER. LEGS ARE OF METAL.

127

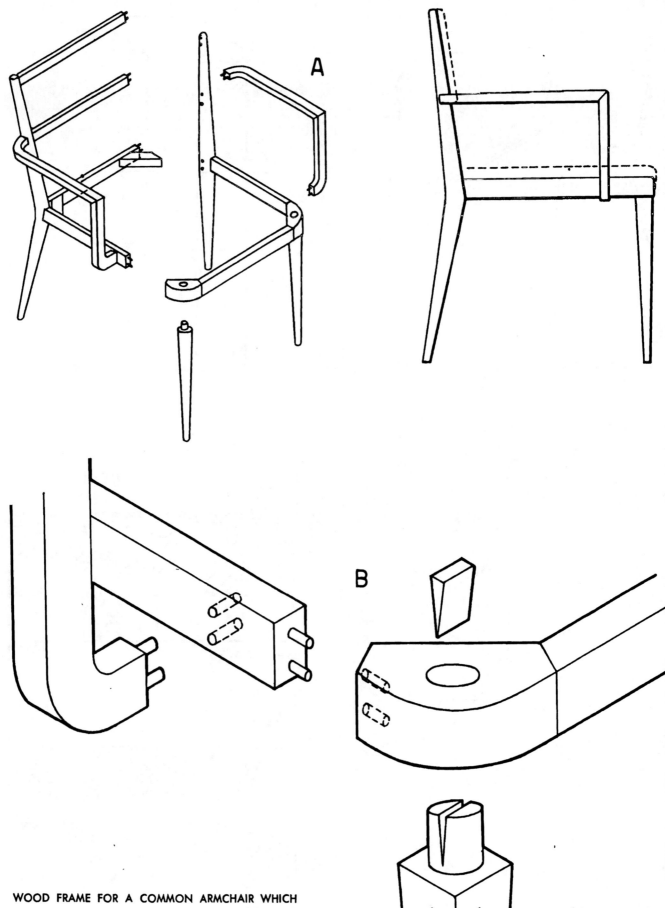

A

B

WOOD FRAME FOR A COMMON ARMCHAIR WHICH
MAY HAVE THE SEAT AND BACK UPHOLSTERED.

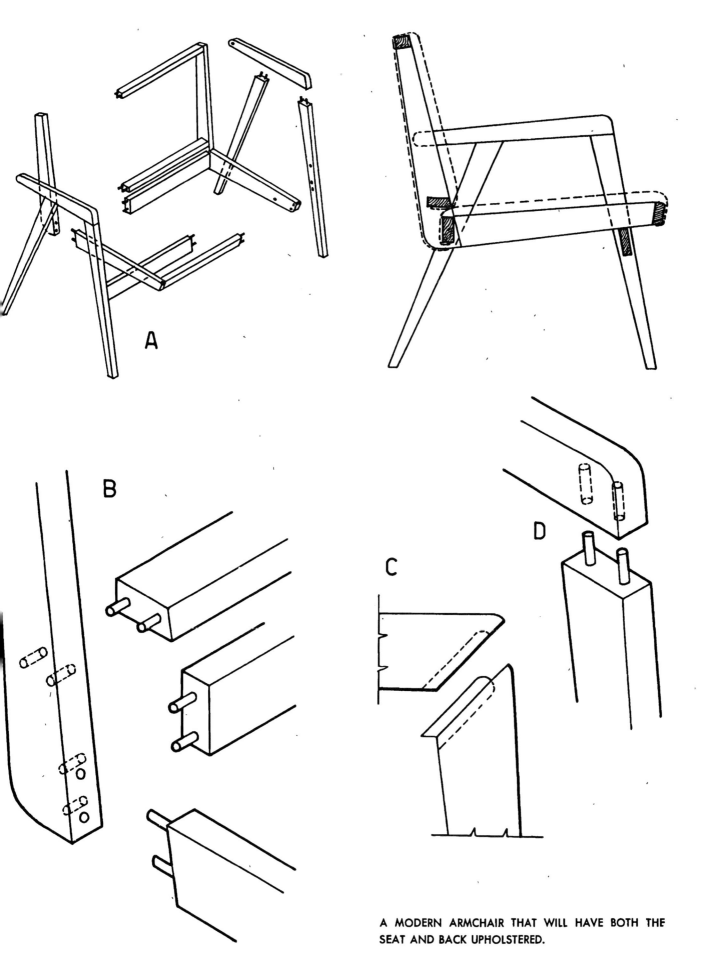

A MODERN ARMCHAIR THAT WILL HAVE BOTH THE
SEAT AND BACK UPHOLSTERED.

A

B

C

D

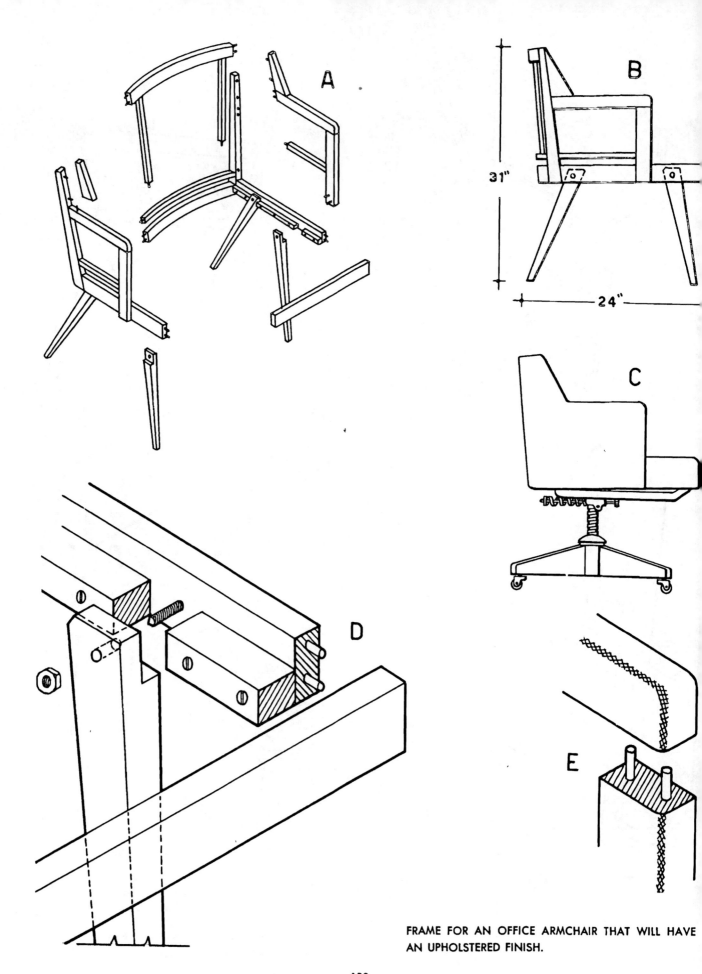

A

B

31"

24"

C

D

E

FRAME FOR AN OFFICE ARMCHAIR THAT WILL HAVE
AN UPHOLSTERED FINISH.

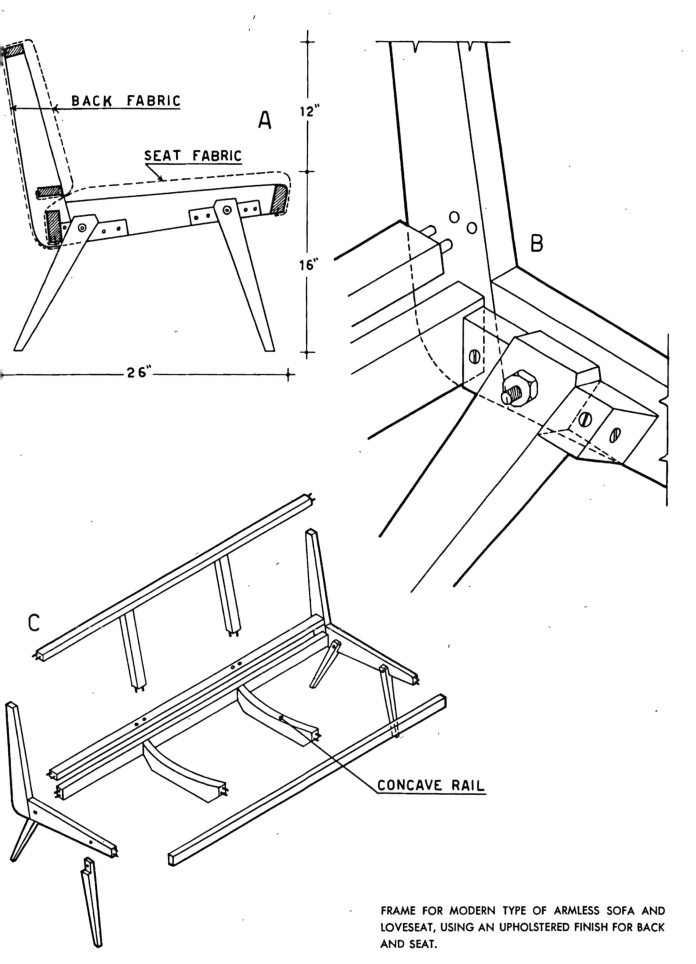

BACK FABRIC

SEAT FABRIC

A

12"

16"

26"

B

C

CONCAVE RAIL

FRAME FOR MODERN TYPE OF ARMLESS SOFA AND
LOVESEAT, USING AN UPHOLSTERED FINISH FOR BACK
AND SEAT.

131

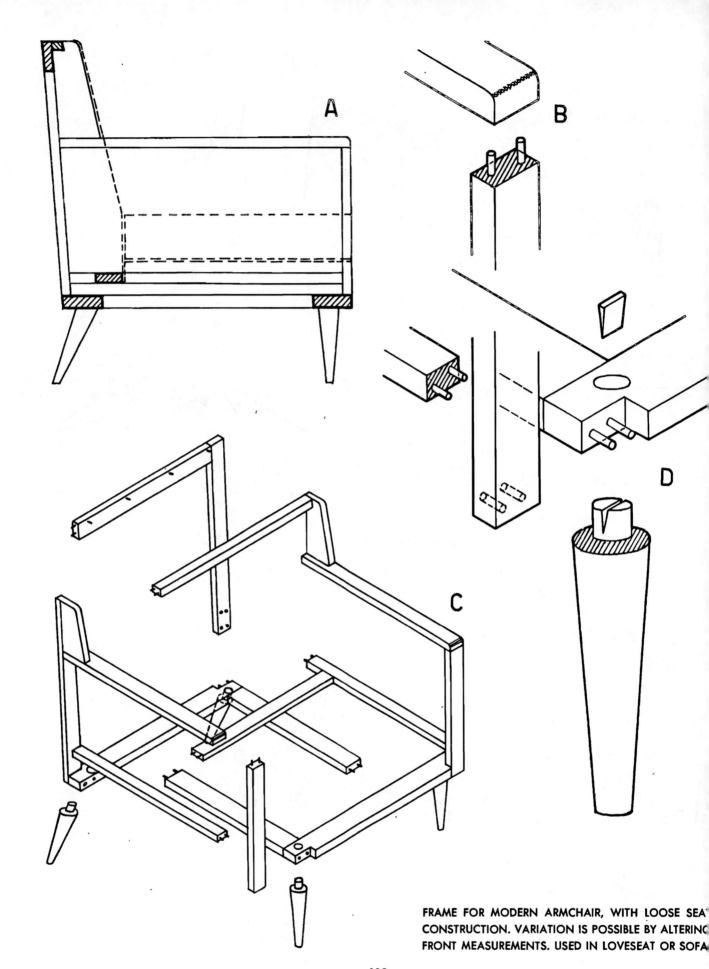

A

B

C

D

FRAME FOR MODERN ARMCHAIR, WITH LOOSE SEA
CONSTRUCTION. VARIATION IS POSSIBLE BY ALTERING
FRONT MEASUREMENTS. USED IN LOVESEAT OR SOFA

UPHOLSTERY MATERIALS

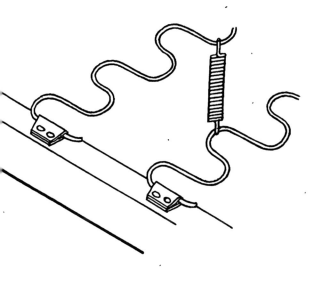

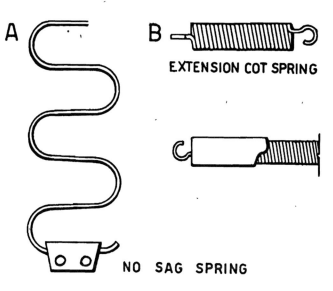

A

B

EXTENSION COT SPRING

NO SAG SPRING

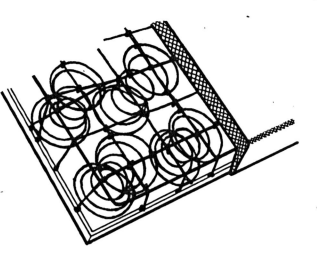

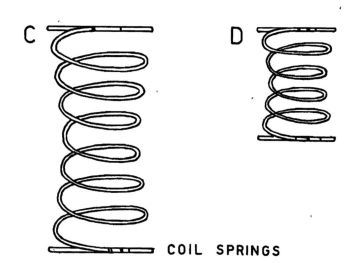

C

D

COIL SPRINGS

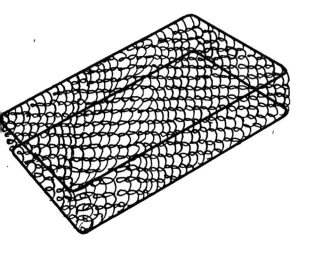

VARIOUS TYPES OF SPRINGS USED IN UPHOLSTERY
WORK.

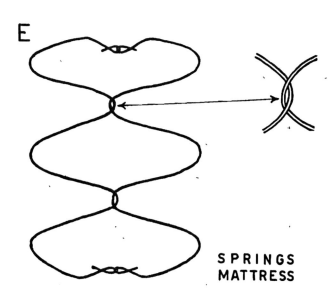

E

SPRINGS
MATTRESS

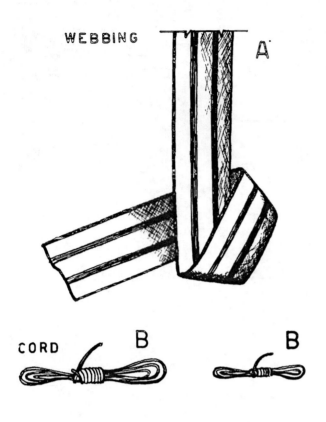

WEBBING

A

CORD B B

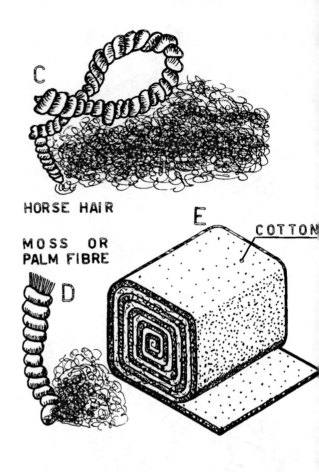

C

HORSE HAIR

MOSS OR
PALM FIBRE

D

E

COTTON

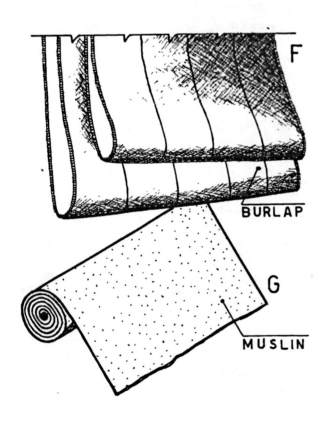

F

BURLAP

G

MUSLIN

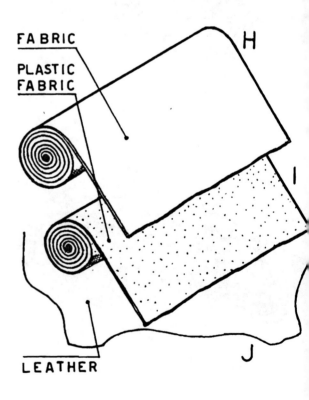

FABRIC

PLASTIC
FABRIC

H

I

LEATHER

J

VARIOUS MATERIALS USED IN UPHOLSTERY.

RUBBERIZED HAIR

A LIGHT AND ELASTIC MATERIAL OF RELATIVE LOW COST WHICH IS USED IN MASS PRODUCTION. IT CAN BE EASILY APPLIED USING STAPLES OR TACKS, AND THE SIZE IS THE SAME AS FOAM RUBBER.

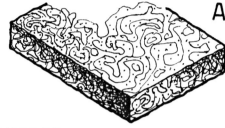

A

FOAM RUBBER

MADE FROM LIQUID LATEX WHICH FORMS A CREAM-LIKE FOAM AFTER BEING PUT THROUGH AIR PRESSURE. IT IS THEN POURED INTO MOLDS OF DESIRED SIZE. IN UPHOLSTERY WORK IT GIVES BETTER RESULTS THAN STUFFING AND IS QUICKER AND EASIER TO USE.

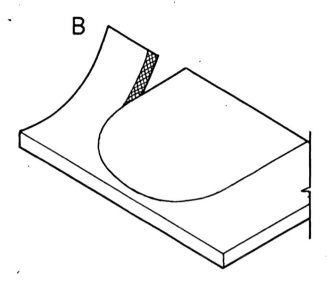

B

CUT FOAM RUBBER WITH SCISSORS FOR CUSTOM WORK, USE BAND SAW FOR STANDARD PRODUCTION. RUBBER SLABS GLUED TOGETHER WITH CEMENT.

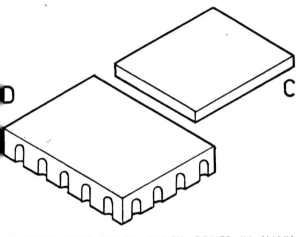

C — SOLID SLAB UTILITY STOCK COMES IN MANY THICKNESSES FROM ¼" TO 1¼".

D — CORED UTILITY STOCK IS DIFFERENT FROM THE SOLID SLAB IN THAT IT HAS A UNIFORM OPEN CORE. ITS THICKNESS VARIES FROM ¾" TO 4½".

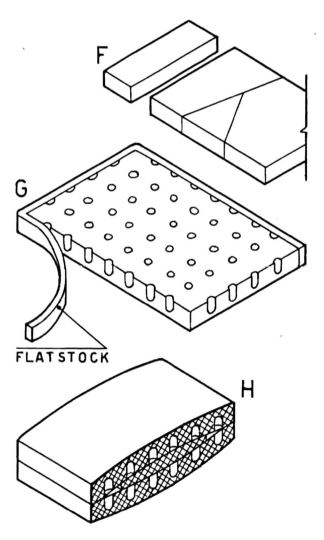

FLATSTOCK

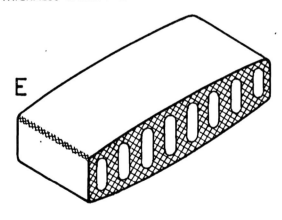

E — FULL MOLDED CUSHION CAN BE MADE IN DIFFERENT SIZES AND SHAPES.

F — SMALL PIECES GLUED TOGETHER TO FORM ONE LARGE PIECE. G — FLATSTOCK GLUED TO A SLAB. H — A FULL CUSHION MADE FROM CORED STOCK.

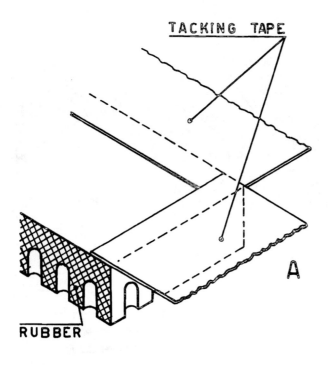

TACKING TAPE

RUBBER

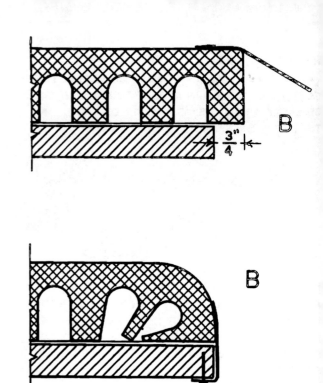

B

$\frac{3"}{4}$

B

METHOD OF APPLYING TACKING TAPE AROUND THE EDGES OF A FOAM RUBBER SLAB USING CEMENT.

IN MAKING CONTOURED EDGES THE FOAM RUBBER SHOULD BE CUT ¾" LARGER THAN THE PIECE BEING UPHOLSTERED.

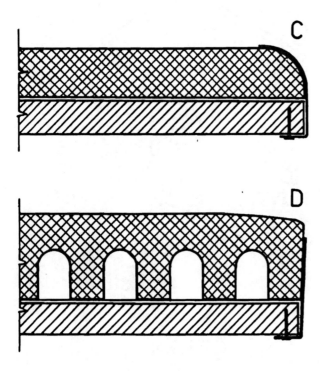

C

D

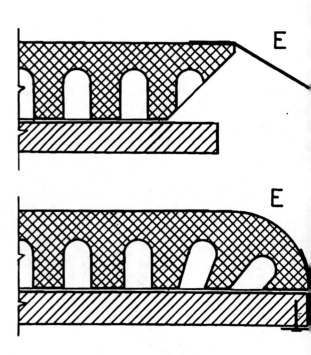

E

E

TWO DIFFERENT USES OF THE TACKING TAPE. THE RUBBER CUSHION IS CUT ¼" LARGER THAN THE PIECE IT COVERS.

ANOTHER WAY OF MAKING A CURVED EDGE.

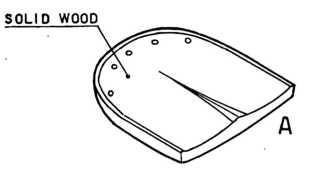

SOLID WOOD

A

PLYWOOD

B

SEATS

THE SEAT DESIGN IS THE MOST IMPORTANT POINT IN UPHOLSTERY WORK FOR UPON ITS CONSTRUCTION DEPENDS THE USEFULNESS OF THE CHAIR OR DIVAN. EACH SEAT MUST BE MADE IN ACCORDANCE WITH THE TYPE OF FRAME TO WHICH IT IS ATTACHED. IT MAY BE MOVABLE OR FIXED, LIGHT OR HEAVY. A WIDE VARIETY OF MATERIALS MAY BE USED.

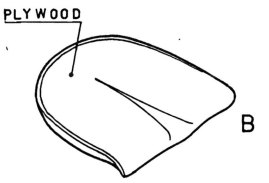

TWO TYPES OF WOOD SEAT THAT MAY BE USED. THE UPPER ONE IS OF SOLID WOOD, THE LOWER OF PLYWOOD.

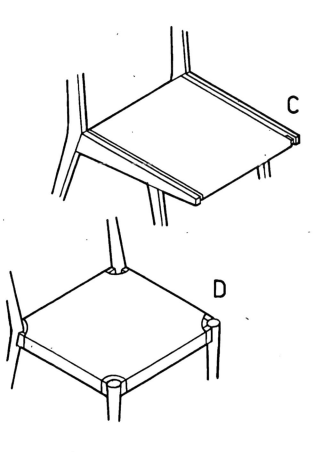

C

D

LEATHER SEATS LIKE THESE ARE EASY TO MAKE.

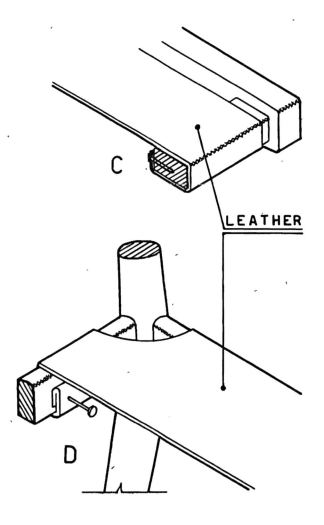

C

LEATHER

D

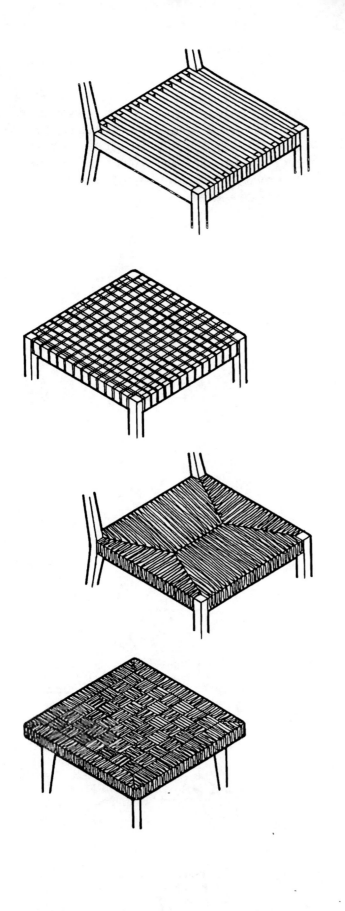

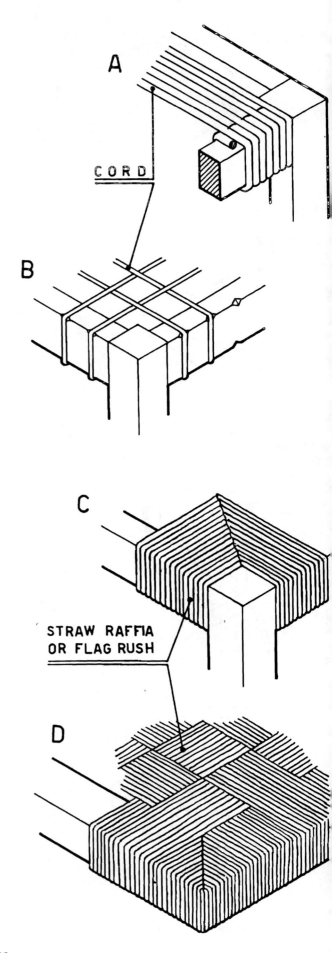

A

CORD

B

C

STRAW RAFFIA
OR FLAG RUSH

D

VARIOUS TYPES OF SEATS THAT CAN BE MADE WITH
CORD, STRAW, RAFFIA OR FLAG RUSH. IN GENERAL,
ANY OF THESE SYSTEMS IS TIME-CONSUMING.

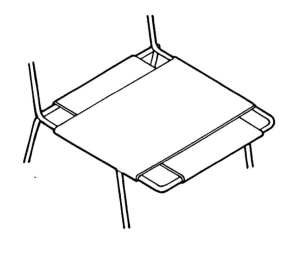

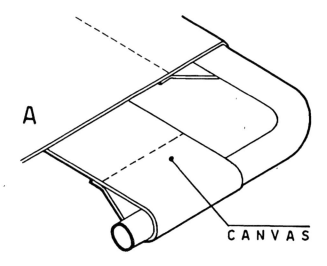

A

CANVAS

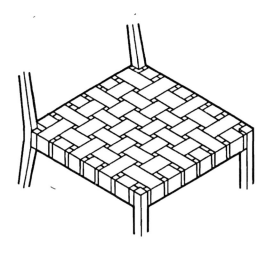

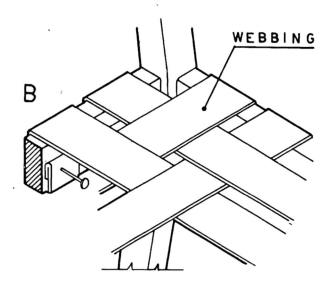

WEBBING

B

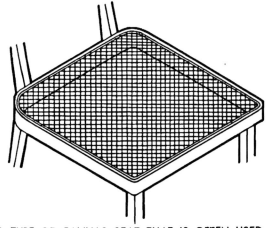

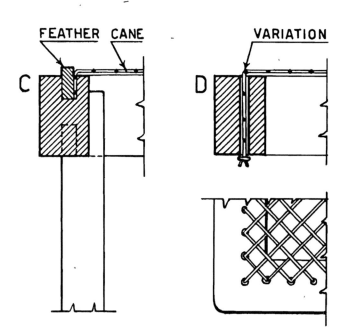

FEATHER   CANE

C

VARIATION

D

A — A TYPE OF CANVAS SEAT THAT IS OFTEN USED
WITH STEEL FRAMES.

B — WEBBING SEAT WHICH IS USED ON MODERN
FURNITURE.

C — CANE MAKES A GOOD TYPE OF SEAT. NOTE THE
ALTERNATE METHOD OF ATTACHING THE CANE
SHOWN IN DIAGRAM D.

139

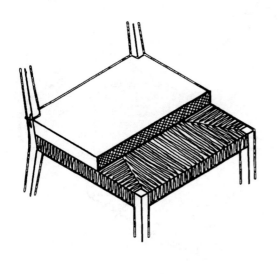

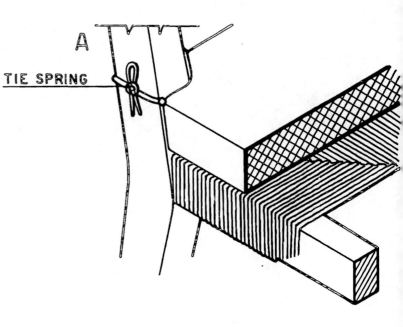

A

TIE SPRING

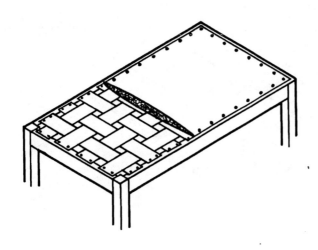

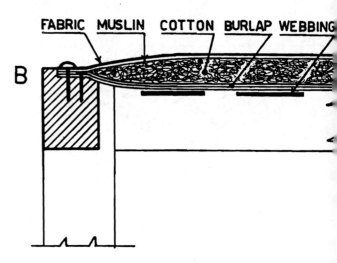

FABRIC MUSLIN COTTON BURLAP WEBBING

B

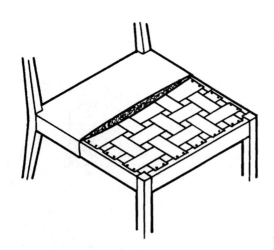

C

THREE DIFFERENT TYPES OF UPHOLSTERED SEAT. "A"
IS AN ARRANGEMENT FOR A REMOVABLE CUSHION,
"B" AND "C" ARE PERMANENTLY ATTACHED TO THE
CHAIR FRAME.

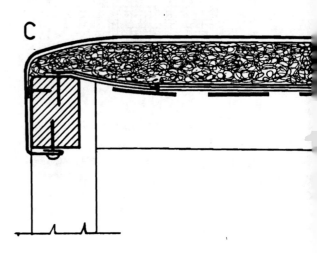

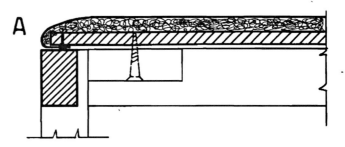

A

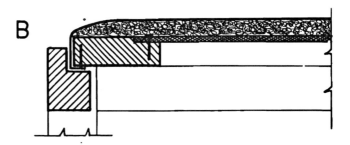

B

FABRIC   COTTON   PLYWOOD

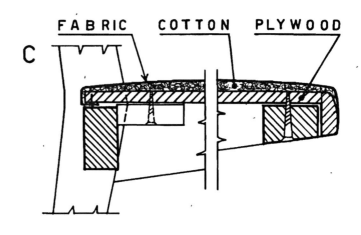

C

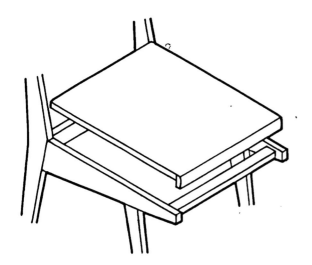

NO SAG SPRING   COTTON   FABRIC

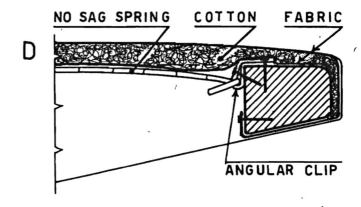

D

ANGULAR CLIP

THESE FOUR SEATS ARE MADE INDEPENDENTLY OF
THE CHAIR FRAME. IN COMMERCIAL WORK, GREATER
SPEED OF ASSEMBLY IS POSSIBLE WHEN THE FRAME
AND SEAT CAN BE MADE INDEPENDENTLY.

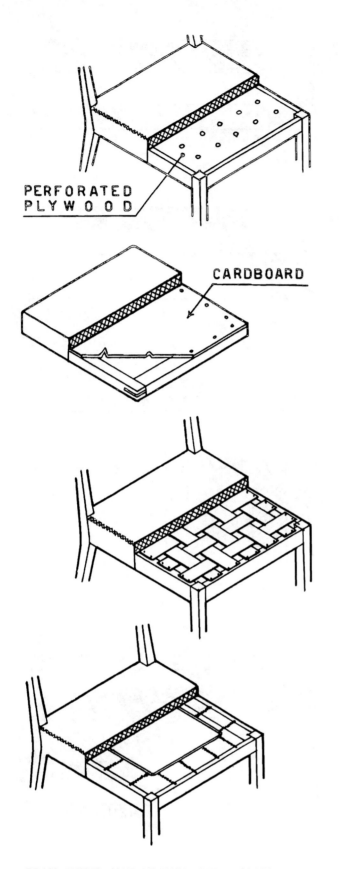

PERFORATED
PLYWOOD

CARDBOARD

FOAM RUBBER MAY BE USED OVER A NUMBER OF
OTHER MATERIALS. PLYWOOD OR CARDBOARD MAY
BE USED AS SHOWN IN "A" AND "B" ABOVE. RUBBER
OVER WEBBING IS USED IN "C"; CANVAS AND
SPRINGS ARE USED IN "D."

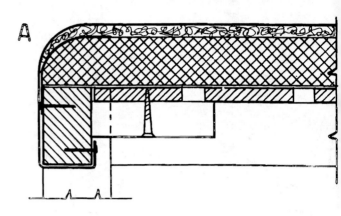

A

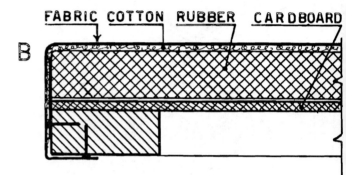

FABRIC COTTON RUBBER CARDBOARD

B

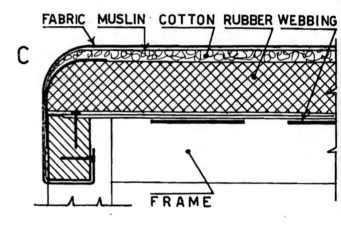

FABRIC MUSLIN COTTON RUBBER WEBBING

C

FRAME

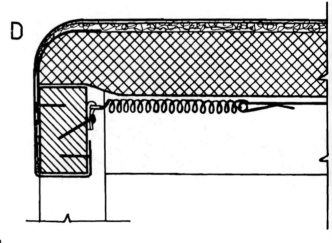

D

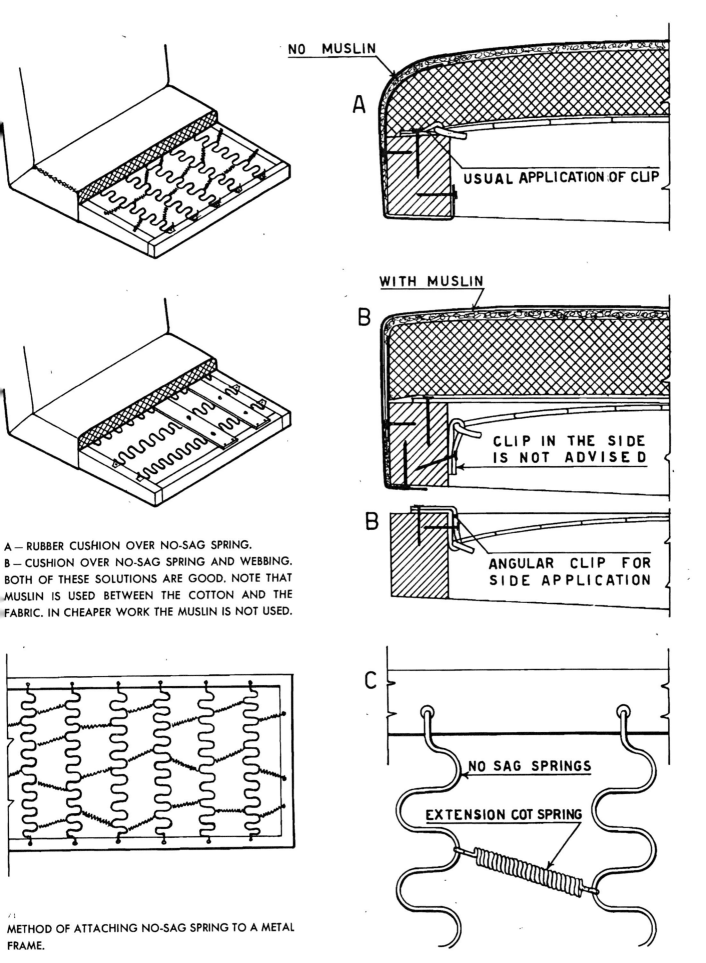

NO MUSLIN

A

USUAL APPLICATION OF CLIP

WITH MUSLIN

B

CLIP IN THE SIDE
IS NOT ADVISED

B

ANGULAR CLIP FOR
SIDE APPLICATION

C

NO SAG SPRINGS

EXTENSION COT SPRING

A — RUBBER CUSHION OVER NO-SAG SPRING.
B — CUSHION OVER NO-SAG SPRING AND WEBBING.
BOTH OF THESE SOLUTIONS ARE GOOD. NOTE THAT
MUSLIN IS USED BETWEEN THE COTTON AND THE
FABRIC. IN CHEAPER WORK THE MUSLIN IS NOT USED.

METHOD OF ATTACHING NO-SAG SPRING TO A METAL
FRAME.

143

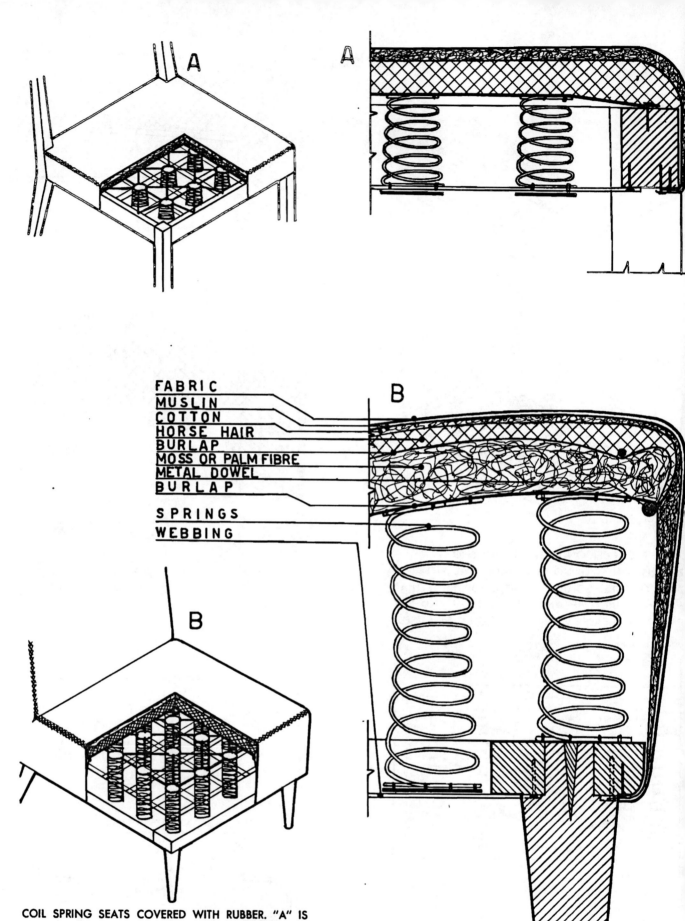

FABRIC
MUSLIN
COTTON
HORSE HAIR
BURLAP
MOSS OR PALM FIBRE
METAL DOWEL
BURLAP

SPRINGS
WEBBING

COIL SPRING SEATS COVERED WITH RUBBER. "A" IS
A TIGHT SEAT. "B" IS A HEAVY SEAT THAT IS SUITABLE
FOR AN ARMCHAIR OR SOFA.

144

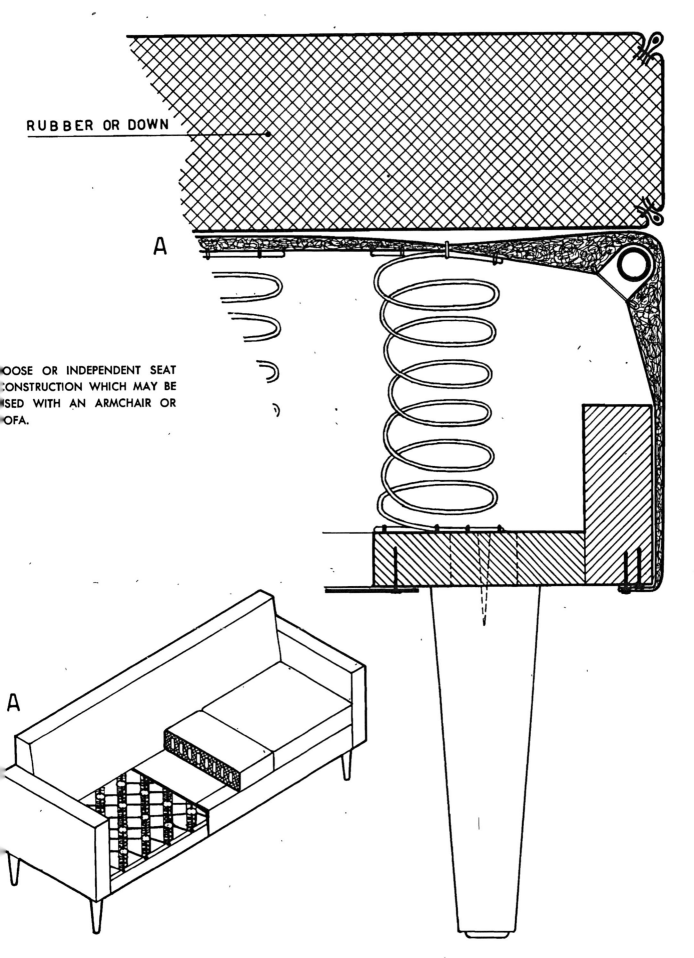

RUBBER OR DOWN

A

LOOSE OR INDEPENDENT SEAT
CONSTRUCTION WHICH MAY BE
USED WITH AN ARMCHAIR OR
SOFA.

A

145

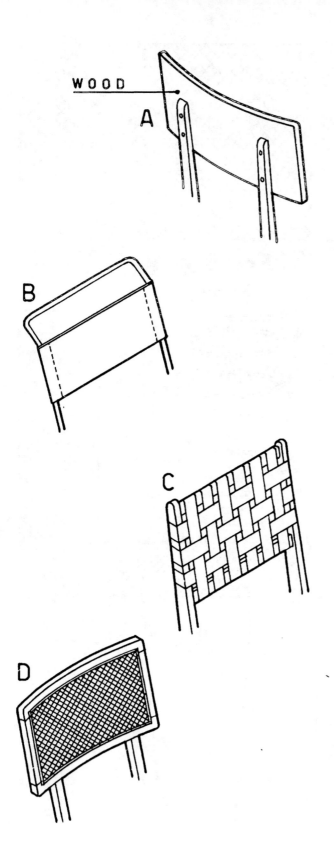

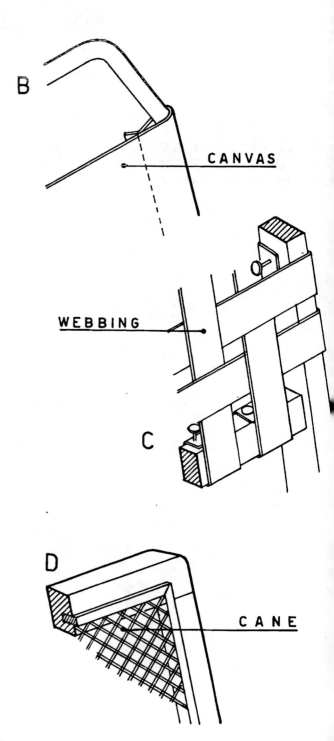

BACKS

THE BACK OF A CHAIR IS USUALLY LIGHTER IN CON
STRUCTION AND MORE RIGID THAN THE SEAT. THER
ARE EXCEPTIONS; SOMETIMES THE SEAT IS OF WOO
AND THE BACK IS UPHOLSTERED. LIKE THE SEAT, TH
BACK MAY BE CONSTRUCTED IN A NUMBER OF WAY.
I HAVE ILLUSTRATED A FEW OF THE BEST METHOD

FOUR TYPES OF BACKS THAT CAN BE USED: "A" IS
MADE OF WOOD; "B" IS OF CANVAS; "C" USES WEB-
BING; "D" IS OF CANE.

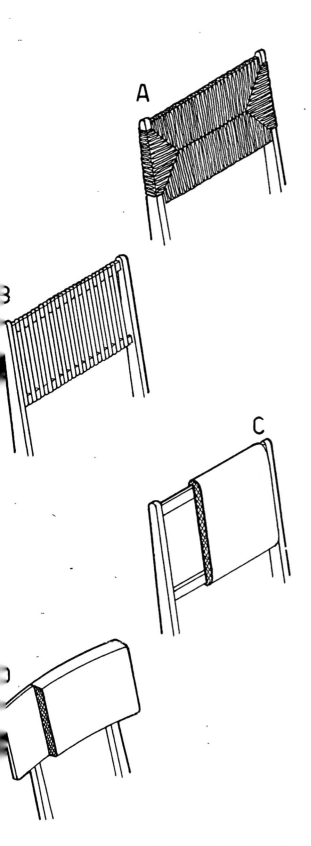

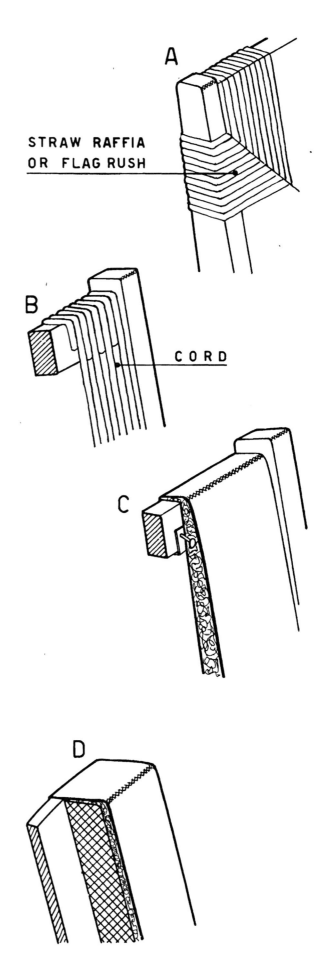

STRAW RAFFIA OR FLAG RUSH

CORD

— STRAW, RAFFIA OR FLAG RUSH USED TO FORM
ACK.
— CORD BACK THAT IS EASY TO MAKE.
— SIMPLE UPHOLSTERED BACK SUITABLE FOR MODERN
JRNITURE.
— WOOD BACK COVERED WITH FOAM RUBBER AND
ABRIC.

147

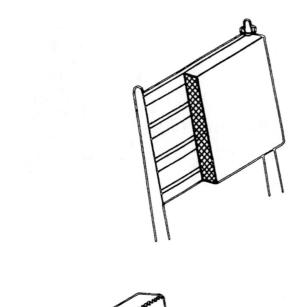

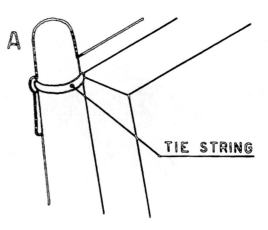

TIE STRING

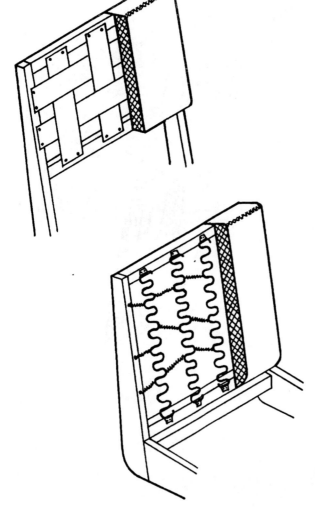

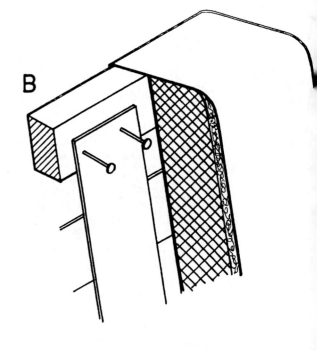

B

C

D

A — REMOVABLE BACK CUSHION ATTACHED WITH A STRING.

B — FOAM RUBBER BACK OVER WEBBING.

C — FOAM RUBBER APPLIED OVER A NO-SAG SPRING.

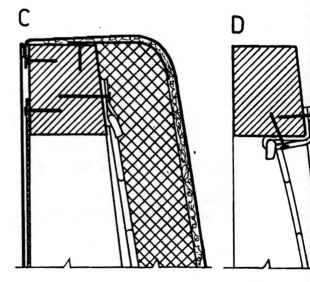

148

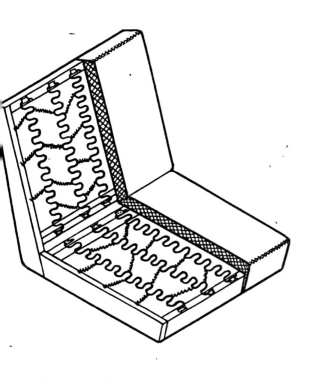

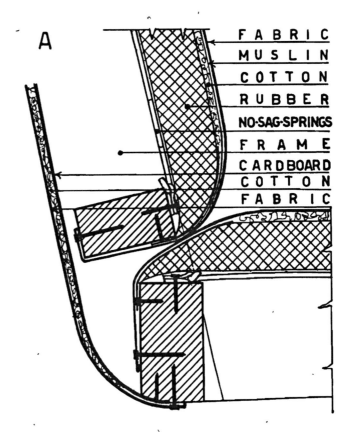

A

FABRIC	
MUSLIN	
COTTON	
RUBBER	
NO-SAG-SPRINGS	
FRAME	
CARDBOARD	
COTTON	
FABRIC	

METHOD OF APPLYING UPHOLSTERY MATERIAL IN THE CORNER FORMED BY THE SEAT AND BACK.

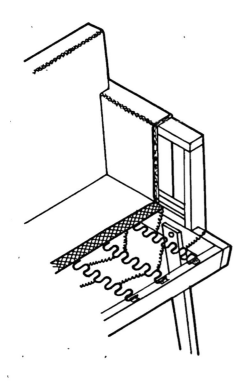

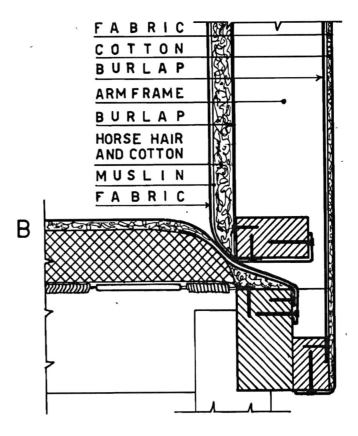

FABRIC	
COTTON	
BURLAP	
ARM FRAME	
BURLAP	
HORSE HAIR AND COTTON	
MUSLIN	
FABRIC	

B

HERE IS ONE WAY OF ATTACHING THE MATERIAL WHERE THE ARM MEETS THE SEAT.

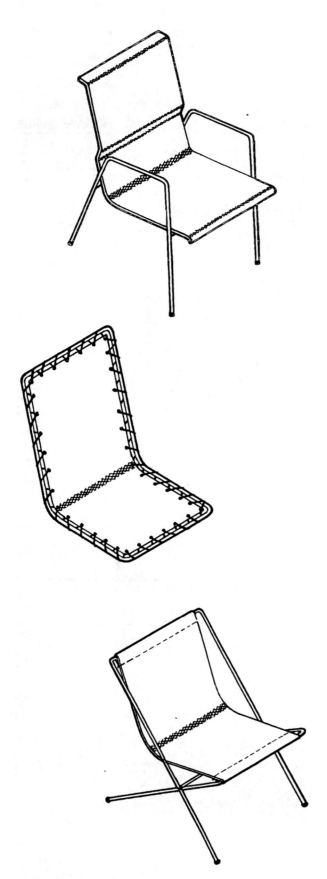

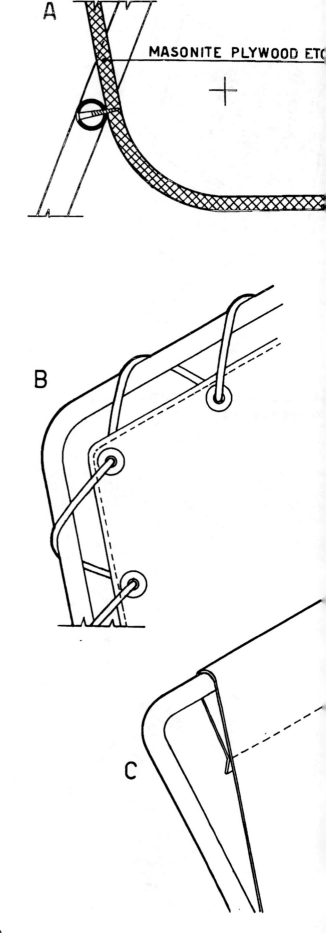

A

MASONITE PLYWOOD ETC

B

C

TYPES OF SEATS AND BACKS MADE OF ONE PIECE OF MATERIAL. "A" MAY BE MADE OF PLYWOOD, MASONITE OR SIMILAR MATERIAL. "B" AND "C" USE CANVAS LACED OR SEWN OVER THE FRAME.

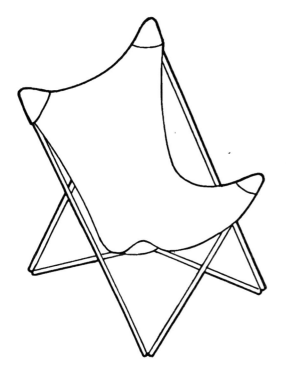

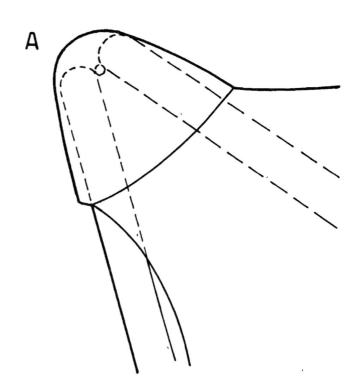

A

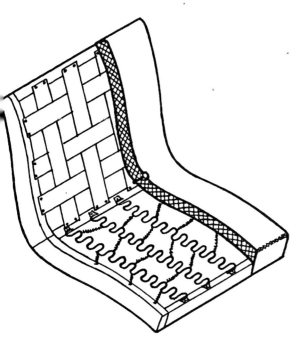

B

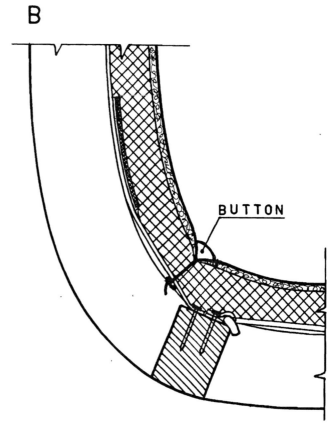

BUTTON

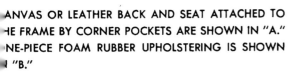

ANVAS OR LEATHER BACK AND SEAT ATTACHED TO
HE FRAME BY CORNER POCKETS ARE SHOWN IN "A."
NE-PIECE FOAM RUBBER UPHOLSTERING IS SHOWN
N "B."

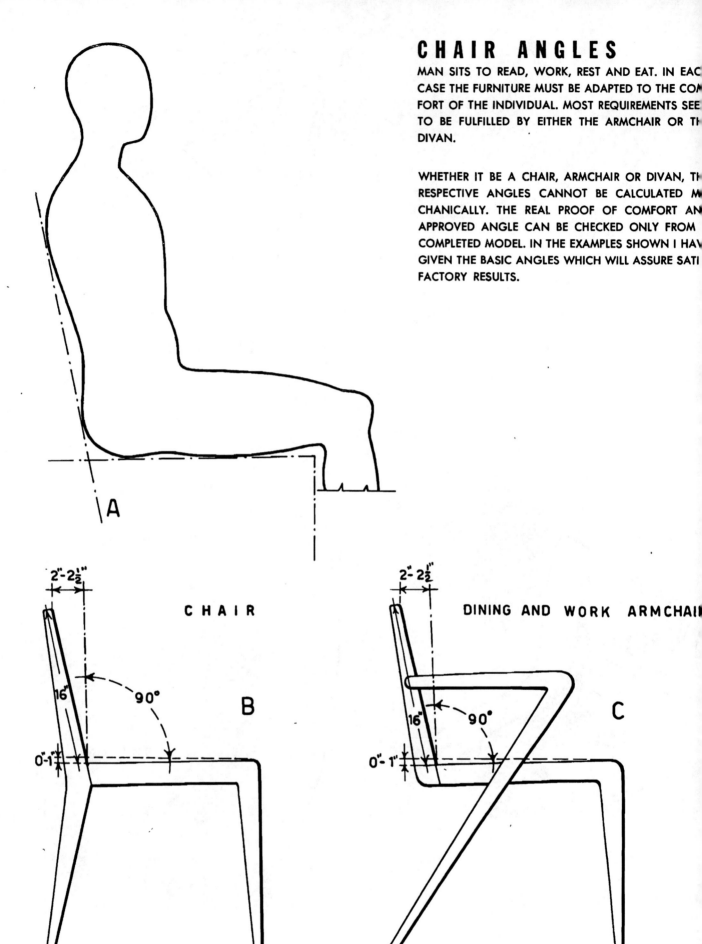

CHAIR ANGLES

MAN SITS TO READ, WORK, REST AND EAT. IN EAC
CASE THE FURNITURE MUST BE ADAPTED TO THE COM
FORT OF THE INDIVIDUAL. MOST REQUIREMENTS SEE
TO BE FULFILLED BY EITHER THE ARMCHAIR OR TH
DIVAN.

WHETHER IT BE A CHAIR, ARMCHAIR OR DIVAN, TH
RESPECTIVE ANGLES CANNOT BE CALCULATED M
CHANICALLY. THE REAL PROOF OF COMFORT AN
APPROVED ANGLE CAN BE CHECKED ONLY FROM
COMPLETED MODEL. IN THE EXAMPLES SHOWN I HAV
GIVEN THE BASIC ANGLES WHICH WILL ASSURE SATI
FACTORY RESULTS.

A

CHAIR

B

DINING AND WORK ARMCHAI

C

ARMLESS CHAIRS

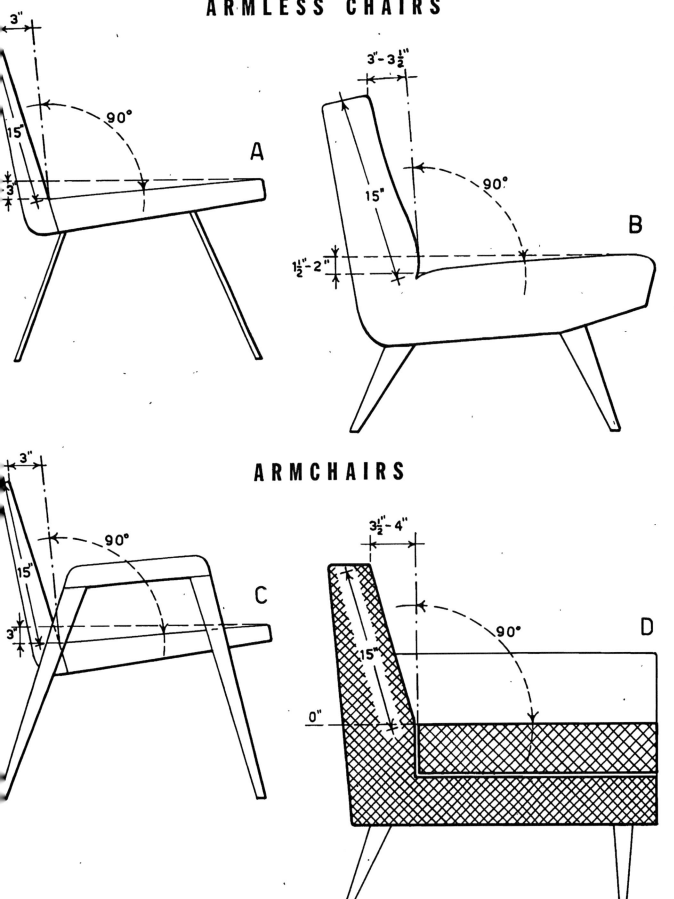

3"

90°

15"

3"

A

3" - 3½"

90°

15"

1½" - 2"

B

ARMCHAIRS

3"

90°

15"

3"

C

3½" - 4"

90°

15"

0"

D

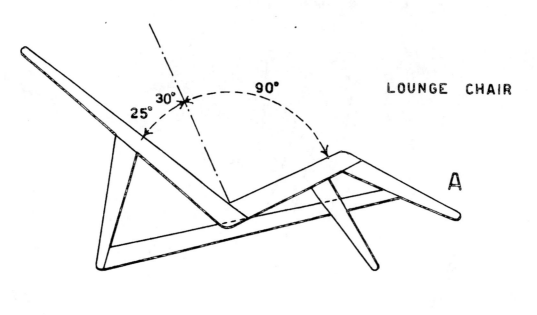

LOUNGE CHAIR

25° 30° 90°

A

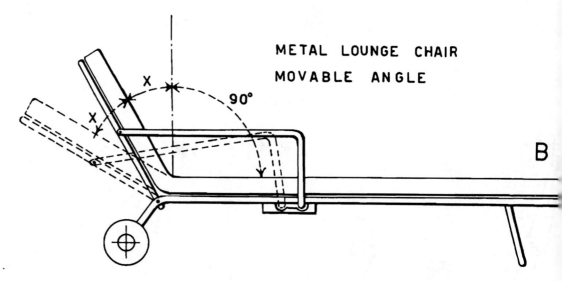

METAL LOUNGE CHAIR
MOVABLE ANGLE

90°

X

B

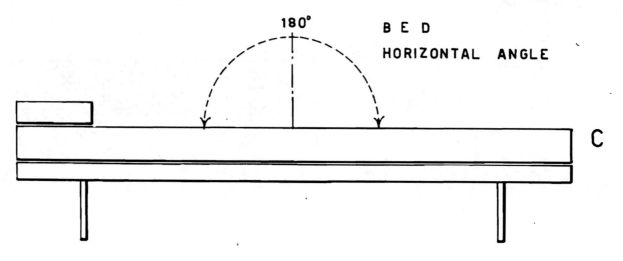

180°

B E D
HORIZONTAL ANGLE

C

FURNITURE FOR THE HOME CRAFTSMAN

IN THIS COUNTRY HUNDREDS OF THOUSANDS OF PEOPLE HAVE SMALL WORK-SHOPS IN THEIR HOMES, WITH THE NECESSARY TOOLS TO MAKE REPAIRS AND TO BUILD VARIOUS USEFUL OBJECTS.

THE MAJORITY OF THESE PEOPLE ARE ALSO INTERESTED IN BUILDING VARIOUS PIECES OF FURNITURE. I HAVE DEVOTED THE LAST 15 PAGES OF THIS BOOK TO A SERIES OF EASY FURNITURE PIECES WHICH THEY CAN MAKE.

I HAVE SIMPLIFIED THE METHOD OF PRESENTATION BOTH IN DESIGN AND IN CONSTRUCTION SO THAT THE READERS CAN READILY UNDERSTAND ALL THE PRO-CEDURES. IT IS POSSIBLE TO BUILD THESE PIECES WITH THE ASSURANCE OF SUCCESS.

PROCEDURE

AFTER YOU HAVE SELECTED THE PIECE OF FURNITURE YOU WANT TO BUILD, THE NEXT STEP IS TO ORDER THE LUMBER. ONE WAY IS TO COPY A LIST OF THE MATERIALS REQUIRED AND ASK ANY LUMBER DEALER TO CUT THE PIECES FOR YOU. ANOTHER WAY IS TO USE LUMBER CUT IN STANDARD SIZES.

IF THE MATERIAL IS PURCHASED IN THE SECOND WAY, IT IS ADVISABLE TO DRAW AN OUTLINE OF THE PIECES DIRECTLY ON THE WOOD. CUT OUT WITH A SAW. PLANE THE SAWED PIECES AND USE A FILE ON THE CURVED SURFACES. MARK AND EXECUTE THE JOINTS OF THE VARIOUS PIECES, CHECKING TO SEE THAT EVERYTHING FITS CORRECTLY. THIS DONE, PROCEED WITH THE ASSEMBLING AS SHOWN IN THE DRAWINGS, USING GLUE AND SCREWS. BE SURE TO FOLLOW THE DIRECTIONS INDICATED IN THE LEGEND.

FINISHING

AFTER BUILDING THE PIECE OF FURNITURE, SANDPAPER ALL PARTS FIRST WITH COARSE SANDPAPER AND THEN WITH FINE SANDPAPER, RUBBING IN THE DIREC-TION OF THE GRAIN. APPLY A COAT OF FIRZITE AND ALLOW IT TO DRY FOR ABOUT EIGHT HOURS; THEN SANDPAPER THE SURFACE AGAIN. WITH A CLEAN BRUSH APPLY TWO COATS OF SATIN LAC (ALLOWING FOUR HOURS BETWEEN COATS), AND FINISH WITH FURNITURE POLISH.

155

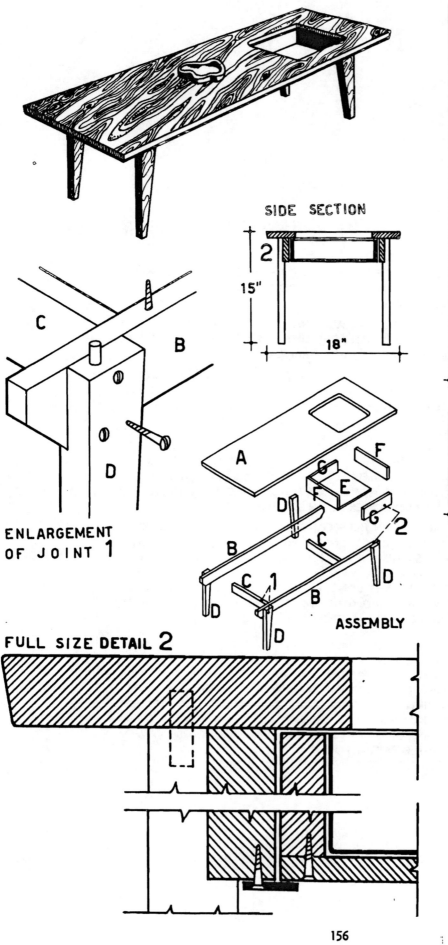

SIDE SECTION

15"

18"

ENLARGEMENT
OF JOINT 1

FULL SIZE DETAIL 2

ASSEMBLY

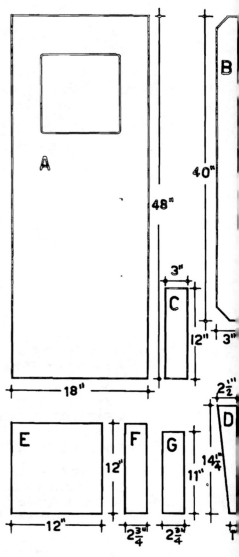

48"

40"

18"

3"

12"   3"

2½"

E   F   G   D

12"

11"

14¼"

12"   2¾"   2¾"

COFFEE TABLE

LIST OF MATERIAL (USE PLYWOOD OR
HARDWOOD).

A — 1 PIECE ¾" THICK AND 48" X 18".
B — 2 PIECES ¾" THICK AND 40" X 3".
C — 2 PIECES ¾ THICK AND 12" X 3".
D — 4 PIECES 1" THICK AND 14¼" X 2½".
E — 1 PIECE ¼" THICK AND 12" X 12".
F — 2 PIECES ½" THICK AND 12" X 2¾".
G — 2 PIECES ½" THICK AND 11" X 2¾".
FOR GENERAL INSTRUCTION SEE PAGE
155.
WHEN YOU HAVE MATERIAL READY FOR
ASSEMBLING JOIN THE PARTS AS FOL-
LOWS:
(1) B WITH C; (2) B WITH D; (3) G WITH
F; (4) GF WITH E; (5) BC WITH FG. SIXTH,
APPLY THE TOP WITH DOWELS AND
SCREWS AND COMPLETE WITH NATURAL
FINISH.

DINING TABLE

ST OF MATERIALS.

— 1 PIECE OF PLYWOOD ¾" THICK AND
4" X 32".

C — FOUR PIPE LEGS WITH FLANGE 27½"
ONG AND 1¼" IN DIAMETER.

OR GENERAL INSTRUCTIONS SEE PAGE
55.

WHEN MATERIAL IS READY FOR ASSEMBL-
NG JOIN THE PARTS AS FOLLOWS:
) B WITH C; (2) A WITH C. YOU WILL
HEN HAVE A SIMPLE MODERN DINING
ABLE. FINISH THE TOP IN NATURAL
NISH. ON THE LEGS USE TWO COATS
F INTERIOR PAINT.

ECTION, DETAIL 1 FULL SIZE

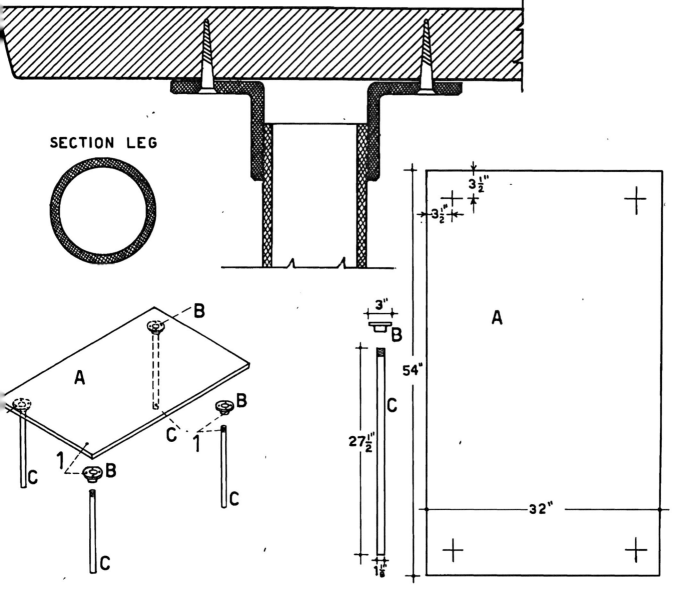

SECTION LEG

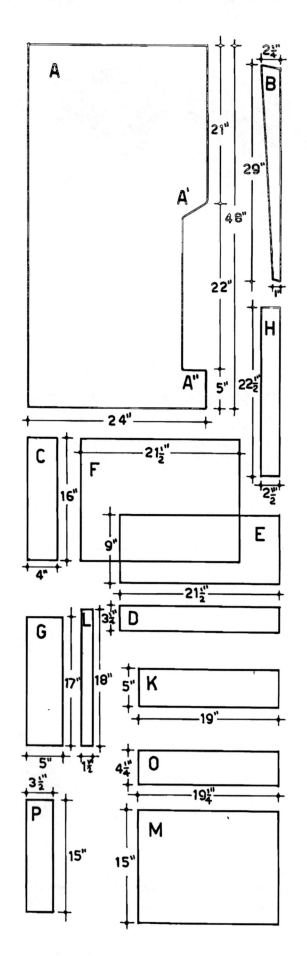

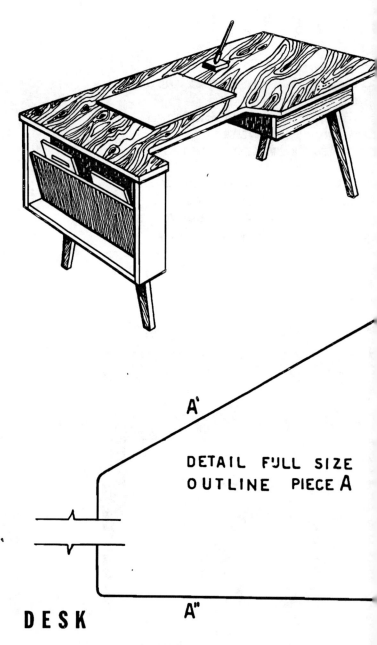

DETAIL FULL SIZE
OUTLINE PIECE A

DESK

LIST OF MATERIALS. (USE PLYWOOD OR HARDWOOD).

A — 1 PIECE ¾" THICK AND 48" X 24". B — 4 PIECES 1¼" THICK AN
29" X 2¼". C — 2 PIECES ¾" THICK AND 16" X 4". D — 1 PIEC
¾" THICK AND 21½" X 3¼". E — 1 PIECE ½" THICK AND 21½"
9". F — 1 PIECE ¾" THICK AND 21½" X 16". G — 2 PIECES ¾" THIC
AND 17" X 5". H — 1 PIECE 1¼" THICK AND 22½" X 2½". K — 2 PIECE
¾" THICK AND 19" X 5". L — 3 PIECES ¾" THICK AND 18"
1½". M — 1 PIECE ¼" THICK AND 19¼" X 15". O — 2 PIECES ½
THICK AND 19¼" X 4¼". P — 1 PIECE ½" THICK AND 15" X 3½".
SEE PAGE 155 FOR GENERAL INSTRUCTIONS.

WHEN MATERIAL IS READY FOR ASSEMBLING JOIN THE PIECES A
FOLLOWS:

(1) C WITH DEF; (2) K WITH GL; (3) H WITH FK; (4) APPLY TOP
WITH C, H, G, K; (DETAIL 2, SEE PAGE 84); (5) APPLY LEGS B WIT
F AND K; (6) (DRAWER) O WITH G P; (DETAIL 3, SEE PAGE 90
(7) M WITH O G; TO COMPLETE DESK. USE NATURAL FINISH A
INDICATED IN GENERAL INSTRUCTIONS.

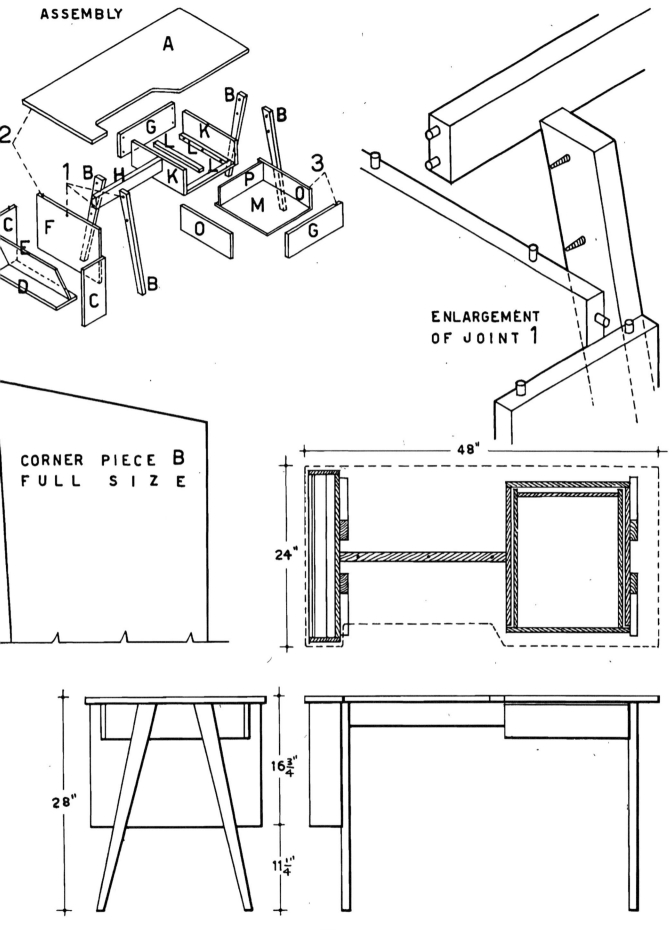

ASSEMBLY

A

B

2

G

K

L

B

1 B H

K

3

C

F

P

O

E

M

D

O

C

G

B

ENLARGEMENT
OF JOINT 1

CORNER PIECE B
FULL SIZE

48"

24"

28"

16¾"

11¼"

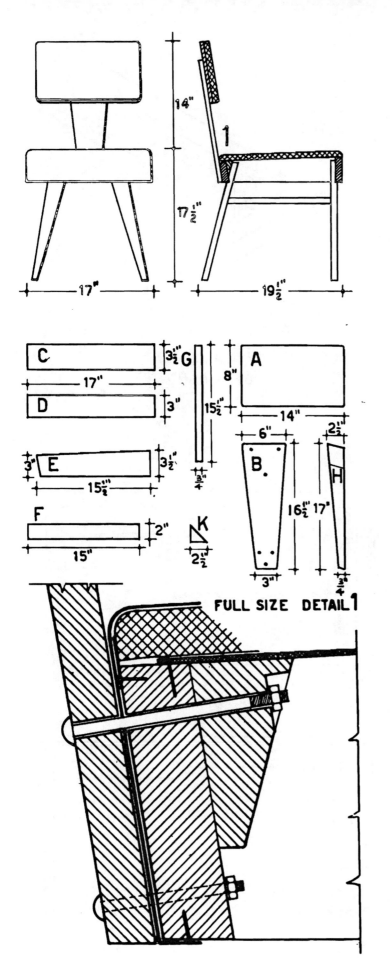

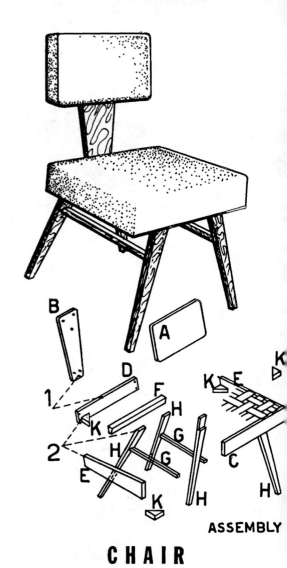

14"

17½"

17"

19½"

C   3½"   G
17"

D   3"

E 3"   3½"
15¾"

F   2"
15"

8"   A
15½"   14"

6"
B   2½"
16½" 17"
2½"
H
3"   ¾"

K
2½"

FULL SIZE   DETAIL 1

ASSEMBLY

CHAIR

LIST OF MATERIALS. (HARDWOOD).

A — 1 PIECE ½" THICK AND 14" X 8". B — 1 PIECE ¼
THICK AND 16½" X 6". C — 1 PIECE ¾" THICK AND 17
X 3½". D — 1 PIECE ¾" THICK AND 17" X 3
E — 2 PIECES ¾" THICK AND 15½" X 3½". F — 1 PIECE
1¼" THICK AND 15" X 2". G — 2 PIECES ¾" THICK
AND 15½" X ¾". H — 4 PIECES ⅞" THICK AND 17"
2½". K — 4 PIECES 1" THICK AND 2½" X 2½" WEBBING
5 YARDS. RUBBER 1 PIECE ¾" THICK AND 27" X 17
FABRIC 1 YARD. 1 BOLT 2¼" LONG AND OTHER 1½
SEE GENERAL INSTRUCTIONS ON PAGE 155.

AFTER MATERIAL IS READY TO BE ASSEMBLED YO
JOIN THEM AS FOLLOWS:

(1) C D WITH "E." (DETAIL 2, SEE PAGE 162 — E
LARGEMENT 2); ATTACH THE CORNER BLOCK "K
JOIN "F" WITH "D", "G" WITH "H." "H" WITH "
D." UPHOLSTER SEAT AND BACK AS SUGGESTED C
PAGES 142 AND 147. JOIN SEAT AND BACK WIT
PIECE MARKED "B" AND YOU HAVE THE COMPLET
CHAIR.

FINISH: COMPLETELY FINISH EXPOSED PARTS BEFO
ASSEMBLING.

ARMLESS CHAIR

LIST OF MATERIALS (HARDWOOD).

A — 1 PIECE ½" THICK AND 11" X 22½". B — 2 PIECES ¾" THICK AND 9" X 2½". C — 1 PIECE ¾" THICK AND 22½" X 1". D — 1 PIECE ¾" THICK 22½" X 2½". E — 2 PIECES ⅝" THICK AND 18" X 2". F — 2 PIECES ¾" THICK AND 24" X 5½". G — 1 PIECE 2" THICK AND 20½" X 2". H — 1 PIECE ¾" THICK AND 22½" X 4½". K — 1 PIECE ¾" THICK AND 22½" X 5½". L — 4 PIECES 1" THICK AND 13" X 3". M — 4 PIECES 1" THICK AND 3½" X 3½". WEBBING 9 YARDS. RUBBER 1 PIECE ¾" THICK AND 38" X 23". FABRIC 1⅔". 4 BOLTS 2¼" LONG. SEE GENERAL INSTRUCTIONS ON PAGE 155.

WHEN MATERIAL IS READY FOR ASSEMBLING JOIN THEM AS FOLLOWS:

F WITH K; ATTACH CORNER BLOCK M; JOIN G WITH H; ATTACH LEGS L. JOIN A WITH B, C, D. APPLY THE UPHOLSTERY WORK AS SHOWN ON PAGES 142 AND 148. ATTACH SEAT AND BACK WITH PIECE E TO COMPLETE ARMLESS CHAIR.

FINISH: COMPLETELY FINISH EXPOSED PARTS BEFORE ASSEMBLING.

CARDBOARD OR WEBBING

FULL SIZE DETAIL 1

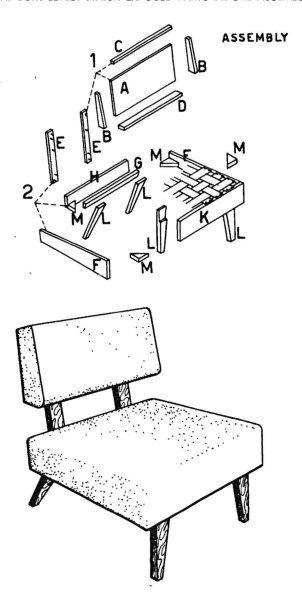

ASSEMBLY

A — 11" — 9"
B — 2½"
C — 1"
D — 2½" — 22½"
E — 18" — 2"
F — 5½" — 24"
G — 2" — 20½" — 22½"
M — 3½" — 3"
H — 4½"
L — 13"
K — 5½"

161

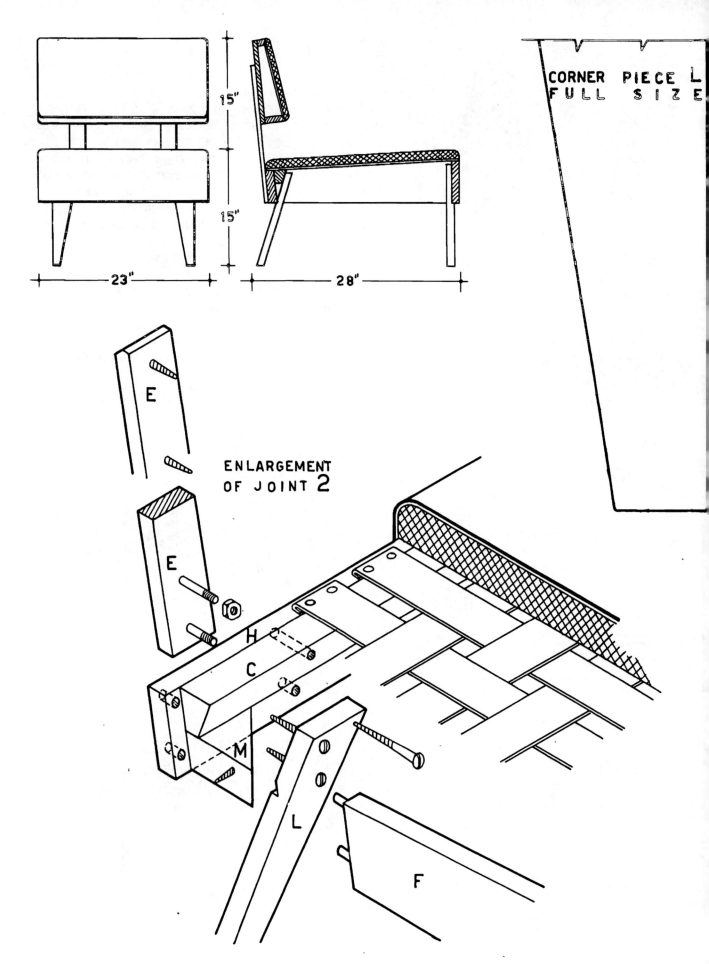

15"

15"

23"

28"

CORNER PIECE L
FULL SIZE

E

ENLARGEMENT
OF JOINT 2

E

H

C

M

L

F

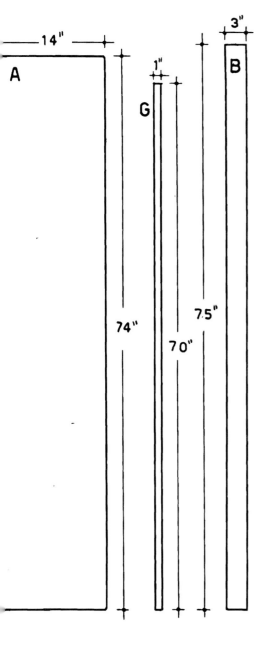

SOFA BED

LIST OF MATERIALS.

A — 1 PIECE ¾" THICK AND 74" X 14". B — 2 PIECES 1½" THICK AND 75" X 3". C — 2 PIECES 1½" THICK AND 31" X 3". D — 2 PIECES 2" THICK AND 18½" X 2". E — 4 PIECES 1¼" THICK AND 10" X 2½". F — 21 PIECES ½" THICK AND 28" X 3". H — 4 PIECES 1½" THICK AND 3" X 3". 1 RUBBER OR NORMAL MATTRESS 4½" THICK AND 75" X 30". THREE RUBBER OR OTHER CUSHIONS 4½" THICK AND 25" X 15". FABRIC 7 YARDS.

FOR GENERAL INSTRUCTION SEE PAGE 155.

AFTER MATERIAL IS READY TO BE ASSEMBLED YOU PROCEED TO JOIN THE PIECES IN THE FOLLOWING MANNER:

B WITH C; ATTACH CORNER BLOCK; ATTACH LEGS E; JOIN G WITH B, C; ATTACH F WITH B AND B TO D; JOIN A TO D; ATTACH MATTRESS AND BACK CUSHIONS TO COMPLETE SOFA.

FINISH THE PART IN VIEW WITH NATURAL FINISH AS INDICATED IN GENERAL INSTRUCTIONS.

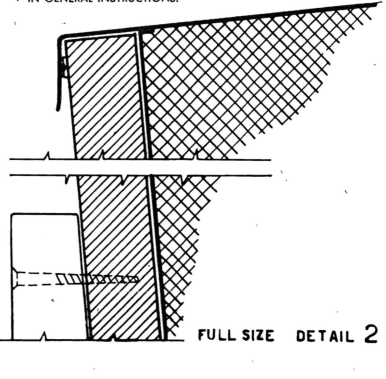

FULL SIZE DETAIL 2

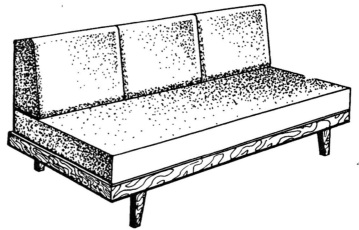

163

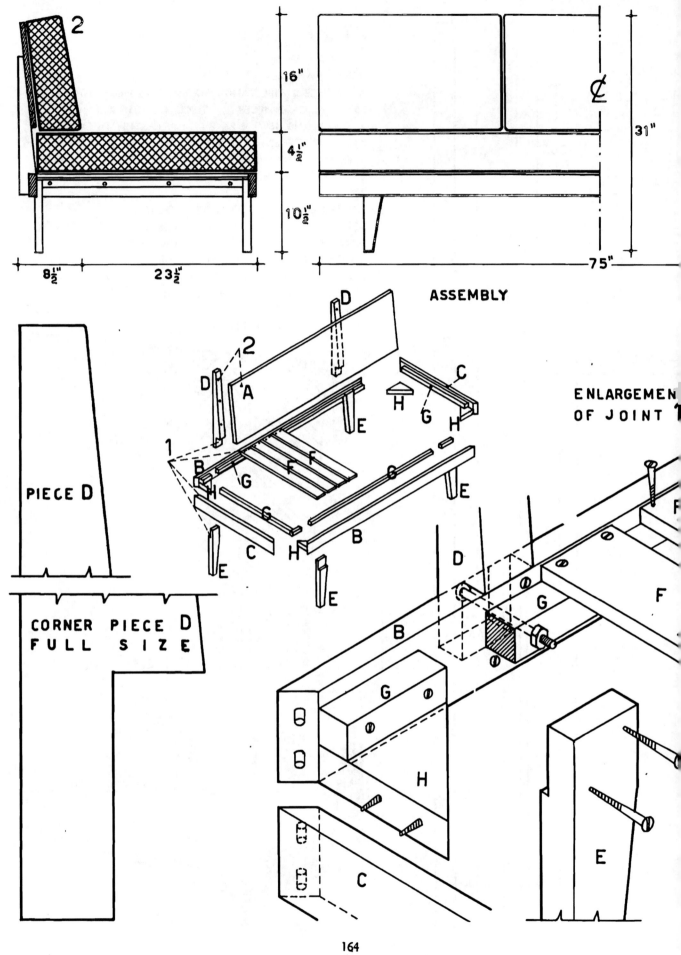

2

16"

4½"

10½"

8½"   23½"

31"

75"

ASSEMBLY

D

2

D

A

E

H

C

G

H

1

B

H

G

F

F

E

C

B

E

E

D

B

G

PIECE D

CORNER PIECE D
FULL SIZE

ENLARGEMEN
OF JOINT

F

F

B

D

G

G

H

E

C

E

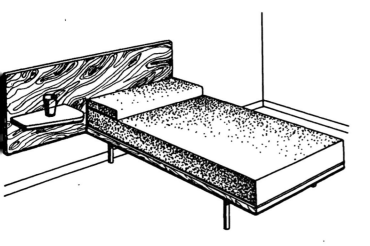

PIECE "A" FIXED ON THE WALL

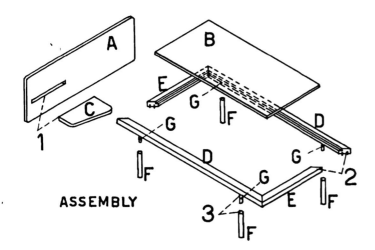

ASSEMBLY

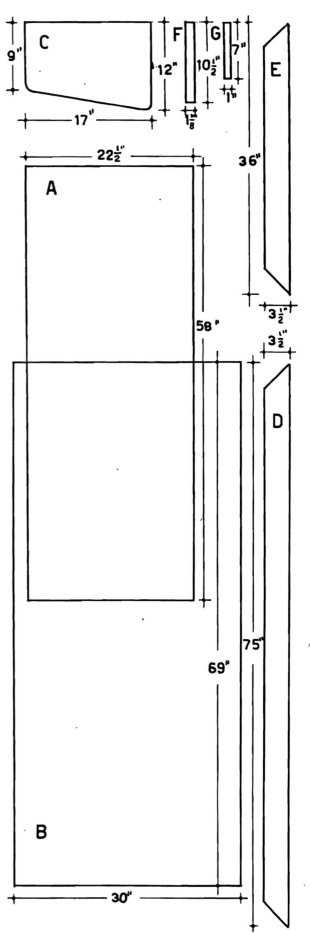

BED

LIST OF MATERIALS. (PLYWOOD OR HARDWOOD)
A — 1 PIECE ¾" THICK AND 22½" X 58". B — 1 PIECE ½" THICK AND
69" X 30". C — 1 PIECE ¾" THICK AND 17" X 12". D — 2 PIECES
1½" THICK AND 75" X 3½". E — 2 PIECES 1½" THICK AND 36" X
3½". F — 4 PIECES METAL PIPE 10½" LONG AND 1¼" IN DIAMETER.
G — 4 PIECES 7" LONG AND 1" IN DIAMETER. H — 1 MATTRESS 5"
THICK AND 75" X 36".

SEE PAGE 155 FOR GENERAL INSTRUCTIONS.

AFTER MATERIAL IS READY YOU PROCEED TO JOIN THEM AS
FOLLOWS:

A WITH C; D WITH E; F, G WITH D (SEE PAGE 86, FIG. B); B WITH
D, E. ADD MATTRESS TO COMPLETE THE BED.

FINISH: USE NATURAL FINISH ON EXPOSED PARTS.

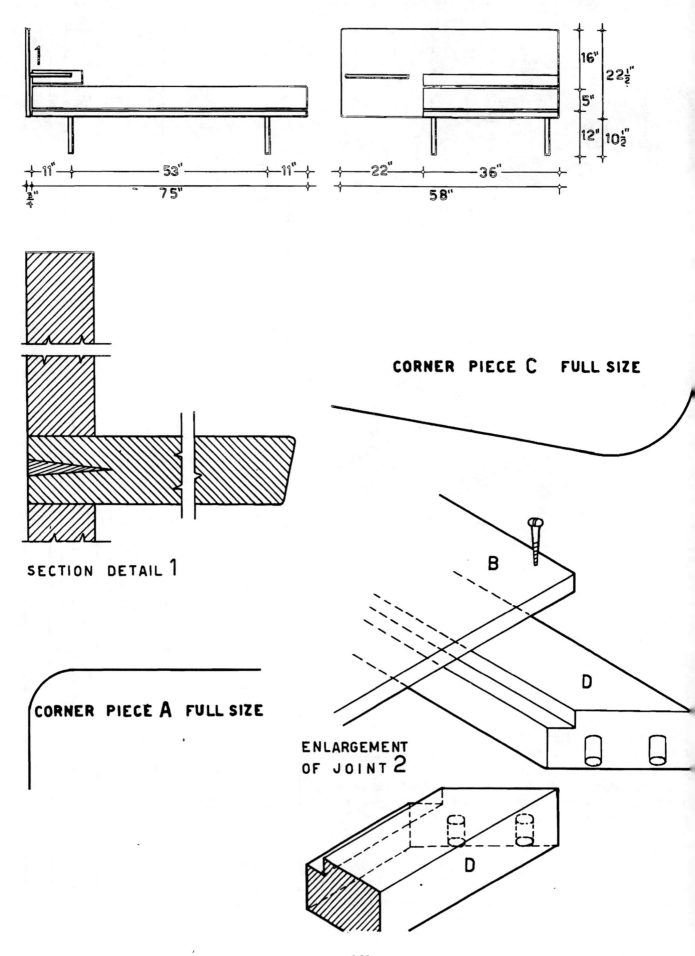

SECTION DETAIL 1

CORNER PIECE C FULL SIZE

CORNER PIECE A FULL SIZE

ENLARGEMENT OF JOINT 2

BOOKSHELVES

LIST OF MATERIALS.

A — 3 PIECES ¾" THICK AND 34½" X 12". B — 2 PIECES ¾" THICK AND 24" X 12". C — 1 PIECE ¼" THICK AND 35½" X 23¼". D — 4 PIECES 1" THICK AND 28" X 1¼". FOR GENERAL INSTRUCTION SEE PAGE 155.

AFTER MATERIAL IS READY TO BE ASSEMBLED YOU PROCEED AS FOLLOWS:

JOIN "A" WITH "B". (DETAIL 2, SEE PAGE 21, FIG. C AND PAGE 28) "A", "B" WITH "C". (DETAIL 3, SEE PAGE 30). ATTACH LEGS "D" TO COMPLETE YOUR BOOKSHELVES.

FINISH: USE NATURAL FINISH AS DIRECTED IN GENERAL INSTRUCTIONS.

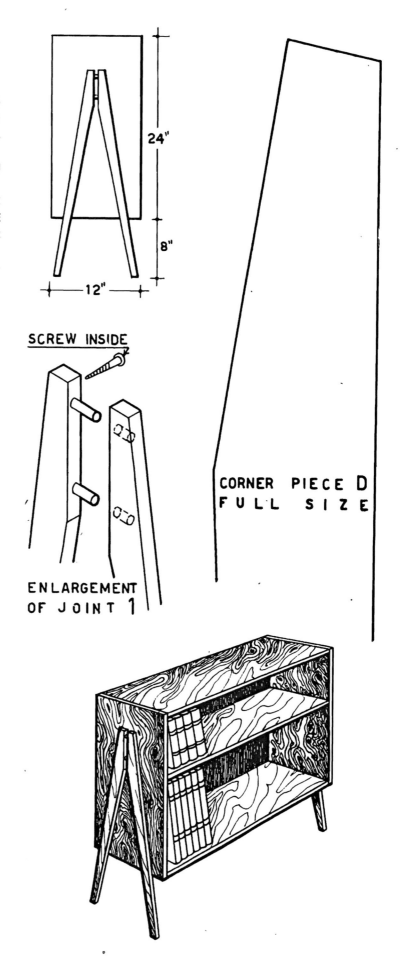

SCREW INSIDE

ENLARGEMENT OF JOINT 1

CORNER PIECE D FULL SIZE

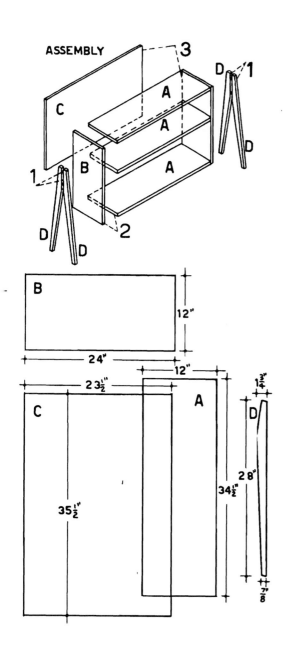

ASSEMBLY

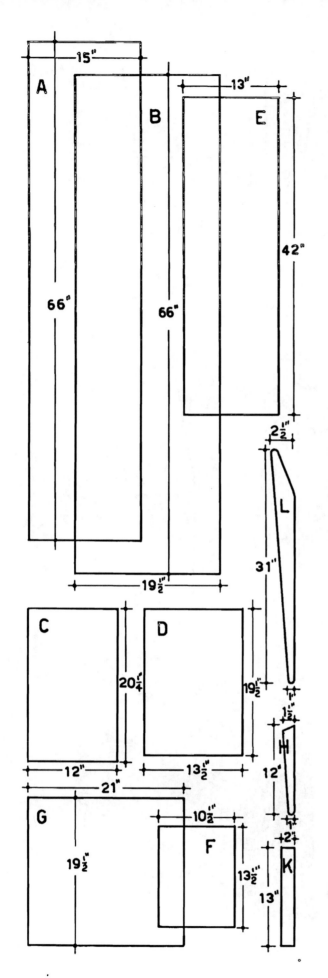

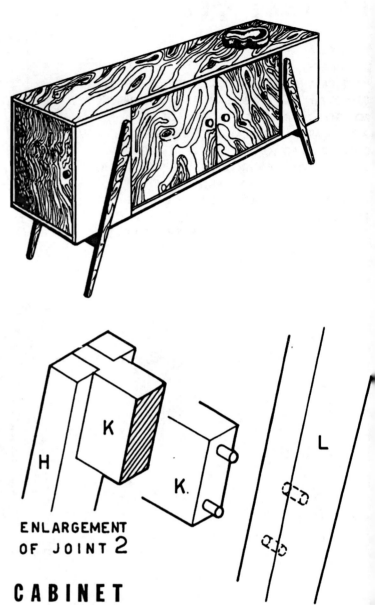

ENLARGEMENT
OF JOINT 2

CABINET

LIST OF MATERIALS.

A — 2 PIECES ¾" THICK AND 66" X 15". B — 1 PIECE ¾" THICK AND 66" X 19½". C — 2 PIECES ¾" THICK AND 20¼" X 12". D — 4 PIECES ¾" THICK AND 19½" X 13½". E — 2 PIECES ¾" THICK AND 42" X 13". F — 4 PIECES ¾" THICK AND 13½" X 10½". G — 2 PIECES ¾" THICK AND 19½" X 21". H — 2 PIECES 1" THICK AND 12" X 1½". K — 2 PIECES 1¼" THICK AND 13" X 2". L — 2 PIECES 1" THICK AND 31" X 2½".

FOR GENERAL INSTRUCTIONS SEE PAGE 155.

AFTER MATERIAL IS READY FOR ASSEMBLING YOU PROCEED AS FOLLOWS:

JOIN "A" WITH "B"; (DETAIL 4, SEE PAGE 21, FIG. C); "F" WITH "B", "D"; "C" WITH "A"; "D". ATTACH SHELVES "E" (SEE PAGE 81, FIG. C); ADD DOORS "D" AND "G". (DETAIL 3, SEE PAGE 57, FIG. A). JOIN "H" WITH "H"-"L". ATTACH LEGS TO COMPLETE THE CABINET. FINISH WITH NATURAL FINISH AS INDICATED IN THE GENERAL INSTRUCTIONS.

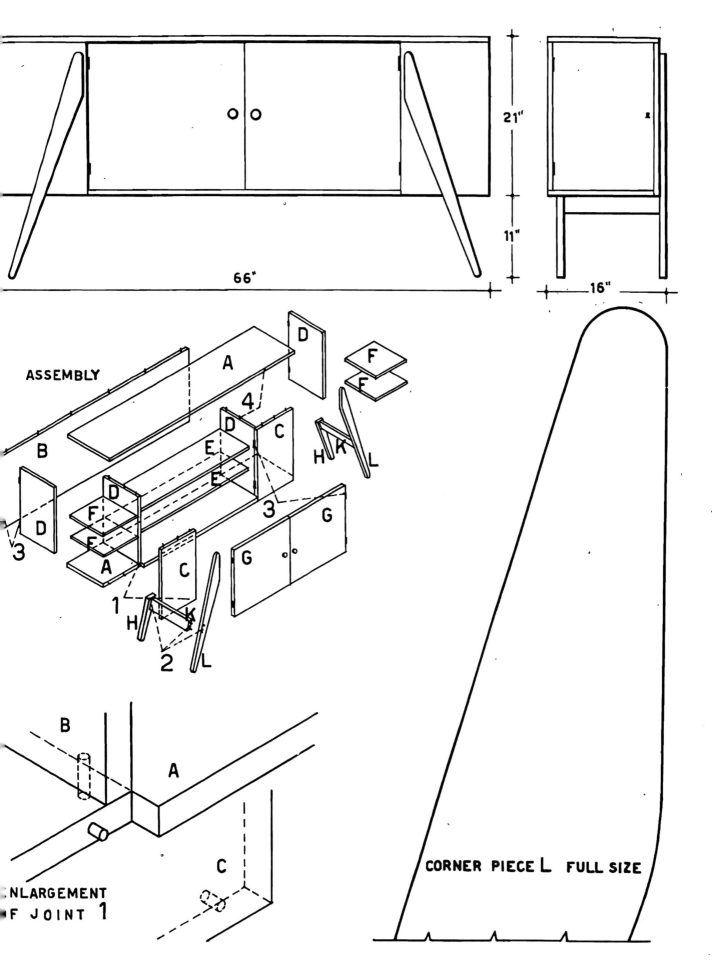

21"

11"

66"

16"

ASSEMBLY

A

D

F

F

B

D

4

E

C

H K L

D

E

D

F

E

3

G

A

C

3

G

G

1

H K

2 L

B

A

C

ENLARGEMENT
OF JOINT 1

CORNER PIECE L FULL SIZE

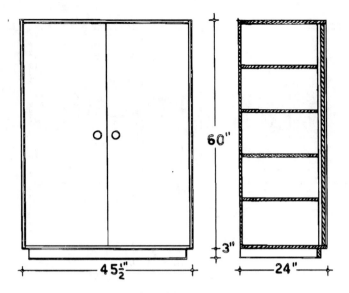

WARDROBE

LIST OF MATERIALS.

A — 2 PIECES ¾" THICK AND 60" X 24". B — 2 PIECES
¾" THICK AND 58½" X 22". C — 2 PIECES ¾" THICK
AND 44" X 24". D — 1 PIECE ¼" THICK AND 59½" X 45".
E — 4 PIECES ¾" THICK AND 22" X 15". F — 1 PIECE ¾"
THICK AND 58½" X 22". G — 1 PIECE 29" LONG AND ¾"
IN DIAMETER. H — 1 PIECE 1" THICK AND 41½" X 3".
K — 2 PIECES 1" THICK AND 22" X 3".

SEE GENERAL INSTRUCTIONS ON PAGE 155.

AFTER MATERIAL IS READY FOR ASSEMBLING PROCEED
AS FOLLOWS:

JOIN "A, C" WITH "A, F, E" (DETAIL 1, SEE PAGE 27,
FIG. C AND PAGE 28); ATTACH BACK "D" (SEE PAGE
30); HANG DOORS "B" (SEE PAGE 57, FIG. A); JOIN
"C" WITH "H, K" TO COMPLETE THE WARDROBE.
INSTRUCTIONS.

FINISH: USE NATURAL FINISH AS DIRECTED IN GENERAL.

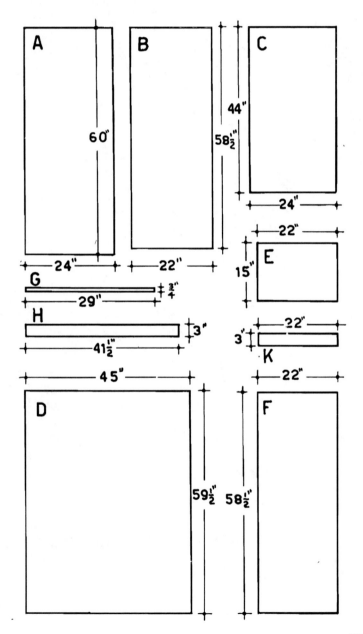

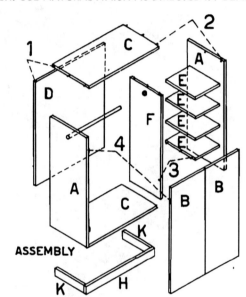

ASSEMBLY

CPSIA information can be obtained at www.ICGtesting.com
Printed in the USA
BVOW05s0127101213

338686BV00007B/43/P